An Essay on Moral Responsibility

An Essay on
Moral Responsibility

Michael J. Zimmerman

Rowman & Littlefield
PUBLISHERS

To Kath

ROWMAN & LITTLEFIELD

Published in the United States of America in 1988
by Rowman & Littlefield, Publishers
(a division of Littlefield, Adams & Company)
81 Adams Drive, Totowa, New Jersey 07512

Library of Congress Cataloging-in-Publication Data

Zimmerman, Michael J.
  An essay on moral responsibility.

  Bibliography: p. 195
  Includes indexes.
  1. Ethics.   I. Title.
BJ1012.Z56   1988   170   87–26391
ISBN 0–8476–7593–9

90   89   88
4   3   2   1

Printed in the United States of America

Contents

Preface

SOME PHILOSOPHICAL PUZZLES are popular; others have very limited appeal. Some puzzles stay stubbornly with you once they have captured your attention; others fade away, once intriguing, but no longer pressing. There is one popular puzzle in particular that has never ceased to nag at me since I became aware of it. It is the familiar puzzle about how anyone could ever be morally responsible for anything, since such responsibility seems to be impossible both on the supposition that determinism is true and on the supposition that determinism is false.

This book is not about that puzzle, but it does concern one element of it. I take up here the question of what moral responsibility is (or would be, were there any). When pondering the puzzle about determinism, I used to take it for granted that I knew pretty well what it is (or would be) to be morally responsible for something. But I discovered that I was wrong. Since embarking on the present project, my views have changed considerably, although by now they have attained a certain stability—and so I present them here.

This book is intended to plug a conspicuous gap in the literature on moral philosophy. Ascriptions of responsibility feature very, very prominently in everyday life, and philosophers, too, have not hesitated to make them. Yet there has been comparatively little systematic effort on the part of philosophers to analyze such ascriptions and there has been no book-length effort, as far as I am aware, to analyze ascriptions of moral responsibility in particular.

I suppose that this book will primarily be of interest to philosophers and students of philosophy. But I hope that it will also engage the attention and interest of those in related disciplines, law in particular. This hope will no doubt be frustrated to a certain extent by the fact that I have endeavored to set matters down in considerable detail. This tends to inhibit readability. In the interest of readability, I have not gone into the sort of detail that I believe to be ideal, from a strictly philosophical point of view. There is a double danger here. First, insofar as I have gone into considerable detail, some potential readers lacking a strong background in philosophy may be discouraged from tackling the material. I would urge such readers to persevere. The most difficult chapter, technically, is the second, and these readers may be able to get what they want out of the book by skipping this chapter and simply reading its synopsis in the second section of Chapter 1, or at least by reading Chapter 2 quickly, without worrying about the details. (Several technical terms, introduced in Chapter 2, are used in later chapters. The Index of Subjects provides the exact location of their introduction.) But second, insofar as I have consciously pulled back from that degree of detail that I believe to be philosophically ideal, I may have committed certain errors that I would otherwise have caught; for pure English prose can be seductive, tempting one to believe that there is accuracy and understanding where, in fact, there is not. But such is the price of compromise. And anyway, there are undoubtedly errors that I would not have caught no matter how precise I had tried to be. One can stare at the issues for just so long, and then one begins to lose one's perspective, so that what once was clear no longer is so. It is unsettling—much like looking at a familiar word for a prolonged period and starting to doubt that it is spelt correctly.

I shall not outline the book in this Preface; I do that in Section 1.2. However, I shall make mention here of three distinctions that I draw in the following pages, distinctions that have very often been overlooked by philosophers but which seem to me of first importance. The first distinction is that which holds between the two types of moral responsibility that I call appraisability and liability. The second distinction is that which holds between the two modes of appraisability that I call direct and indirect. And the third distinction holds between what I call culpability (a type of appraisability) and wrongdoing. The failure to attend adequately to these distinctions undermines much that has been written on the topic of moral responsibility—including earlier published work of mine. When one holds these distinctions clearly before one's mind, one is constrained to reject a good deal that is involved in the common practice of ascribing responsibility—of praising, blaming, rewarding, and punishing. For example, the first distinction implies that even if a terrorist, who has blown scores of innocent people to bits by detonating a bomb in a crowded airport, is very much to blame in terms of appraisability, it remains an open question whether or not he is to blame at all in terms of liability— that is, whether or not he is deserving of overt censure or punishment. The second distinction implies that this terrorist is no more to blame than he would have been had his bomb failed to detonate. And the third distinction implies that the terrorist may even be praiseworthy rather than blameworthy—indeed, that he may even be more praiseworthy than, say, a dedicated famine-relief worker. Moreover, insofar as liability is grounded in appraisability, this third distinction implies that our institution of punishment is to a large extent ill-founded—not because no one can ever deserve punishment, but simply because most of those whom we do punish would appear not to deserve it. These people are, in effect (though not commonly acknowledged to be, and certainly not acknowledged by the law to be), victims of what the law calls strict liability statutes.

These are fairly radical implications. Insofar as the distinctions have merit, as I believe they do, and insofar as they have these (and many other such) implications, as I again believe they do, we must revise much of our common practice of ascribing responsibility. That is the central theme or, if you like, the moral of this book.

Acknowledgments

Robert Audi, Donald Hubin, and Douglas Husak all supplied detailed critical comments on the entire book in one or another of its earlier versions. I am extremely grateful to them for these comments, which were invariably penetrating and constructive. Many other individuals helped in one way or another with various portions of the material included in the book. In particular, I thank the following: Raziel Abelson, Felicia Ackerman, George Agich, Richard Brandt, Selmer Bringsjord, Dan Brock, Philip Devine, Alan Donagan, Rem Edwards, Fred Feldman, Michael Gorr, John Greco, David Hilbert, Shelly Kagan, Lowell Kleiman, Peter Klein, Eric Kraemer, John Ladd, Peter McInerney, Thomas Moody, Edmund Pincoffs, Itamar Pitowsky, Philip Quinn, Allen Renear, Ernest Sosa, Mark Strasser and Margaret Walker. I thank, too, the students in my graduate seminars on responsibility given at Brown University in 1982 and 1985. Finally, I should say that the seminal work of Joel Feinberg has been and remains a source of great inspiration to me. Given the collaborative nature of philosophy, I cheerfully hold all of the aforementioned responsible for the contents of this book.

A fellowship received from Rutgers University in the summer of 1980 helped me start work on the issues addressed in this book; attendance at an institute on human action, funded by the National Endowment for the Humanities and directed by Robert Audi, helped me to continue work on these issues; a sabbatical received from Brown University in the fall of 1984 helped me to complete a first draft of the book. I gratefully acknowledge these contributions.

Portions of several previously published papers appear either *verbatim* or slightly modified in the following pages. These papers are listed in the Bibliography as Zimmerman (1982, 1985a, 1985b, 1986a, and 1987a). I am grateful to the editors of the *Pacific Philosophical Quaterly*, the *Philosophical Quarterly*, the *American Philosophical Quarterly, Noûs*, and *Ethics* (published by the University of Chicago) for permission to reproduce this material.

1

INTRODUCTION

1.1 Varieties of Responsibility

THE TERM "RESPONSIBLE" and its cognates are richly ambiguous, a fact which has been widely noted.[1] I find it useful to distinguish broadly between what I shall call *causal responsibility,* on the one hand, and *personal responsibility,* on the other. In addition, personal responsibility may be either *prospective* or *retrospective.*

If someone says that the short-circuit was responsible for the fire, he would normally be understood to mean simply that the short-circuit caused the fire. Causal responsibility just is event-causation; that which is responsible is an event (in this case, the short-circuit), and that for which this event is responsible is another event (in this case, the fire).[2]

If someone says that the lifeguard is responsible for the swimmers' safety, he would normally be understood to mean that it is the lifeguard's obligation to make sure that the swimmers are and remain safe. Here, "responsible" expresses what I call prospective, personal responsibility.[3] It is personal, in the sense that that which is responsible is a person; it is prospective, in the sense that that which the lifeguard is responsible *for* lies in the future. When someone is said to have a responsibility to do something, this is another way of saying that he bears prospective responsibility for the action in question; a responsibility, in this sense, is an obligation. The obligation may be moral, or legal, or imposed in virtue of some other type of rule (*e.g.,* a rule of chess that requires one to move one's bishop only diagonally); and thus prospective, personal responsibility may be moral, or legal, or whatever. When someone is said to be a responsible person, this is another way of saying that he takes his responsibilities seriously.[4]

If someone says that the lifeguard is responsible for the swimmers' deaths, he would normally be understood to mean that the lifeguard is to blame for the swimmers' deaths. Here "responsible" expresses one

1

variety of what I call retrospective, personal responsibility. It is personal since, as before, that which is responsible is a person; it is retrospective, in the sense that that which the lifeguard is responsible *for* lies in the past.

The terms 'prospective' and 'retrospective' are not ideal. What I have called prospective responsibility need not, in fact, be prospective, although it cannot be retrospective. Someone S may be obligated at time T to perform action a at time T', and it may be that T is identical with T'. Worse, what I have called retrospective responsibility not only need not be retrospective, but there is reason to think that it can be prospective. That is, there is reason to think (as we shall see in Chapter 3) that it is possible that S be 'retrospectively' responsible at T for performing a at T', and yet that T be *earlier* than T'. But, having said this, I should immediately add that, *typically* (even if not necessarily), when there is occasion to *ascribe* what I have called prospective responsibility, that for which the agent is responsible does lie in the future; and, *typically* (even if not necessarily), when there is occasion to *ascribe* what I have called retrospective responsibility, that for which the agent is responsible does lie in the past. Thus the terms 'prospective' and 'retrospective' are certainly suggestive; and I know of none better.[5] I shall continue to use them as indicated, but I urge the reader not to be misled by them.

When I say that personal responsibility, whether prospective or retrospective, is responsibility that some person bears for some event, I am using the term "event" broadly. For one can be responsible for states as well as changes, and for long, drawn-out processes as well as for instantaneous happenings. An event, as I am using the term, is anything that takes place in time and essentially involves some individual object.

Blameworthiness is not the only form in which retrospective, personal responsibility may be manifested. For instance, if someone says that the anonymous donor is responsible for the charity's success, he would not normally be understood to mean that the donor is to blame for the success; indeed, he would normally be understood to mean that the donor deserves praise for the success. And, in general, praise may express moral or legal or aesthetic (or whatever) approval, just as blame may express moral or legal or aesthetic (or whatever) disapproval. Thus retrospective, personal responsibility may be moral or legal or whatever, just as prospective, personal responsibility may be—although it is interesting to note that our language much more readily sanctions "the lifeguard is *morally* responsible for the swimmers' deaths" than it does "the anonymous donor is *morally* responsible for the charity's success," the reason for which escapes me.

It should be acknowledged that the original statement about the donor (namely, "the anonymous donor is responsible for the charity's success") *could* be used simply to express a certain fact about causal responsibility, to wit, that the donor was the (main) cause of the success. But this is unlikely; the "is" of the statement would normally be replaced by a "was," if this were meant.[6] Of course, if we were talking about a deceased donor, this telltale mark would not be available to us. That is, "the anonymous donor was responsible for the charity's success" could be used equally as well to express causal as to express retrospective, personal responsibility; only the context of the statement's utterance would allow us to make a decision on this matter. (Similarly, although this is less likely, the statement "the lifeguard was responsible for the swimmers' deaths" could be used simply to express causal responsibility.) In saying this, I am not contradicting the claim made earlier that causal responsibility is a relation that binds *events* to events; for, I believe, where causation is predicated in this way of an agent, it may be more informatively predicated of an event which involves the agent.

It is possible, of course, that the original statement about the donor serve a dual purpose, that of expressing a fact that concerns both personal and causal responsibility. That is, one who ascribes responsibility to the donor for the charity's success might be ascribing a hybrid personal-*cum*-causal responsibility, claiming that the donor both bears (retrospective) personal responsibility and bore causal responsibility for the success. Indeed, I believe that such a dual purpose is often operative in such ascriptions. In such cases one must be very careful to distinguish the two aspects of the purpose; for personal responsibility is not to be confused with causal responsibility and, especially, one should not take it for granted (as is often done) that personal responsibility requires causal responsibility.[7]

In addition, it must be acknowledged that ascriptions of causal responsibility can sometimes have a function (in fact, a prospective function) which ascriptions of retrospective, personal responsibility can also sometimes have—that of pointing out to us how we should act in the future.[8] But, again, we must not let this lead to misunderstanding, to a confusion of causal with retrospective, personal responsibility. Just consider this dialogue in a recent Andy Capp cartoon (*The Providence Journal-Bulletin*, Nov. 1986):

Vicar to Andy (who is stumbling, red-nosed): "Tch! Tch—! Just look at y'self, lad. It's the beer, and the beer alone, that's responsible for the mess you're in. Don't you realise that?"
Andy (sobbing on vicar's shoulder): "Thanks, Vicar—*hic*—you're the very first person who's said it isn't all *my* fault!"

We should note, too, yet another fact that can confuse the unwary, and that is that praise and blame may be ascribed figuratively in cases where it is only causal responsibility that is at issue. Someone may, for instance, blame the weather for the bad crops; as far as I can tell, this amounts to no more than ascribing causal responsibility to the weather for an unto-ward event. Especially confusing, in this context, are those cases where an agent is "blamed" for a certain untoward event, but where in fact only causal responsibility is at issue (or where the only evidence is of causal, and not of personal, responsibility).[9]

Various authors have subdivided the concept of retrospective, personal responsibility in various ways.[10] Some of these subdivisions will be reflected in what follows, some not. But there is one subdivision that I believe to be absolutely critical, but which has, for the most part, gone unnoticed.[11] This concerns the distinction between what I shall call *appraisability* and *liability*. An agent is appraisable if he is deserving of a certain type of judgment; an agent is liable if he is deserving of a certain type of treatment. Both types of responsibility have an essential tie to praise- and blameworthiness, but to praise- and blameworthiness of different types. In the case of appraisability, the type of praise and blame at issue is *inward*; it constitutes making a private judgment. In the case of liability, the type of praise and blame at issue is *overt*; it constitutes acting in a certain way, a way which purports to give public expression to a private judgment. Thus, while appraisability and liability are both varieties of retrospective, personal responsibility, and while both these varieties have essential ties with praise- and blameworthiness, they are to be sharply distinguished; for the types of praise and blame at issue, and indeed, as we shall see, the types of worthiness also, differ considerably.

My concern in this book is with *moral, retrospective, personal respon-sibility,* in the forms of both *appraisability* and *liability* (though primarily the former). It is these types of responsibility that I shall seek to clarify. Other types of responsibility, even those which admit of a moral variety, will not be discussed, except incidentally and as they pertain to those types that concern me here. In this connection, it is worth noting that there will be little occasion to discuss prospective responsibility. It is often claimed that there is a strong tie between prospective and retrospec-tive responsibility of the following sort: retrospective responsibility arises out of a failure to meet one's prospective responsibility, and such failure gives rise to new prospective responsibilities, themselves the potential occasion (if not met) for further retrospective responsibility, and so on. Or, to put it more roughly but perhaps more clearly: a failure to meet one's obligations gives rise to blameworthiness and also to new obliga-tions, which are themselves the potential occasion (if not met) for further blameworthiness, and so on.[12] But, while this is of course so, not too much should be made of it, for two reasons. First, although the failure to meet one's obligations can indeed occasion blameworthiness, it need not; for wrongdoing does not automatically confer culpability—a theme that I shall be plugging constantly throughout the book. Secondly, while blame-worthiness can indeed be incurred by way of failing to meet one's obligations, it need not; for culpability does not imply wrongdoing—another theme that I shall be constantly plugging. It is also often claimed that retrospective responsibility gives rise to prospective responsibilities, that being at fault imposes an obligation of reparation. But again, while this can be so, it need not be so (a matter that I shall take up in the final chapter). There seem to me, indeed, to be no interesting, strictly logical ties between prospective and retrospective responsibility.

One other limitation should be noted. I shall be concerned only with responsibility that may be ascribed to *individual* persons, although I shall discuss the ascription of such responsibility in group situations. Admittedly, entire groups are sometimes themselves talked of as persons, even in moral (though more often in legal) contexts, and sometimes retrospective, personal responsibility is ascribed to them. I suspect that, if this can be done at all meaningfully in the moral arena, then all such ascriptions of responsibility are reducible to ascriptions of responsibility to individuals; but I shall not seek to prove this and shall not concern myself with this issue further.[13]

Much philosophical discussion concerning that notion of responsibility with which I shall here be concerned has taken the following form: we know what it means to say that someone is morally responsible for something, and we know that freedom of the will and of action is a precondition of such responsibility; but it is not clear whether or not we ever act freely, and so it is not clear whether or not we are ever in fact morally responsible for anything. And the debate has usually[14] revolved around the free will-determinism controversy. But that is not how I shall proceed here. I do not presume that we have an adequate grasp of the notion of moral responsibility; on the contrary, my task will be to tighten our grasp of it. That is, I want to come to a better, fuller understanding of this notion; for, in my experience, it proves to be very slippery, and it is dangerous to think that we may employ it unexamined in our discussion of free will, determinism, and such. But, like those who have employed this concept in the debate on free will and determinism, I shall assume that freedom of the will and of action is essential to moral, retrospective, personal responsibility. In fact, I propose to take this assumption very seriously indeed. When one adheres strictly to this assumption, some rather startling conclusions emerge.

I assume that there *is* a notion (or, better, two notions—those of appraisability and liability) to be understood; this has seldom been denied.[15] I shall try to give a detailed account of what conditions are necessary and sufficient for someone's bearing (retrospective) moral responsibility for something.[16] I shall *not* assume that anyone ever is in fact morally responsible for anything. This is worth emphasizing, since I certainly do not wish to presuppose a particular solution to the free will-determinism controversy. My goal here is simply that of coming to understand the concept of moral responsibility, which is of course something that can be achieved even if it happens that no one is in fact (or ever has been, or ever will be, or even, in some senses of "could," ever could be) morally responsible for anything. But, having said this, I should immediately acknowledge that I do believe that many people often are morally responsible for some things—indeed, this belief motivates the entire enterprise—and I shall often talk as if the belief were correct.

1.2 Synopsis

Since what follows is fairly long and detailed, since it will often prove fairly difficult to work through, and since my discussion of responsibility presupposes, and so must await the presentation of, certain preliminary material in Chapter 2, I think it best to provide here an outline of what is to come in the rest of the book. This will be very brief, touching only on the highlights of what follows, and will be completely free of the clutter of qualifications and modifications.

Background. The present inquiry into moral responsibility presupposes a certain theory of human action. The pertinent parts of this theory are presented in Chapter 2. This presentation is inevitably very compact, rough, and blunt; a separate, book-length treatment of the theory is required for it to be adequately presented.[17]

I take action to be the bringing about of an event, and I take the bringing about of an event to consist in a volition's causing that event. I present this traditional view in Section 2.1; it is a view which, though often criticized, is, I believe, fully defensible. A volition is simply a type of decision or choice that some event occur, involving the belief that whether or not the event occurs is, in some sense, "up to one"; in the terminology that I shall use, one wills an event only if one believes that one is in strict, standard control of it.

There are various ways to bring about an event. One may bring it about *tout court;* or one may help to bring it about (this happens when one's volition is "a cause," but perhaps not "the cause," of the event); or one may contribute to it (this happens when the event is a consequence, but perhaps not a causal consequence, of one's volition). In addition, one may participate in group action, in the sense that the event that occurs as a consequence of one's volition occurs also as a consequence of someone else's volition.

The concept of an attempt is tied to that of an action. In one sense, an attempt just is a volition; in another, an attempt occurs only when a volition is efficacious. The concept of an omission is also tied to that of an action. Generally, an omission is the nonperformance of an action that one can or could perform; one can also intentionally omit to do something, and one can engage in group omission.

It is important to distinguish these various concepts, for they are all pertinent to the ascription of responsibility. One can be responsible in various ways for an event, or for bringing it about, or for attempting to bring it about, or for omitting to bring it about; and one can be responsible for the consequences of all these sorts of things. But one cannot be responsible for any of them unless one enjoys a certain sort of freedom. In Section 2.2 I distinguish two types of freedom, which I call strict and broad. A person acting under coercion (at gunpoint, for example) is not broadly free to do other than that which he is coerced to do; but, strictly, he is free to do otherwise (and thereby run the risk of getting "wasted," in that awful TV vernacular). On the other hand, no one is strictly free to jump over the moon, however hard he might have trained. I argue that there are senses in which both strict and broad freedom come in degrees, but also that there is an important sense in which strict freedom does *not* come in degrees.

One can distinguish freely doing something from being free to do it; and one can make many related distinctions. Those which are pertinent to the ensuing discussion of responsibility are drawn up in Section 2.2. One particularly important distinction is that between direct and indirect freedom. An agent is directly free only with respect to his volitions; he is indirectly free with respect to the consequences of those volitions with respect to which he is directly free. Indirect freedom is parasitic on direct freedom; it is contained in direct freedom, in the sense that an event's occurring as a consequence of an agent's volition is wholly "up to nature," except insofar as the agent is free with respect to the volition itself.

Finally, in Section 2.3, various types of control are distinguished. One enjoys standard control over an event just in case one is free with respect both to its occurring and to its not occurring. One enjoys curtailed control over an event just in case one is free with respect to its occurring but not with respect to its not occurring. And one enjoys complete control over an event just in case one has control both over it and over all events upon whose occurrence its occurrence is contingent. Again, I make these distinctions here because they are pertinent to the later discussion of moral responsibility.

Appraisability. In Chapter 3, I turn to an account of that type of moral responsibility that I call appraisability. It is this type that lies at the heart of my inquiry.

Appraisability is the worthiness of appraisal, the deservingness of being inwardly praised or blamed. In metaphorical terms, it is the condition of being such that there are "credits" or "debits" in one's "personal ledger," so that one is worthy of being judged to have such credits or debits. If one has credits, one is laudable; if one has debits, one is culpable. My aim is to draw up a detailed account of the conditions under which one incurs laudability and culpability.

I start in Section 3.1 with culpability. I point out that, just as one may enjoy direct or indirect freedom with respect to an event, so one may be directly or indirectly culpable for it. I claim, roughly, that one is directly culpable for willing an event (one can never be directly culpable for anything but a volition) just in case one strictly freely willed it in the belief that one would thereby do wrong. I then state in detail what I mean by this. (I do not yet defend the claim; that comes in Chapter 4.) In so doing, I distinguish between callousness (roughly, foreseeing but not intending wrongdoing), malice (roughly, intending wrongdoing), and satanic wickedness (roughly, intending to do wrong for the sake of doing wrong). I point out that direct culpability varies in degree according to whether the agent is merely callous, or malicious, or satanically wicked. It also varies according to the seriousness of the wrongdoing envisaged and the perceived likelihood of doing wrong. I claim that it does *not* vary according to the degree of freedom which the agent enjoys; for strict freedom does not come in degrees (in the relevant way), and, I claim, broad freedom is irrelevant to ascriptions of appraisability.

I then turn in Section 3.2 to direct laudability and claim, roughly, that one is directly laudable for willing an event just in case one strictly freely willed it for the sake of doing right, but not in the belief that one would thereby do one's duty. There is an asymmetry between the accounts of direct culpability and direct laudability, inasmuch as only the "positive" analogue to satanic wickedness confers laudability on the agent; the analogues to malice and callousness do not. This constitutes a pretty strict account of the conditions of direct laudability; I seek to defend it in Chapter 4. I point out that direct laudability comes in degrees—not, of course, in virtue of the distinction between the analogues to callousness, malice, and wickedness, but just in terms of the perceived degree and likelihood of doing right.

I stress "perceived." My view is that direct laudability and culpability are *not* functions of doing right and wrong, but of willing to do (what one *perceives* as) right and wrong; and so one can be laudable (culpable) without doing right (wrong), and one can do right (wrong) without being laudable (culpable). It is clearly appropriate to characterize this view as an *internalist* view of appraisability.

In Section 3.3 I turn to a discussion of indirect laudability and culpability. I argue for a claim that I take to be most important, namely, that indirect laudability and culpability are essentially empty, being wholly parasitic on direct laudability and culpability. Just as one may be indirectly free with respect to an event and yet one's freedom does not substantially extend beyond the volition of which the event is a consequence and with respect to which one is directly free, so too one may be indirectly appraisable for an event and yet one's appraisability does not substantially extend beyond the volition of which the event is a consequence and for which one is directly appraisable. The occurrence of events as a consequence of one's volitions does not occasion any further entries in one's ledger beyond those already occasioned by the volitions themselves. This leaves us with a certain leeway as to how to account for indirect appraisability. I distinguish various positions, stating my preference for what I call the Internalist Position, a thesis that reflects my internalist account of direct appraisability and highlights the essential emptiness of indirect appraisability. I then point out that one may be appraisable in many ways for a single event and also appraisable in many ways at one and the same time.

There is a middle ground between laudability and culpability; I call it indifference-worthiness and discuss it in Section 3.4. This is a sort of neutrality which matches, not the absence of an inscription in one's ledger, nor the inscription of a "credit" and a "debit" which "cancel each other out," but rather the inscription of a "zero" (neither a "credit" nor a "debit") in one's ledger.

I conclude the main part of Chapter 3 with a summary in Section 3.5 of my findings as to the conditions of appraisability. I reiterate: a person is substantially appraisable for an event just in case he is directly appraisable for it. I then include a final section (3.6) on the distinction between a justification and an excuse. I note that there are two basic types of excuse—a radical one, which erases culpability by erasing appraisability; and a regular one, which erases culpability but not appraisability—and I argue that one can have both a justification and an excuse for an event. I also point out that, insofar as one can be culpable without doing wrong, having a justification for what one does does *not* automatically defeat an ascription of culpability. Finally, I distinguish between dejustification and disentitlement, the analogues to justification and excuse that concern laudability.

Objections and amplification. In Chapter 4, I entertain objections to the account of appraisability given in Chapter 3 and, in so doing, endeavor to amplify that account.

First, in Sections 4.1 and 4.2, I deal with the claim that the preceding account of appraisability is defective in its implications with respect to ignorance and negligence, insofar as it seems to imply that one cannot be appraisable (in particular, culpable) for actions performed in ignorance or negligently. I point out that the claim is mistaken. While it is true that, according to the account, there are ways in which ignorance and negligence (or, rather, something akin to negligence, which I call neglect) cannot be culpable, there are also ways in which they can be culpable. In the course of the discussion, I distinguish various modes of ignorance and negligence and also distinguish negligence from rashness and recklessness.

I turn in Section 4.3 to the objection that my account of appraisability implies that one is as appraisable for failed attempts as for successful ones, and that this claim is false. I acknowledge the implication but argue that the claim is not false.

In Section 4.4, I argue that appraisability for omissions is always indirect. I then consider the claim that one cannot be responsible for one's omissions and the consequences thereof, or that at least one cannot be *as* responsible for them as one is for one's actions and the consequences thereof. I conclude that there is no reason to accept this claim.

It is often contended that, when one shares responsibility for an event with another person, one's responsibility is diminished simply in virtue of this fact. My account implies otherwise, and in Section 4.5 I entertain the objection that it ought not to do so. I acknowledge that one's responsibility *can* be diminished in cases of group action and omission, but I argue that it *need* not be. In the course of this discussion I touch on the question of intervening agency, and again I argue that no diminution (let alone elimination, as is sometimes claimed) of responsibility is necessarily occasioned by this phenomenon.

I next consider, in Section 4.6, the objection that compulsion (that is, the lack of broad freedom) can affect appraisability, and yet my account implies otherwise. I argue that, while compulsion might on occasion diminish wrongdoing, it does not diminish culpability if the agent does not regard it as diminishing wrongdoing. For broad unfreedom, when not accompanied by strict unfreedom, does not entail that the agent literally must do what he does; and if he strictly freely, but broadly unfreely, does something that he regards as wrong, then he is culpable.

I then turn, in Section 4.7, to a discussion of the power of mental disorders to excuse. I note that it is quite clear that sometimes they do excuse, but it is also quite clear that sometimes they do not excuse. I note further that, when they do excuse, this is so simply by virtue of their involving excusing conditions already explicitly accommodated by my account of appraisability, and hence that the account requires no modification in this regard.

It might be thought that appraisability is a matter of an evaluation of one's character, that the entries in one's personal ledger amount to a character report. In Section 4.8, I argue that this is not so, that appraisability attaches to one's self as opposed to one's character, and that there is no essential connection between appraisability and character. But I acknowledge that there can be a contingent connection, in that sometimes one can be responsible for one's character—although, for the most part, one's character is beyond one's control and hence not something for which one is generally appraisable. However, I point out in Section 4.9 that, in so saying, I do not wish to deny that an agent's character is open to moral evaluation, even that part of his character that lies beyond his control; I wish merely to observe that such evaluation is not a matter of what I have called appraisal. Indeed, an agent may manifest many virtues and vices that are simply not pertinent to laudability and culpability, although they are admirable and reprehensible in some other way. It is most important to note this limitation to the evaluation involved in appraisal. Otherwise, one is likely to make the mistake either of denying the link between responsibility and control and then ascribing responsibility too liberally, or of insisting on the link between responsibility and control and then denying the admirability and reprehensibility of the virtues and vices.

But is control a condition of responsibility? It is to this question that I turn in Section 4.10, and I argue that standard control (which requires, in the current vernacular, alternate possibilities) is not necessary for responsibility, although curtailed control (*i.e.,* freedom) is necessary. I point out that, if this is so, the traditional debate between so-called compatibilists and incompatibilists (on whether or not determinism is compatible with freedom of will or action) is little affected.

Finally, in Section 4.11 I raise the question of what the relation is between appraisability and luck. Recently it has been argued that moral responsibility eschews luck (for where there is luck there is no control) but that, luck being ineliminable, it follows that moral responsibility is nonexistent. I reject this argument by distinguishing two types of luck—resultant and situational—and pointing out in just what respects they are ineliminable (complete control is an impossibility, but control *tout court* is not) and just how this might affect ascriptions of appraisability. The existence of resultant luck, I acknowledge, implies the essential emptiness of indirect appraisability, but not the nonexistence of direct appraisability. I am unsure how the existence of situational luck affects ascriptions of appraisability; but, if it has an effect at all, it is that our everyday ascriptions are far too few, not far too numerous—granting, that is, that people sometimes (indeed, often) do act strictly freely.

Liability. Chapter 5 is concerned with that second species of retrospective responsibility that I call liability. In Section 5.1, I state that one is liable for an event just in case one deserves, in virtue of being appraisable for it, either to experience pleasure or pain or, more particularly, to be overtly praised or blamed for it. Overt praise and blame are public expressions of private appraisal; I call them commendation and censure and distinguish two types, which I call weak and strong. Strong censure involves acting on the intention to make someone suffer as he is deemed to deserve. Punishment, in the full-blown sense, is a type of strong censure. (An analogous point holds for reward and strong commendation.)

A major question is what it means to ascribe desert to someone in such contexts. It is this which occupies my attention in Sections 5.2 and 5.3. In Section 5.2, I distinguish between various modes of desert ("deserves," "deserves not," "does not deserve," "does not deserve not") and point out that there is often a significant difference to be noted between two superficially similar statements (*e.g.*, between "he does not deserve to be censured" and "he deserves not to be censured"). I then inquire into the connection between desert and rights, noting that desert sometimes, but not always, confers rights. And I point out that considerations of desert constitute just one of the elements that go toward the overall justifiability of a course of action and that they are in principle overridable.

I then turn my attention in Section 5.3 to what it would mean to say that someone deserves, in virtue of being culpable, to suffer or to be censured. (I call this the thesis of moral retributivism, which is to be distinguished from the thesis of logical retributivism, according to which one cannot punish someone whom one believes inculpable.) I point out that there are grave difficulties in understanding the claim, difficulties having to do with time of desert and of suffering, way and source of suffering, and, above all, matching degree of suffering to degree of culpability. But I also point out that these difficulties are not confined to this claim but also affect the claim that someone deserves, in virtue of being inculpable, not to suffer or to be censured. (I call this the thesis of moral protectionism.) I leave unresolved the issues of whether moral retributivism is true and of whether moral protectionism is true, although I state my strong inclination to accept the latter. I then briefly discuss two related issues—those of mercy and strict liability. With respect to the former, I distinguish several types of mercy and discuss how mercy is to be distinguished from forgiveness. With respect to strict liability, I distinguish two types of what I call strict victimization, point out why such victimization appears to be morally repugnant, and then emphasize what I take to be a very important fact, namely, that much of current legal punishment in effect constitutes strict victimization and is, for this reason and to this extent, morally repugnant.

Finally, in a departure from the detailed format which has gone before, I end, in Section 5.4, with a sweeping discussion of when it is that punishment is overall justified. My aim in this final section is to emphasize the fact that, even if retributivism and protectionism are both true, it can sometimes happen that the culpable (and so, too, the liable) ought not to be punished and the inculpable (and so, too, the nonliable) ought to be punished. In this context, many of the conditions earlier deemed irrelevant to appraisability (and so, too, to liability) can come into play. Especially, luck can make a difference.

1.3 Implications of the Inquiry

As I have intimated already in this chapter and also in the Preface, and as will become increasingly obvious in Chapters 3, 4, and 5, many of the conclusions that I shall be drawing concerning the nature of moral responsibility will appear quite radical. I take this to be an important feature of the book, although it should not be thought that I started work on it with the purpose of being provocative. On the contrary, my goal has always been simply to try to lay out in detail and with precision what the nature of moral responsibility is and what its ties with other concepts are. It was only after I began my inquiry that its radical implications began to emerge, and frankly, I resisted many of them for quite some time, insofar as they undermine much of our common practice of ascribing responsibility—including much of my practice, as I have habitually engaged, and sometimes inconsistently continue to engage, in it.

It must be noted that these implications are *not* to be attributed to my adopting certain esoteric assumptions about the nature of action, freedom, or whatever. While I have said that the material following Chapter 2 presupposes the material in Chapter 2, and while I acknowledge that much of the material in Chapter 2 is both technical and controversial, this point must now be put in perspective. First, the accounts of action and of freedom presented in Chapter 2 are certainly technical and, in their detail, both novel and controversial—I have no wish to deny this—but, in their broad outline, they are far from new. On the contrary, an account of action according to which action involves some mental cause of some (usually) physical event—and the account that I present is of this sort— has proved to be, in the history of the philosophy of action, far and away the most popular sort of account. Moreover, it seems to be the sort of account that common sense endorses. (Of course, it has had its detractors, but then what philosophical theory has not?) In addition, an account of freedom of action according to which such freedom is anchored in freedom with respect to the mental element in action—and the account that I present is of this sort—is a natural corollary to the mental-cause account of action and, while it has not been adopted by all those who accept the mental-cause account, it has been accepted by a great many. Secondly, and even more importantly, while the conclusions which I draw concerning moral responsibility do, in their detail, presuppose the account that I give of action and of freedom, in many instances these conclusions, in their broad outline, presuppose these accounts *not at all*. On the contrary, the conclusions can be traced to the following general assumptions: that moral responsibility requires freedom; that direct freedom is to be distinguished from indirect freedom; that culpability is to be distinguished from wrongdoing; and that appraisability is to be distinguished from liability. These four assumptions must, I think, be accepted *even if* the particular accounts of action and of freedom that I propose are rejected; and I shall contend that these four assumptions *alone* yield many of the radical results to which I have alluded.

So let there be no mistake about this. If the conclusions that I draw are to be rejected, this cannot be accomplished by a curt dismissal of the particular accounts of action and of freedom that I adopt. It can only be accomplished by finding fault with the four assumptions mentioned or with my reasoning from these assumptions. As for my reasoning from these assumptions, this will be presented at the appropriate points in later chapters. As for the assumptions themselves, while I confess that I do not know how to render the first plausible to someone who does not already find it so, I shall defend it against its best-known attacks in Sections 4.9 and 4.10. Moreover, this assumption seems to be one so extremely widely held among philosophers and nonphilosophers alike that I do not hesitate to make it myself. I shall try to say something to render the other three assumptions plausible, although this attempt too seems to me somewhat otiose in that almost everyone will, I think, accept them on reflection.

I have said that many of the conclusions that I reach undermine much of our common practice of ascribing responsibility (of praising, blaming, rewarding, and punishing). They do this in two ways. Sometimes they imply that our common practice is too liberal, in that we ascribe responsibility where there is none (or ascribe a greater degree of responsibility than is warranted). Such conclusions I shall call *deflationary* (with respect to our common practice). Sometimes they imply that our common practice is too conservative, in that we fail to ascribe responsibility where there is some (or ascribe a lesser degree of responsibility than is warranted). Such conclusions I shall call *inflationary* (with respect to our common practice). Of course, it is an interesting question why our common practice should thus diverge from the conclusions that I draw insofar as these conclusions are apparently yielded by apparently unexceptionable assumptions. I do not pretend to have an answer to this question, however; I shall rest content simply with highlighting the divergence. I could go further and claim that, insofar as the assumptions in question are obvious, they must be implicitly accepted by any (thinking) person who ascribes responsibility, so that our common practice is doubly indictable: not only is it *mistaken,* but it is *false to its own presuppositions*. But, while I think that this charge has much to be said for it, I shall not press it; for it is not clear to me just what is involved in an assumption's being "implicitly accepted," and it suffices for my purposes simply to demonstrate the mistaken nature of much of our common practice of ascribing responsibility.

Notes

1. See, *e.g.*, Hart (1968), pp. 211–2; Baier (1970), pp. 103–7; Glover (1970), p. 19; Audi (1974), p. 2.

2. *Cf.* Hart (1968), pp. 214–5, on what he calls 'causal responsibility.'

3. *Cf.* Hart (1968), pp. 212–4, on what he calls 'role-responsibility'; Baier (1970), p. 104, on what he calls 'task-responsibility.'

4. *Cf.* Hart (1968), p. 213; Audi (1974), p. 2, on what he calls 'dispositional responsibility'; Haydon (1978) for an elaboration of this account.

5. Others have used them thus. See, *e.g.*, Feinberg (1970), p. 25; Morris (1976), pp. 118–19.

6. See Hart (1968), p. 215. *Cf.* Beardsley (1969), p. 39; Feinberg (1970), p. 130ff.

7. *Cf.* Edwards (1969), Chapter 4, where the distinction between personal and causal responsibility is not made sufficiently clear.

8. *Cf.* Baier (1985), pp. 11–12.

9. On the various types of blame, see Kenner (1967) and Kleinig (1973), pp. 69–70.

10. For example, Baier (1970) discusses what he calls 'accountability,' 'answerability,' and 'liability.' Some of these categories are employed also by: Hart (1968), pp. 211–12; Audi (1974), p. 2; Fletcher (1978), p. 459; and others. And Hart also talks of 'capacity-responsibility.'

11. A recent example: Donagan (1977), pp. 54–55. But see: Brandt (1958), p. 8; Beardsley (1969), especially p. 35; Feinberg (1970), Chapter 2; Glover (1970), pp. 56–57; and Jensen (1984), p. 324.

12. *Cf.* Baier (1985), pp. 6–7.

13. *Cf.* Downie (1969); Bates (1970–71); and Lewis (1972). For an apparently contrary view, see Cooper (1968, 1969); Feinberg (1970), p. 248ff.; Held (1972b); and French (1984). I say "apparently" because the initial appearance may be misleading. For example, Held has recently articulated a view according to which the sort of responsibility that may be ascribed to groups is fundamentally different from the sort of responsibility that may be ascribed to individuals. See Held (1986).

14. But not always. See Taylor (1976).

15. But see Matson (1956).

16. At least, I shall try to do so for appraisability. I shall treat liability in somewhat less detail in Chapter 5.

17. I have undertaken this in Zimmerman (1984).

2

BACKGROUND

MORAL RESPONSIBILITY of the variety that is at issue in this book is responsibility that a person bears toward some event. And it arises only in the context of free action. Some account, therefore, of events and of free action is required as background to our discussion of moral responsibility.

In this chapter I shall present material in brief, rough, and blunt fashion. It is indispensable to a full understanding of what follows later, but a complete presentation and defense of it cannot be undertaken here. Such a treatment of much of the material has been undertaken elsewhere, however.[1]

2.1 Action

Events. I take events to be finely grained, abstract, proposition-like entities that directly concern individual things. For example, the sun's shining is an event, as are Socrates' sitting, his walking, and his dying; but red's being a color and two plus two's equalling four are not events. Insofar as they are finely grained, events are numerous. Many distinct events may occur at the same time and place. For instance, Jones's raising his arm, his flipping the light switch, his illuminating the room, and his alerting the prowler may all, on occasion, co-occur; but they will remain distinct. Such a treatment of events may appear to multiply their number beyond necessity; I deny this. In particular, even where Jones's flipping the light switch, his flipping it with gusto, his flipping it in haste, and so on, all co-occur and are all distinct, we may say that only one flipping occurs (thus preserving at least one way in which we would normally count events). Insofar as they are abstract, events exist necessarily, but they may or may not occur. The sun's shining on Boston exists (and hence is available for contemplation, discussion, and so on), but

16

does not occur, when it is nighttime in Boston, or when Boston is covered by cloud. Recurrence may be taken literally; that is, one and the same event may occur, then cease to occur, then occur again (all the while existing, of course).

I do not pretend that we *must* take events to be finely grained and abstract; a treatment of them as coarsely grained or as concrete may be defensible. But I do claim these advantages for the treatment that I advocate: it can be worked out in considerable detail; it allows for a precise account of certain logical relations (such as implication, conjunction, disjunction, negation, and so on) between events; it allows us to dispense with talk of events being "under a description" (which is necessary only where they are coarsely individuated); and it allows us to dispense with a distinction between event-types and event-tokens (which is necessary only where events are taken to exist only when they occur).

Action. Roughly, a person acts just in case he brings about an event; and he brings about an event just in case some volition of his is causally efficacious in an apppropriate way. Somewhat more precisely (where S is an agent, e an event, and T and T' times):

(P2.1)* S brings about e relative to T and T' if and only if, for some event f,
             (a) S wills f at T, and
             (b) this volition is the cause of e's occurring at T'.

The simplest sort of illustration of such bringing about is where e is identical with f. For example, let e and f be S's arm's rising; then S raises his arm just in case he brings about his arm's rising, and this occurs when he wills its rising and this volition is the cause of its rising. This account of action—while conforming with the traditional, volitional approach—is still very imprecise. I shall not fill in the details here, but the following points should be noted.

First, on this picture of action, the person's bringing about e is the action; e is *not* a consequence of the action but is, in a sense, "internal" to it; I call e the "issue" of the action. Still, e is, of course, a consequence of the person's *volition*. (I shall discuss the notion of a volition shortly.) Moreover, what is the issue of one action may be a consequence of another; for example, a death is the issue of a killing but a consequence of a shooting.

Second, no particular relation between e and f is specified in (P2.1). While it would be too restrictive to say that e and f *must* be identical (as they were in the arm-raising example)—for this would be almost tantamount to saying that all action is intentional action—, it is in fact too

---

*All proposition numbers are preceded by "P."

liberal to leave the relation between e and f completely open. But there is no need to pursue this here.

Third, the relation between T and T' is left unspecified. Clearly, T cannot be later than T', but must it be earlier? I shall henceforth assume that it must.

Fourthly, a notion, related to but distinct from that at issue in (P2.1), may be roughly accounted for thus:

(P2.2) S helps to bring about e relative to T and T' if and only if, for some event f,
           (a) S wills f at T, and
           (b) this volition is a cause of e's occurring at T'.

The distinction between (P2.1) and (P2.2) of course consists in the distinction between something's being "the" cause and something's being "a" cause of something else. This is a familiar distinction. For example, under normal conditions, if I raise my arm, then some volition of mine is the cause of my arm's rising. But if my arm is very heavy (loaded down, perhaps, with weights), then I may need some help with raising it; and, if such help is forthcoming and my arm rises, then my volition will be "a" cause—a causally contributory factor—but perhaps not "the" cause of the rising. Just how to make this distinction between "a" and "the" cause precise is quite unclear to me; I am not even sure whether it can be done in a purely nonnormative fashion, or whether the distinction is somehow normatively dependent on the context in which it is to be employed. Still, the distinction is a common and important one, and it is one to which I shall return later in this chapter.

Fifthly, another notion, related to but distinct from those at issue in (P2.1) and (P2.2), may be roughly accounted for thus:

(P2.3) S contributes to e relative to T and T' if and only if, for some event f,
           (a) S wills f at T, and
           (b) e's occurring at T' is a consequence of this volition.

The distinction between (P2.1) and (P2.2) on the one hand, and (P2.3) on the other, lies in the term "consequence." In the cases so far given (of arm-raising, killing, and so on) all the consequences have been causal, but there are cases where they are perhaps not causal. For example, an event f may be said to be a consequence of an event e if the former would not have occurred (then and there) had not the latter occurred (then and there)[2]—as, for example, when Smith, as a consequence of Jones's urging, relents and patches up his differences with Brown; but for Jones's urging, Smith would not have relented. This "but for" sense of "consequence" is perfectly proper, and it remains so even if (as I think[3]) the notion of a *causal* consequence is distinct from this notion of a "but for" or—as I shall call it—*simple* consequence. And if the notions of a simple consequence and a causal consequence are distinct, we may distinguish two types of contribution: bringing about (or helping to bring about), where the issue of the action is a causal consequence of the volition, and simple contribution, where the issue is a simple consequence of the volition.

Finally, group action is possible in the following sense: an event may be a consequence both of a volition of some agent S and also of a volition of some distinct agent S'. That is, both S and S' may *contribute to* some event e; indeed, both S and S' may *help to bring about e*. I am not sure whether both S and S' may *bring about e*, in the sense that *each* of them brings it about (rather than in the sense of their bringing it about *together*, which is certainly possible[4]): this depends on how the notion of being-"the"-cause is to be construed, and especially on whether more than one event may be "the" cause of some event. At any rate, it should be noted that group action comes in various modes: it may be either *sequential* or *simultaneous*, and it may be either *overfull* or *brimming*. It is sequential if the individuals involved act *seriatim*, as in the assassination of Caesar; otherwise it is simultaneous, as in Caesar's pall-bearing.[5] And it is overfull if one of the volitions concerned is such that, while the outcome (*i.e.*, the common consequence of the volitions, the issue of the group action) is a *causal* consequence of the volition, it is not a *simple* consequence of the volition; otherwise it is brimming.[6]

Volition. Clearly, the concept of volition plays a crucial role in the foregoing account of action. There is absolutely nothing unduly mysterious about this concept. I take a volition simply to be a *decision* or *choice* (not necessarily based on deliberation but still practical in nature and made in light of certain background beliefs) that some event occur, a decision which is *accompanied by an intention* that it (the decision) be causally efficacious with respect to the event in question.[7] Volition, then, is a *propositional* attitude. But one may, for short, speak of willing an *event e*; this may be taken to mean that one wills that e occur.

There is a division among those who champion volitions as essential to action. Some view them, as I do, as a type of decision[8] (it is simply because not all decisions are volitions that I use the technical term "volition"), while others view them as a type of desire-*cum*-belief.[9] This is no place to try to defend in detail the claim that volitions are decisions rather than complexes of desires and beliefs, but I shall list here some of the reasons for making this claim. First, volitions *qua* decisions help make sense of practical reasoning; they constitute the endorsement of one course of action in preference to others—and thus are *choices*—, such endorsement being the intended and typical conclusion of practical reasoning. (This is not to say that all action is the deliberate product of practical reasoning. Even in the limiting case of pure spontaneity, however, I would claim that a choice is involved, a spontaneous opting for this rather than that.) Second, volitions *qua* decisions help explain the phenomenon of weakness of will; such explanation seems not to be afforded by appeal to the agent's strongest desire(s)(-*cum*-beliefs). Third, volitions *qua* decisions help explain action in light of incommensurate desires; where the agent has various conflicting desires, which he does not find commensurable, the explanation of action again seems not to be afforded (solely) by appeal to his desires(-*cum*-beliefs). Fourth, volitions *qua* decisions essentially involve, as I shall shortly elaborate, intention, while desires and beliefs do not; thus they help explain the essential intentionality of action. Fifth, an agent need not desire to do everything that he sets out to do, unless "desire" is used very broadly (as "want" often is); much of what we do, we do reluctantly. Finally, since freedom of action seems *not* to require alternate possibilities (see Section 4.10), one needs an alternative account of what is required, and one way to attempt this is to invoke the concept of freedom of *will* (see the next section of this chapter), where willing is understood in terms of decision-making. It is worth noting, also, that an appeal to volitions *qua* decisions in the explanation of action does not preclude an appeal to desires and/or beliefs; for volitions are themselves often (but, and this is part of my point, not always) to be explained in terms of desires and/or beliefs. Of course, even if all of this is granted, none of this shows that action *requires* volitions *qua* decisions, but only that much action involves them. But here I would just say that, if one accepts that action requires volitions, one gets a simpler, unified theory of action. Is there nonetheless reason to reject the claim? Perhaps unthinking and/or habitual action would appear to provide such reason. I tend to think that it does not—but I shall return to this in a moment.

There are several modes of volition. One may will an event e, $e.g.$, one may will that one's arm rise; one may will e for the purpose of some event f, $e.g.$, one may will that one's arm rise in order that Smith be thereby alerted, or one may will that one's mouth remain closed in order that one thereby fulfill a promise not to talk for five minutes, and so on; and one may will e for the sake of f (that is, will e for the purpose of f and f for the purpose of nothing further). If one is successful, then e will be the issue of an action but not, strictly speaking and under normal conditions, an action itself. (One wills one's arm's rising, and not one's raising one's arm; for the latter, being an action, already comprises a volition.)[10] But f, being the intended consequence of e (at least, in those cases where it is not identical with e), may or may not be an action.

I take it that, if the following is true:

(P2.4) S wills e for the purpose of f,

then so too are the following:

(P2.5) S considers both e and f,

(P2.6) S intends both that e occur and that f occur,

(P2.7) S believes (at least dispositionally) that he has control both
              over e and over f.

These implications deserve discussion.[11]

The claim that (P2.4) implies (P2.5) is in fact problematic. It is here
that the phenomena of unthinking and habitual actions pose questions.
When we perform such actions, are we completely oblivious of what it is
we intend to do, or is our attentiveness merely diminished? I am not sure
what the proper answer to this question is. But note that, however it is
answered, we are not constrained to reject the claim that action requires
volition; we are constrained, at most, to reject the claim that (P2.4)
implies (P2.5). At least, this is how I think the matter should be viewed.
While I acknowledge that the issue is controversial, there seems to me
nothing incoherent in the claim that one is oblivious (or, at least, not
fully, occurrently mindful) of what one intends to do, and I would add to
this that there is nothing incoherent in the claim that one is oblivious (or,
at least, not fully, occurrently mindful) of what one decides to do. The
phrase "unconscious decision" does not strike me as self-contradictory.
If it is not, then, in the interest of a unified theory of action, I would urge
that all action, even unthinking and habitual action (granting that such
"action" really is genuine action—and I would grant this), involves a
volition *qua* decision, even though the agent is oblivious (or, at least, not
fully, occurrently mindful) of the volition in question. And so, if we are
sometimes not at all mindful of what we intend to do but act anyway,
then, while the claim that action requires volition is not to be rejected,
the claim that (P2.4) implies (P2.5) is to be rejected or, at best, revised;
but if we are always mindful (albeit often only dimly) of what we intend
to do when we act, then I see no reason for such rejection or revision.

The claim that (P2.4) implies (P2.6) is important. Since action requires
volition, and volition intention, we may say that, whenever one acts, one
intends to do something (although we cannot say that, whatever one does,
one does intentionally or even intends to do).[12] For example, even if I
accidentally knock over the coffee-pot when reaching for a second cup of
coffee, I will have intentionally reached out for that second cup. This is
close to saying what others, adopting a coarsely grained ontology of
action, say when they assert that every action is "intentional under some
description."[13] This is *not* to say that every action is "desired under some
description." As noted before, it seems that one need not desire to do
everything that one sets out to do; for one may act reluctantly. But even
what one does reluctantly, one may do intentionally. Intention, then,

even if not desire, is, I believe, necessary to all action; and traditional moral concern with what it is that the agent intends when he acts is right on target. The theme that "it's the thought that counts" will be seen to be a prominent one in the "internalist" theory of moral responsibility that follows.

The claim that (P2.4) implies (P2.7) is also important. Freedom may be an illusion, but it is an inescapable one. Something like this implication has been asserted by very many philosophers.[14] The sort of control that I have in mind I shall, in Section 2.3, describe as *strict, standard* control. If S is in control of e, then e is, in a rough but intuitive sense, "up to him." Carl Ginet has put the point well as follows:

Realizing, as I do, that I do not at the moment *have* a choice between floating off the floor to hover in mid-air and not doing so, I can do nothing now that would constitute either choosing to do so or choosing not to do so. However vividly I might imagine hovering, however seriously I might say to myself "No, I won't do it just now," and whatever feelings of relief or regret I may have for a pleasure missed, it will all be a farce and not really choosing not to hover, in any sense, as long as I am aware that it simply is not open to me now to hover off the floor.[15]

Finally, a distinction must be drawn between S's willing e and S's being willing that e occur. One way to understand the latter (clearly not the only way—what follows is a narrow construal, and so semistipulative— but it is a way that will prove very important later) is roughly as follows:

(P2.8) S is willing at T that e occur at T' if and only if, for some event f, S wills f at T, in the belief that
          (a) e's occurring at T' will or may be a consequence of this volition, and
          (b) e's occurring at T' would be less likely if he were not to will f at T.[16]

And, insofar as (P2.4) implies (P2.6), I take it that it also implies:

(P2.9) S is willing both that e occur and that f occur.

Attempts. There are, I believe, two main sorts of attempts. An attempt, in the broad sense, just is a volition; in a narrower sense, an attempt is an efficacious, and at least partly successful, volition. Efforts are attempts of the latter sort. For instance, a paralyzed person may, in the broad sense, try (make an attempt) to raise his arm (if he is unaware of his paralysis), in the sense that he may will his arm's rising; in the narrower sense, he is unable even to try. In the narrower sense, a person may be said to have attempted to lift a heavy object if he has succeeded in doing so or, at least, succeeded in doing something (perhaps only bracing his muscles) toward this goal.

Omissions. Despite the prominence of the term "act of omission," omissions ought not to be thought of as actions of a certain sort. One often acts, but need not act, when one omits to do something. Roughly:

(P2.10)   S omits to bring about e if and only if S can, but does not, bring about e.

At least, this may be called the basic sense of "omit." More restrictive senses may be identified by supplementing this account in various ways; e.g., one may be said legally to omit to do something just in case one omits, in the basic sense, to do it but ought, legally, to do it. The sense of "can bring about e" in (P2.10) is that of being strictly free to bring about e. This notion will be discussed more fully in the next section.

Intentional omission is more complicated. It cannot be accomplished (I believe, but shall not here argue) without intentionally doing something in the place of that which one omits to do. Thus all intentional omission indirectly involves volition. Indeed, we may say:

(P2.11)   If S intentionally omits to bring about e, then there is some event f such that S wills f for the purpose of not-e,

where "not-e" signifies a "negative event," viz., the negation of e.[17] For example, if one intentionally omits to bring about the light's going on (that is, one intentionally omits to turn on the light), then one intentionally brings about (and thus wills) some event f for the purpose of the light's not going on. (One may, for instance, intentionally remain seated, thus making it impossible for one to turn on the light.)

We often talk of the consequences of omissions. These are simple consequences of the negative events—the not-doings—which omissions comprise; they are events whose occurrence the agent fails to prevent by virtue of his omission. For example, if I omit to extinguish a cigarette, the ensuing fire is a simple consequence of my omission; I could have prevented the fire but did not; it would not have occurred but for my not extinguishing the cigarette. Some claim that the consequences of omissions are *causal* consequences, but I find this dubious.[18] At any rate, it is clear that the consequences of omissions may be morally significant.

Not only may omissions have other events as consequences, they may (in virtue of the not-doings which they comprise) be consequences, either causal or simple, of other events. The manner in which they may be causal consequences of other events differs somewhat from the manner in which "normal," "positive" events may be causal consequences. For instance, an omission may be the consequence of a volition, as in the case of intentional omission, but *only* by way of a "normal" event. If I intentionally omit to turn on the light, then some volition of mine causes some "normal" event (e.g., my hand's remaining at my side), and this "normal" event is (in the circumstances) causally incompatible with my turning on the light. Hence, the negative event of my not turning on the light is a causal consequence (*via* a somewhat circuitous route) of my volition, and in virtue of this my omitting to turn on the light may also be said to be such a consequence.[19]

Finally, as with group action, there can be group omission. This occurs when two or more people, who could engage in group action, do not do so. As before, such omission may be sequential or simultaneous, overfull or brimming, although it should be noted that there cannot be group omission which is both sequential and brimming. If someone S has already omitted to do something to prevent a certain outcome, and if his doing this was necessary for the outcome's not occurring (which, by hypothesis, it was, since the group omission is brimming), then no other person S' can subsequently omit to prevent this outcome; for no one is any longer in a position to prevent the outcome, and yet (according to (P2.10)) being in such a position is required for the omission to prevent it.

2.2 Freedom

Two types of freedom. There are at least as many senses of "free" as there are of "responsible," but one can isolate two senses of the former which are particularly pertinent to that one sense of the latter (*viz.*, moral, retrospective, personal responsibility) which is the present focus of discussion. I shall call these *strict freedom* and *broad freedom*.

Consider this familiar example. A man walks into a bank, goes up to a teller, points a gun at the teller, and orders him to hand over all the money in the till. The teller then does so—but does he *freely* do so? I suggest that we say: yes, in the strict sense; no, in the broad sense. That is, if the teller, in defense of his action, were subsequently to say, "I had no (other) choice; there was nothing (else) I could do," we should recognize what he says to be, broadly speaking, true but, strictly speaking, false.[20]

In my view, what informs freedom of action, whether strict or broad, is freedom of the will. Roughly:

(P2.12) S freely brings about e relative to T and T' if and only if, for some event f,
           (a) S freely wills f at T, and
           (b) this volition is the cause of e's occurring at T'.

In addition, just as (P2.12) is analogous to (P2.1), so accounts of freely helping to bring about, analogous to (P2.2), and freely contributing, analogous to (P2.3), may be given.

If one strictly freely wills an event, then (and only then) one's volition is, in a sense, "truly one's own"; one is, in a sense, the "source" of one's volition (and hence of the action that comprises it). This is true of the teller in the foregoing example, even though he was strongly coerced to act as he did and even though he would have preferred not to be in a situation where he "had to" hand over the money.

Just what strict and broad freedom consist in is, of course, an exceedingly complex question. For the most part, the former has been the focus of the debate between compatibilists and incompatibilists (although it has often not been adequately distinguished from the latter, especially by compatibilists); and the latter has been at least part of the focus of social theorists. I believe that I have some idea as to how best to analyze the concept of strict freedom; but I favor an incompatibilist analysis, and I certainly do *not* want to insist on its accuracy here, for *nothing* that I shall say will presuppose the truth of incompatibilism. And I really have very little idea as to how to analyze the concept of broad freedom. Clearly, broad freedom is lacking when one chooses between (perhaps merely apparent) alternatives, all of which are repugnant to a certain degree and in a certain way to oneself. But just what *sort* of repugnance is at issue, I am not at all sure. The teller found both handing and not handing over the money repugnant and, for this reason, acted broadly unfreely. But does someone act broadly unfreely when he finds both staying in and getting out of bed in the morning repugnant? Is this just a minor episode of broad unfreedom, or not an episode of broad unfreedom at all? How does one tell? Or again, if someone makes you an offer that you "cannot" refuse—and I mean an offer, not a threat—is your broad freedom thereby diminished or eliminated?[21] I do not know how to answer these questions.[22]

Moreover, it is difficult to know how to classify certain cases of apparent unfreedom. I assume that machines operate and that lower animals act strictly unfreely and thus that, if we are essentially like machines or like lower animals, then we act strictly unfreely also.[23] The question is whether we are essentially this way or, if not, whether we ever act as if we were. I suppose that certain conditions can render us strictly unfree on occasion—brain surgery, perhaps; or hypnosis; or certain neuroses or obessions—but it is difficult to tell. Certain neuroses or obsessions, at least, would appear to render us broadly, rather than strictly, unfree, operating in a manner similar to that of coercion (however exactly that operates). And there are other cases where we would diagnose unfreedom—such as buying a drink, having been subjected to subliminal advertising; or such as taking on, and apparently cheerfully acting on, the ideals of one's captors—but where it is unclear whether it is strict, broad, or some other type of unfreedom that is at issue.

Whatever the proper analyses of strict and broad freedom, it is clear that the latter is in a sense dependent on the former. Let us suppose that hypnotism robs one of strict freedom,[24] and let us now suppose that the teller in our original example was hypnotized into handing over the money. Any threat with which the teller was faced must then have been quite idle; it cannot have operated so as to have forced him to hand over the money, since (by hypothesis) he strictly had to do so anyway. Or suppose that the teller was hypnotized into *not* handing over the money. The threat must again have been quite idle; for again it cannot have operated so as to have forced him to hand over the money. Of course, the threat may well not have been idle in the sense of scaring the teller out of his wits; but the poor man will not have *acted on* his fear (he will not, that is, have made a choice on the basis of his fears), since his volition was manipulated by the hypnosis. At least, this is how matters seem to me, although I confess to being quite ignorant of the details of the operation of hypnosis and, thus, am reluctant to insist that it robs one of strict freedom.

I would be even more discontent than I am with my inability to clarify these issues concerning freedom if I were unable to provide any account of strict freedom and if I thought an account of broad freedom essential to an account of appraisability. But neither of these is the case. I have tried elsewhere to give an account of strict freedom,[25] and I shall argue in Section 4.6 that, despite popular belief, moral responsibility is *not* a function of broad freedom. I retain, of course, the conviction that it is a function of strict freedom; that is, that one is morally responsible for nothing of which one is not at least in part the source. This conviction, which is a very common one and which serves to fuel the debate between compatibilists and incompatibilists, is one for which I know of no positive argument, although I shall seek to defend it in Sections 4.9 and 4.10.

Further dimensions of freedom. Freedom, whether strict or broad, also varies along several other dimensions.

First, one may not only *freely* will, or bring about, something; one may be *free to* do so. (More particularly, one may be *free from* any constraints *to* will or bring about something. Sometimes, of course, one may be said to be free from certain constraints, but not from others, to do something, and here the explicit mention of the constraints involved is useful. But by "free to" I mean "free from *any* constraints to," and here the explicit mention of constraints is otiose. Note that "can," in one of its most important senses, may be used to express this sense of "free to."[26]) How are these two modes of freedom related? We can say at least this:

(P2.13)   If S freely wills e at T, then
           (a) S is free at T to will e at T, and
           (b) S wills e at T.

But we cannot accept the converse of (P2.13).[27] And we should note that the time of freedom may be distinct from the time of the volition with respect to which one is free; for example, I am free now to (will to) drive to Boston tomorrow.

We may also say the following:

(P2.14) S is free at T to bring about e relative to T' and T'' if and only if, for some event f,
            (a) S is free at T to will f at T', and
            (b) if S were to will f at T', then he would bring about e relative to T' and T''.

Moreover, there are various, more restrictive notions which may be accounted for, on the basis of (P2.14), roughly in the following manner: S is free to bring about e X-ly just in case, for some event f, S is free to will f and, if he were so to will, he would bring about e X-ly. A particularly important variation of this is the following:

(P2.15) S is free at T to bring about e intentionally relative to T' and T'' if and only if
            (a) S is free at T to will e at T', and
            (b) if S were to will e at T', then he would bring about e intentionally relative to T' and T''.

We should also note that freedom may come in stages, as it were, insofar as S may be free at T_1 to bring about some event f_1 and, if he were to do this, it would put him in a position at T_2 to bring about some other event f_2 and, if he were to do this, it would put him in a position to bring about something else and. . . . and so on, until finally the agent is free at T_n to bring about some event f_n. In such a case, we may say that S is free at T_1 to *approximate* f_n. (For example, I am free to approximate my thirst's being quenched if I can now get up from my desk, go to the kitchen, open the cupboard, pick out a glass, turn on the faucet, fill the glass with water, and raise the glass to my lips. The successful accomplishment of each stage (and there are also many intermediate stages, of course) puts me in a position to accomplish the next.) Finally, notice that analogues to (P2.14), (P2.15) and to what has just been said about approximation may be given in terms of *helping to bring about e* and of *contributing to e* (compare and contrast (P2.2) and (P2.3) above with (P2.1)).

It is convenient to talk of S's being free *with respect to e*. Just what this amounts to depends on whether e is a volition, a consequence of a volition, or an action.

Suppose that e is S's willing f. Then S is free with respect to e just in case S is free to will f. And we may say that S is free with respect to not-e just in case S is free to will something other than f.[28] Freedom with respect to a volition may be either *immediate* or *remote*. If, when S is free at T to will e at T', T' is later than T, then S's freedom is remote; if T' is identical with T, then S's freedom is immediate. (Thus, in the thirst-quenching case, my freedom with respect to my willing my thirst's being quenched was remote when I was at my desk but immediate when I raised the glass to my lips.)

Suppose that e is some potential consequence of a volition of S's. Then S may be free with respect to e in a number of different ways. If he is free to bring about e, then his freedom with respect to e may be said to be *primary*; if he is free to help bring about e, then his freedom with respect to e may be said to be *supplementary*;[29] if he is free to contribute to e, then his freedom with respect to e may be said to be *contributory*. (Thus, my freedom with respect to my thirst's being quenched was primary; had I needed help, it would have been merely supplementary; had the help required the free volition of another, then perhaps it would have been merely contributory.[30]) Again, if S is free to bring about e (or to help to bring it about, or to contribute to it), then his freedom with respect to e may be said to be *adjacent;* if he is only free to approximate e, then his freedom with respect to e may be said to be *distant*. (Notice that, whether S's freedom with respect to e is adjacent or distant, it *must* be remote. See the commentary on (P2.1) above.) Or again, if S is free to bring about e (or to help to bring it about, *etc.*) intentionally, then his freedom with respect to e may be said to be *transparent;* if he is free to bring it about (or to help to bring it about, *etc.*) only unintentionally, then his freedom with respect to e may be said to be *opaque*. (Thus my freedom to quench my thirst was transparent; if I thereby unwittingly caused certain chemical reactions to occur in my body, my freedom to do that was opaque.) Finally, if S is free to bring about (*etc.*) something other than e, then S may be said to be free with respect to not-e.

Suppose that e is S's bringing about f (or his helping to bring it about, *etc.*). Then S may be free with respect to e in all of the ways just mentioned: whatever type of freedom he enjoys with respect to the volition concerned (immediate or remote) he may be said to enjoy also with respect to $e;$ and whatever type of freedom he enjoys with respect to f (primary or supplementary or contributory, adjacent or distant, transparent or opaque) he may be said to enjoy also with respect to e. Notice that freedom with respect to an action may be *temporally hybrid*, in that S may be immediately free with respect to the volition but (of necessity) remotely free with respect to the issue. Finally, if S is free to bring about something other than f (or free to help to bring it about, *etc.*), then S may be said to be free with respect to not-e.

Just how important these various dimensions of freedom are will vary from context to context. The remoter the freedom, the worse, when one needs to get something done in a hurry. Primary freedom is more important than merely supplementary freedom when one cannot rely on outside cooperation. The more distant the freedom, the worse, when one's energy ebbs. And transparent freedom can be very important, as has in effect been noted by a very large number of philosophers who have emphasized the liberating power of knowledge. If all I have to do to win a fabulous prize is to inscribe "36, 25, 112, 4" on a card but am ignorant of this, in that while I know that some such inscription will allow me to win I do not know that it is this particular sequence that will do so, then whatever opaque freedom I may have with respect to the inscription is almost wholly useless to me.[31]

Undoubtedly yet further dimensions of freedom could be distinguished; but I shall limit myself to the foregoing, since only these will feature later (except for one to be mentioned shortly). Even so, it is clear—although this is seldom noted, even by philosophers—that there is an enormous variety of ways in which an agent S may be free with respect to an event e, and I have done no more than give a sketch of this here. The sketch is of course predicated on the central assumption, stated in (P2.12) above, that S freely brings about e just in case he brings about e in virtue of freely willing some event f. Some philosophers deny that it makes sense to talk of freedom of the will and claim that it makes sense only to talk of freedom of action or of man. They are drawn to this for one of two reasons. Either they reject the concept of volition; but in my opinion the concept is perfectly defensible, although I shall not seek to defend it here.[32] Or they accept the concept but believe that it is senseless to employ it in this way. Among the latter philosophers are many compatibilists who favor saying something like this: S is free to bring about e just in case, if S were to will e, he would bring about e. (It is often not clear whether this is supposed to be an account of strict, or of broad, freedom.) And then they say: we cannot talk of being free to will e, for this would involve some such senseless iteration of "will" as in "if S were to will to will e, he would will e." A swift rebuttal of this position is possible. First, there is no obvious nonsense involved in talking of willing to will, although assuredly most volitons are not themselves directed on volitions and freedom of the will could not in general *require* this without setting up an infinite regress of willing. Secondly, the proposed account of the freedom to bring about e is woefully inadequate.[33] Finally, even if the proposed account of the freedom to bring about e were adequate, there is no need to think that some parallel sort of account is required of the freedom to will e—especially since willing is not itself acting.

One final distinction may be made here. It is implicit in the central assumption just noted but should be made explicitly. Freedom with respect to a volition may be said to be *direct* (unless such freedom exists only by virtue of freedom with respect to another volition); freedom with respect to a consequence of a volition, because it can be attained only *via* freedom with respect to a volition, may be said to be *indirect*; freedom with respect to action is *ontologically hybrid*—both direct (with respect to the volition involved) and indirect (with respect to the issue involved).

(Thus my freedom with respect to my willing my thirst's being quenched was direct; with respect to my thirst's being quenched (and my stomach's reacting, and any and all other consequences), it was indirect; and with respect to my quenching my thirst, it was ontologically hybrid.) The picture, then, is this. Freedom of action is anchored in freedom of the will. Indirect freedom is parasitic upon direct freedom. An agent's freedom with respect to some consequence f of a volition e of his extends no further than e itself; his freedom with respect to the former is wholly contained in his freedom with respect to the latter; except insofar as he is free with respect to e, he is not free with respect to f's being a consequence of e and thus not free with respect to f.

It is very important to note that, while the particular theory of action which I presuppose here is perhaps controversial in many ways—and perhaps particularly so with respect to its reliance on the concept of volition—, it would seem that the point just made concerning the parasitic nature of indirect freedom *must* be accepted on *any* plausible theory of action. After all, however it is that we inject ourselves into the world, the freedom with which we do so has bounds; the consequences of this injection lie beyond these bounds. This general point is represented in the following simple diagram:

$$\bullet e \text{---} \circ f_1 \text{---} \circ f_2 \text{---} \circ f_3 \text{------------} \circ f_n \text{----------------}$$

In the diagram, e is that event (on my theory, a volition, but perhaps something else on some other theory) that is subject to an agent S's direct manipulation, that is, with respect to which S is directly free; f_1, f_2, etc. are the consequences of e. (Of course, there could be a branching of consequences, but there is no need here to complicate the diagram in order to accommodate this possibility.) Now, in virtue of being free with respect to e, S is of course free with respect to f_1, f_2, etc. (as long, perhaps, as these are not also the inevitable consequences of some other event with respect to which S is not free). But S's freedom with respect to f_1, f_2, etc. is wholly parasitic on his freedom with respect to e; he is not *directly* free with respect to them; they are beyond his control except insofar as he is free with respect to e. Thus, if we are to focus on that with respect to which S may be said to be *substantially* free, we need to look only at e; f_1, f_2, etc.—that chain of events emanating from e—may be left out of the picture, dismissed as merely parasitic. (Hence the representation in the diagram of e as "full" but of f_1, f_2, etc. as "empty" or "hollow.") As we shall see, this parasitic nature of indirect freedom, its strict ontological superfluity, has extremely important implications concerning moral responsibility.

Finally, the matter of *degrees* of strict and broad freedom needs to be addressed. We may distinguish between two "modes" of degrees of freedom—*intrinsic* and *extrinsic*—and, in my opinion, the following is true: broad freedom comes in degrees both intrinsically and extrinsically, while strict freedom comes in degrees extrinsically but not intrinsically. What do I mean by this?

First, the extrinsic mode. Clearly, there is a sense in which, if S is free with respect to both e and f and S' is free with respect to e but not f, then S is (ceteris paribus) freer, or free to a greater degree, than S'. S is (ceteris paribus) free with respect to more and, hence, more free than S'. This holds for both strict and broad freedom. In this extrinsic way, both strict and broad freedom may be increased or decreased by events.

Second, the intrinsic mode. This is a matter of there being a variation in the degree of freedom which an agent enjoys with respect to one and the same event. Since one may find certain courses of action more or less repugnant, broad freedom clearly comes in degrees in this intrinsic way. That is, the more (or less) repugnant an action is to an agent (in whatever sense of "repugnant" is appropriate here), the less (or more) broadly free the agent is with respect to that action. Thus, if S finds bringing about e only mildly repugnant while S' finds bringing about f very repugnant, then, S is (ceteris paribus) free to a greater degree than S'. S is (ceteris paribus) more free with respect to e than S' is with respect to f and, hence, is in a sense more free than S'. However, I do not believe that strict freedom varies in degree in this intrinsic way. That is, I do not think that an agent can be more or less strictly free with respect to an event, and so I also do not think that an agent can more or less strictly freely will or bring about an event; intrinsically, strict freedom is an all-or-nothing affair.[34] Or so it seems to me. I am not sure how this might be proven. It might be objected that strict freedom is just a matter of having genuine alternatives and that, the more alternatives one has, the freer one is. But this objection seems to me probably to be based on a confusion of the intrinsic with the extrinsic mode. Of course, this might not be so; it might be based on the view that, to be strictly free with respect to e, an agent must be strictly free with respect to some event other than e, and the more such events, the freer he is with respect to e itself. This is an interesting claim; it coherently incorporates the extrinsic into the intrinsic mode. But it seems false to me, for two reasons. First, I am inclined to think that being strictly free with respect to e does not require being strictly free with respect to any event other than e.[35] I shall return to this matter of "alternate possibilities" in the next section. Secondly, even if I am wrong in this, I cannot see that strict freedom with respect to e increases with the number of events other than e with respect to which one is also free. Commonly, at least, the claim that strict freedom of action requires being able to do "other than" one does is left at just that—that there be an alternative—and is not appended with the rider that the more alternatives there are, the freer one is with respect to the action in question. And I see no reason to append such a rider here. Thus

I shall assume (while acknowledging that much more could and should be said on the matter) that, intrinsically, there are no degrees of strict freedom.

2.3 Control

It is commonly said that moral responsibility presupposes not just freedom but control. What is the relation between freedom and control?

There is a standard sense of "control" that is captured in the following formula:

(P2.16) S has standard control over e if and only if
      (a) S is free with respect to e, and
      (b) S is free with respect to not-e.[36]

If S has standard control over e, then e is, in a sense, "up to him" (except in one type of case). Standard control may, of course, be strict or broad, direct or indirect, immediate or remote, transparent or opaque, adjacent or distant, primary or supplementary or contributory.[37] (If S's standard control over e is not primary, then it would be misleading to think of e as being "up to S"; in this type of case, it is best to think of e as being "*partly* up to S.") Understanding control in this way is also consistent with a more refined model of control according to which control consists partly in the operation of some feedback mechanism whereby the agent somehow monitors his progress toward some goal.[38] For instance, it may be that I can drink a glass of water only because I can reach out my arm, then register that this component of the action has been successfully completed, then open my fingers, then register this, then grasp the glass, then register this, and so on. If such intermediate registration of intermediate successes is required for the successful completion of some entire complex action, then so be it. This fact is accommodated by the possibility that freedom be both indirect and distant.

Many philosophers appear to understand freedom to be equivalent to standard control. That is, they take it that, if S is free with respect to e, then S is free with respect to not-e, and *vice versa*.[39] I think that this is a mistake. This issue of "alternate possibilities" is one that I shall take up in detail in Section 4.10. But at this point I shall note simply that it is not obvious that freedom is equivalent to standard control and that we should not rule out the possibility that control may be curtailed, rather than standard, in the following sense:

(P2.17) S has curtailed control over e if and only if
      (a) S is free with respect to e, but
      (b) S is not free with respect to not-e.

If S is free with respect to e but not with respect to not-e, then e cannot be said to be "up to him," although, if it occurs, it may still be said to be "truly his." Of course, curtailed control, like standard control, may be strict or broad, direct or indirect, and so on. (In saying that control may be only curtailed control, I may be stretching the term "control" beyond its normal limits. Certainly, I agree that standard control is a more standard sense of "control."[40] But I do not think that much rides on this.)

Control is often said to come in degrees. There are two main ways to accommodate such talk. First, if it is broad control that is at issue, then, since broad freedom may vary in degree with respect to one and the same event, there may be corresponding degrees of broad control with respect to one and the same event.[41] But since there cannot (intrinsically) be degrees of strict freedom, strict control cannot similarly inherit degrees. Secondly, whether it is strict or broad control that is at issue, we often talk of our having (or, usually, lacking) "real," "full," or "complete" control over an event in the sense of having control both over it and over all those events upon whose occurrence its occurrence is contingent.[42] Somewhat more precisely:

(P2.18) S has complete control over e if and only if
            (a) S has control over e, and
            (b) for all events f of which e is a consequence, S has control over f.

Control over an event e may thus be said to approach completeness to a greater or lesser degree, depending on which events f (of which e is a consequence) are in one's control. (Of course, there are problems here. First, it may seem that one is, on this understanding of completeness, never in complete control of any event. I would agree; see Section 4.11. Secondly, it is not at all clear how the degrees of approaching such completeness are even in principle to be determined, insofar as it is not at all clear what is the appropriate way to "assemble" for this purpose those events f, of which e is a consequence.) The type of completeness may be said also to vary according to the type or types of consequence (causal or simple) at issue.

We should note that, even in the absence of complete control, if S has standard, primary control over e, then e is, in an important sense, "up to him." Thus e may still be, in this sense, *fully* in S's control even if it is not *completely* in his control.[43] Of course, if e is not completely in S's control, then certain events of which e is a consequence are not up to S but, rather, up to someone else or merely "up to nature." But this does not imply that e itself is not up to S.[44] My arm's rising here and now requires the cooperation of nature and is thus not completely in my control; nonetheless, it is fully in my control, in that whether or not it rises here and now is up to me.

Finally, we may talk of exercising control. *Exercising* control over *e* is related to *having* control over *e*, as *freely* willing or bringing about *e* (*etc.*) is related to *being free* with respect to *e*. If I have control over my arm's rising and I raise my arm, then, typically, I have exercised my control over my arm's rising.[45]

NOTES

1. See Zimmerman (1984), *passim.*

2. Note that, if it is thought incorrect to say that every event is a consequence of itself, then this rough formula requires refinement.

3. "But for" consequences are such that the events of which they are consequences are *necessary* conditions of them; this leaves open the possibility that there are no *sufficient* conditions of them. On the other hand, I believe that, whenever one event is a causal consequence of another, there is a sufficient condition (involving the latter event) of the former event. (In this connection, note that an incompatibilist account of freedom of action requires that free actions be causal consequences of no event; but clearly they may be consequences, in the "but for" sense, of some event.) Some clear examples of events which are "but for" but not causal consequences of other events are given in Kim (1973), pp. 570–71. Also I think that the consequences of omissions are consequences of this same sort, as I shall shortly have occasion to note again. Compare Donagan (1977), p. 48. Contrast the more liberal uses of "cause" in: Feinberg (1970), Chapter 7, especially pp. 135, 155–58, 160–61, 165, and 179; Ayer (1984), pp. 13–14.

4. (P2.1) would need revision in order to accommodate this possibility, but I shall not try to provide such revision here. For an extended treatment of such joint action, see Tuomela (1984).

5. It can be both, in that some of the individuals involved may act *seriatim* and some not. (Perhaps some of Caesar's assassins stabbed simultaneously.)

6. Several clarificatory comments are in order here. First, there is clearly a very close relation between the concept of overfull group action and the concept of causal overdetermination, although just what the latter concept amounts to is not something that I shall discuss here. Secondly, while I believe that there can be overfull group action (because I believe that a causal consequence need not be a simple consequence—compare note 3), this is not something that I shall seek to prove here. If I am wrong, this simply means that the concept of overfull group action is never instantiated. But, thirdly, what might be an example of overfull group action? Perhaps ten persons bearing Caesar's pall when five could do the job. Why might this *not* be an example of overfull group action? Because it is not clear that the contributions of the nonsuperfluous five are, or can be, the *same* when only five bear the pall as when ten do. At any rate, it is clear that the contributions *need* not be the same, and so, fourthly, overfull group action is to be distinguished from *oversupplied* group action, of which the just cited example of superfluous pall-bearers is an illustration. Oversupplied group action is group action where there are more agents involved in the group action than are needed to produce the outcome; that is, a proper subset of the agents involved could manage on their own to produce the outcome. Fifthly, it is clear that group action can be neither *underfull* nor *undersupplied;* for in neither case would the outcome occur. Finally, and perhaps most importantly, it is clear that group action can be overfull or oversupplied with respect to one outcome but not with respect to another. For example, perhaps only five are needed to bear the pall, but ten are needed to do so without staggering.

7. Perhaps it is better to say that a volition is *not* accompanied by the intention that it *not* be causally efficacious, rather than that it *is* accompanied by the intention that it *be* causally efficacious. For, while I think that a volition is *typically* accompanied by the latter intention, perhaps it is only *necessarily* not accompanied by the former. Why? Well, if it were *necessarily* accompanied by the latter, this would seem to imply that whoever wills something has the concept of a volition, and thus (by my account) that whoever acts has this concept. And it is implausible to think that small children have this concept, even though it is plausible to think that they act. But perhaps best of all is a compromise here, according to which we should say that those who lack the concept of a volition can only act in a weak sense, while those who have it can act in the full sense.

8. See, *e.g.,* Sellars (1976).

9. See, *e.g.,* Davidson (1963), pp. 4, 5, 12; Baier (1965), p. 193; Goldman (1970), pp. 67–68, 72–76; Goldman (1976).

10. It may be suggested that there is no need to think that the *object* of a person's volition is the issue of his action, rather than the action itself, even if it is accepted that the action *comprises* the volition whose *consequence* is the issue in question (and, clearly, not the entire action itself). There is some truth to this. I have said that a practical decision, to rank as a volition, must be accompanied (but see note 7) by an intention that it be causally efficacious; and so we may say, roughly, that whenever one decides that one's arm should rise in a manner which is tantamount to *willing* that one's arm should rise, one *intends* to *raise* one's arm. It *can,* of course, happen not only that one has this "second-order" intention, but also that one makes a "second-order" *decision* to raise one's arm.

11. Another implication of (P2.4): *S* wills *f.* This implication is assumed in the statement of (P4.6) in Section 4.2.

12. In fact, there are two intentions operative in willing *e:* the "first-order" intention that *e* occur, and the "second-order" intention that the decision that *e* occur be causally efficacious with respect to *e.* See note 10.

13. See, *e.g.,* Davidson (1971), p. 46.

14. See, *e.g.,* Kant (1785), p. 116, together with Paton's commentary on p. 42; also Wolff (1973), p. 200. *Cf.* Kenny (1966), p. 648; Audi (1973), pp. 395–96; Castañeda (1975), pp. 134–36, 312; Davis (1979), p. 75.

15. Ginet (1966), p. 93. On the implication of (P2.7) by (P2.4), see van Inwagen (1983), p. 153ff. Contrast: Dennett (1984), p. 113; Waller (1985). Despite Ginet's example, it may be thought that (P2.4) at best implies that *S* does *not* believe that he *lacks* control over *e* and *f.* After all, can one not "have a go" at something that one neither believes to be in one's control nor believes not to be in one's control, perhaps simply in order to find out whether or not it *is* in one's control? The answer to this is: yes, but that does not show that (P2.4) does not imply (P2.7). For when one "has a go" in such a case, one does not *intend* to accomplish the thing in question, one merely *hopes* to accomplish it. Of course, perhaps one does intend to *attempt* to accomplish it, but then one believes the attempt to be in one's control.

It is worth noting that there may well be a distinction between having a dispositional belief and having a disposition to believe, as argued in Audi (1982). If this is true, perhaps much of what I say here and elsewhere about (dispositional) belief ought rather to be put in terms of the disposition to believe. But this is a complication that I shall henceforth overlook.

16. It is far from clear to me what is involved in the belief that an event is *more or less likely* to occur if some other event occurs; but it is clear to me that we all often have beliefs of this sort. *Cf.* Rescher (1983), pp. 7, 9, and 95.

17. A complication: while the present treatment of events as abstract entities allows for a straightforward use of "not" in "not-*e*," it is still not clear just what entity is designated by "not-*e*." For instance, suppose that *e* is Smith's hand rising. What, then, is not-*e*? Presumably: Smith's hand not rising. But what is *this*? Is it: its not

being the case that Smith's hand rises? If so, then it is not, strictly, an event. Or is it: Smith's being such that his hand does not rise? If so, then it is an event (partly because it entails that Smith exists). But I shall not pursue this here and shall, for simplicity's sake, assume that "negative events" are genuine events.

18. As does Baier (1985), p. 14. See note 3. Contrast Harris (1980), Chapter 3.

19. In saying this, I am of course not saying that the "can"-component of omission—*i.e.*, in the present case, the fact that I can turn on the light—is itself a causal consequence of my volition.

20. *Cf.* Aristotle, *Nicomachean Ethics,* Book III, Chapter 1, on types of voluntariness; Fitzgerald (1968), pp. 129–130; Goldman (1970), p. 209; Kleinig (1973), p. 94; Kenny (1978), pp. 35–36; Gosselin (1979), section 2; Greenspan (1979), p. 232*n.*; Ayer (1984), p. 8. Some philosophers (many but not all of them compatibilists) seem to reject the distinction, some shunning broad freedom (see Dworkin 1970), p. 373; Frankfurt (1973); Berofsky (1980); Thorp (1980), pp. 8–9), some shunning strict freedom (see Nesbitt and Candlish (1973); Audi (1974), p. 4; Dennett (1984), p. 133). But the distinction seems to me inherent in our everyday thinking and thus to be pretheoretically plausible—even if, theoretically, it might seem to be a distinction upon which incompatibilists in particular would wish to insist. (And anyway, it should be noted that some notable compatibilists accept the distinction. See Glover (1970), pp. 116–17; Kenny (1978), p. 38.)

21. On this issue, see: Nozick (1969); Gert (1972); Held (1972a); Bayles (1972, 1974); Frankfurt (1973); Lyons (1975); Benditt (1977); VanDeVeer (1977).

22. This is not to say that I have no suspicions as to how they should be answered. It seems to me that broad unfreedom involves repugnance with respect to the *situation* in which one finds oneself, and thereby with respect to what one does in this situation. This is a common observation (*cf., e.g.,* Thalberg (1978), p. 217); but, as it stands, it is very rough, and I shall not pursue it here. Still, it does seem to me to suggest that neither the person in bed nor the person faced with a very attractive offer is broadly unfree to any degree.

The most promising discussions of broad unfreedom with which I am familiar are those contained in Nozick (1969) and Audi (1974). But neither author provides an analysis of the concept. Perhaps broad freedom is analyzable in terms of strict freedom along something like the following lines: S is broadly unfree to bring about e just in case S is strictly unfree to bring about e without f (some undesirable event) occurring. (*Cf.* van Inwagen 1984, p. 10.) But in the absence of just what sort of undesirability is at issue, this suggestion remains no more than promising.

23. Contrast Dennett (1984).

24. I am not at all sure that it does, for I am not at all sure how hypnotism operates. I am not alone in this. *Cf.* London (1969), Chapter 4.

25. Zimmerman (1984), Chapter 11.

26. Since omission does not require action, there is no straightforward sense to be given to either "S is free to omit to bring about e" or "S freely omits to bring about e." Insofar as all omission to bring about e implies that the agent can bring about e, such use of "is free to" and "freely" is redundant. (See (P2.10) above.) Of course, it might happen on occasion that an agent omits to bring about e by freely bringing about f.

27. For strict freedom, something like what in Zimmerman (1984), Chapter 11, I call "effectuation" is, I think, required in this connection.

28. Such use of "not-e" is problematic, as mentioned in note 17. The locution "something other than f occurs" must of course be understood to imply that f does not occur. (It is prudent to point this out explicitly, especially given the finely grained ontology of events presupposed here.) Similarly, willing something other than f (that is, willing that something other than f occur) requires not willing f (that is, not willing that f occur).

29. The distinction between primary and supplementary freedom is, of course, just

as hard to draw as that distinction in which it is rooted, namely, the distinction between "the" and "a" cause. Suppose that I can now continue to write. Is my freedom with respect to continuing to write primary or supplementary? One is inclined to say: primary. But notice that it of course relies on the "cooperation" of nature and of others—I must not be interrupted. Suppose that, with the help of others which has been assured me, I can now lift a heavy object. Is my freedom with respect to the object's rising primary or supplementary? One is inclined to say: supplementary. (And if I could lift the object with, but only with, their help, and they just will *not* help, then I am simply *not* free at all with respect to its rising.) But I confess to having no general criterion to help adjudicate these issues.

30. On this last point, see note 3.

31. *Cf.* Goldman (1970), p. 203; Dennett (1984), p. 115ff.

32. But see Zimmerman (1984), Section 10.2.

33. See Chisholm (1976), p. 57.

34. *Cf.* Gosselin (1979), section 2; Thorp (1980), pp. 8–9.

35. Of course, *believing* that one is free with respect to some other event *is* required. See Section 2.1.

36. Instead of "*S* has control over *e*" we might say: "*S* is in control of *e*," "*e* is under *S*'s control," or "*e* is not beyond *S*'s control." Note that to say that *S* is in standard control of *e* is not, of course, to say that *S* is free with respect to the conjunctive state of affairs *e* and not-*e*. Note also that I claim only that (2.16) captures *a* standard sense of "control." There are standard senses of "control" that are not essentially tied to freedom at all. *Cf.* Dennett (1984), Chapter 3.

37. Or some hybrid of these dimensions. Such a hybrid would occur if, for example, *S*'s freedom with respect to *e* were primary but with respect to not-*e* merely supplementary.

38. *Cf.* Dennett (1984), p.72.

39. A recent example, in a very long line of examples: Ayer (1984), p. 2.

40. *Cf.* Fischer (1982), pp. 24, 31–32, and 37, where "control" is clearly used in the standard sense and where it is said that someone who is in what I call curtailed control of an event may be "in charge of" that event but is not "in control of" it.

41. Again, there may be complications concerning hybrids, as where *S*'s broad freedom with respect to *e* is of a greater degree than his broad freedom with respect to not-*e*.

42. *Cf.* Feinberg (1970), p. 35.

43. *Cf.* Dennett (1984), p. 54.

44. See note 29.

45. *Cf.* Baier (1985), p. 14, on having and using causal power. I say "typically," because, as noted, the converse of (P2.13) is not *necessarily* true. See note 27.

3

APPRAISABILITY

MORAL APPRAISABILITY has to do with that type of *inward* moral praising and blaming that constitutes making a private judgment about a person.[1] I think that it is helpful, at least initially, to describe such praising and blaming metaphorically. There is an abundance of available metaphors. Praising someone may be said to constitute judging that there is a "credit" in his "ledger of life," a "positive mark" in his "report-card of life," or a "luster" on his "record as a person"; that his "record" has been "burnished"; that his "moral standing" has been "enhanced." Blaming someone may be said to constitute judging that there is a "discredit" or "debit" in his "ledger," a "negative mark" in his "report-card," or a "blemish" or "stain" on his "record"; that his "record" has been "tarnished"; that his "moral standing" has been "diminished."[2] Someone is praiseworthy if he is deserving of such praise; that is, if it is correct, or true to the facts, to judge that there is a "credit" in his "ledger" *(etc.)*. Someone is blameworthy if he is deserving of such blame; that is, if it is correct, or true to the facts, to judge that there is a "debit" in his "ledger" *(etc.)*. It is important to note that, in the context of *inward* moral praise and blame, *worthiness* of such praise or blame is a strictly nonmoral type of worthiness; it is a matter of the truth or accuracy of judgments. This is to be contrasted with that type of worthiness which constitutes worthiness of *overt* moral praise or blame. I shall return to the latter type of worthiness in Chapter 5, where overt praise and blame will be discussed. In this chapter it is only with appraisal, with inward praise and blame, that I shall be concerned.

To appraise someone in the manner just indicated is to "measure the man." It is to evaluate *him* in a certain way; it is *not* to evaluate his character or his personality. (For more on character, see Section 4.8.) Moreover, it is to evaluate him with respect to a particular episode in his life; it is to make a judgment as to his *moral worth*, but only insofar as this is constituted by the episode in question. It is not as if the person's entire "moral life" were on the line when he is appraised; a good person may be blameworthy on occasion, and a bad person praiseworthy, and it is only one entry in the ledger, not the entire ledger, that is at issue. Still, each such episode—each entry in the ledger—is relevant to an overall assessment of his moral life, that is, to determining his moral worth in general.[3]

Of course, the metaphor is only a metaphor. There are no ledgers, report-cards, or records of the sort mentioned—unless some vault in the heavens, guarded by God, contains them, and this is certainly *not* something that I am presupposing here. But even if there are no such records, it remains a fact that certain events occur and that a person's moral worth is a function of these events. A person can be praiseworthy or blameworthy without anyone's being aware of this, without anyone's taking note of it, without anyone's actually praising or blaming him. Indeed, the metaphor of the ledger can be misleading unless it is handled very carefully. Normally, when an ordinary person keeps a ledger, *he* makes the entries and he has a *purpose* in doing so; the entries are not somehow automatically recorded in the ledger, he being simply its custodian. But, if there were a ledger of life, its entries would not be made by anyone, nor would there be a purpose to the entries. (In saying this, I am again ignoring theological issues.) Rather, the entries would be automatically recorded; they would appear simply by virtue of certain events occurring (events of which the person's moral worth is a function). In this connection, we must particularly guard against thinking that inward praising and blaming are analogous to the *making* of entries in the ledger; on the contrary, they are analogous to *judging there to be* such entries.

Thus the metaphor, even if initially suggestive, must be handled with extreme caution. Moreover, it must be recognized that a person may have a *number* of "moral records," to only *one* of which moral praise and blame are pertinent. For example, a person may have the "record" of being a habitual wrongdoer but, as we shall shortly see, this may be irrelevant to his blameworthiness. Or, again, a person may have a long "record" of vicious activity but, as we shall see in Section 4.9, this may also be irrelevant to his blameworthiness. And so the metaphor is, at best, only *suggestive*. It is no substitute for a detailed account of the phenomena of inward praise- and blameworthiness.

And so, let us now undertake such a detailed account. In order to distinguish that worthiness of inward praise and blame associated with appraisability from that worthiness of overt praise and blame associated with liability, I shall employ some terms in a manner which I hope accords with much, but which I do not pretend accords with all, of everyday usage. I shall call worthiness of inward praise *laudability* and worthiness of inward blame *culpability*. I shall begin with an examination of culpability.[4]

3.1 Direct Culpability

Culpability may be *direct* or *indirect* in a manner which correlates with direct and indirect freedom. (See pp. 29–30.) In this section I shall be concerned exclusively with direct culpability.

Doing wrong. Just as an agent is directly free only with respect to his volitions, so he is directly culpable only for his volitions. A first approximation of what I take to be the conditions of direct culpability may be put as follows:

(P3.1)   *S* is directly culpable for willing *e* if and only if *S* strictly freely willed *e*, in the belief that, by virtue of so willing, he would do wrong.

This requires some careful unpacking.

First, direct culpability of course constitutes a species of what I have called moral, 'retrospective,' personal responsibility. Recall that in Chapter 1 I denied that such responsibility is in fact *necessarily* retrospective. We are now in a position to see what such a denial amounts to, at least with respect to appraisability. We may ask: if *S* wills *e* at *T* (that is, roughly, if *S* decides at *T* that *e* should occur) and is directly culpable for this, *at what time* is he culpable for this? In this context, what this question amounts to is this: at what time is it correct, or true to the facts, to blame *S* inwardly for willing *e* at *T*? The answer clearly is: at that time at which it is true that (to speak tenselessly) *S* wills *e* at *T*. Now, it is relatively uncontroversial that, if *S* wills *e* at *T*, then it is true at *T* and forever thereafter that *S* wills *e* at *T*. Thus at least this may be said to be true: if *S* wills *e* at *T* and is culpable for this, then he is culpable at *T* and forever thereafter for it. This is not to speak harshly, but merely accurately.[5] One must not confuse appraisability with liability. It seems harsh to say that, if *S* wills *e* at *T* and is *overtly* blameworthy for this, then he is at *T* and forever thereafter *overtly* blameworthy for it. But we have to do here, not with overt, but with *inward* blameworthiness. Indeed, if there can be true propositions about the free volitions and actions of persons in the future, then we should also admit that persons are *forever* (period) (that is, not just forever after, but also forever before) culpable for those volitions for which they are culpable. I shall take no stand here on whether in fact a person is forever culpable for that for which he is culpable; for I shall take no stand on whether there can be true propositions about the free volitions and actions of persons in the future. But the very fact that it is at least plausible to believe that such propositions can be true prompts me not to talk of "retrospective" responsibility as essentially retrospective, or even as essentially nonprospective. However, insofar as actual ascriptions of such responsibility are *typically* retrospective, I shall continue to call such responsibility retrospective. In this spirit, in (P3.1) I have used the past tense with "willed" and I shall continue so to use it, for this is the most natural tense to use here. (It is just that I disavow the claim that this is the tense that *must* be used.)

Second, I should note that by "wrong" I mean that which is *morally* wrong *all things considered* (and thus not that which is merely *prima facie* morally wrong, or morally wrong in a certain respect). Of course, if (P3.1) is to be at all useful, such wrong must be understood to be in principle identifiable *quite independently* of any question of blame. Here we meet with some controversy. Some philosophers contend that, far from culpability being analyzable in terms of wrongdoing, wrongdoing is to be analyzed in terms of culpability.[6] Others appear to contend that neither is analyzable in terms of the other, for the reason that there is no distinction between them, that is, that to say that one has done wrong is just to say that one is culpable for something. Now, of course, I deny both these claims. While I have no knockdown argument for my denial, perhaps the following observations will help to render it plausible to those who do not already find it so.

Suppose that Jones comes upon a car accident; the driver is unconscious. Being a member of the "TV generation," Jones expects the car to explode at any moment, and so he rushes to the driver and drags him clear of the wreck. The result: the driver is paralyzed for life (whereas he would not have been if Jones had left him where he was), and the car does not explode. Now, did Jones do wrong? One is initially pulled in two directions and finds oneself inclined toward some such bumbling compromise as this: "Well, Jones did do wrong in a way, but he did what he thought was right, and that's all that can be expected of him. After all, one ought to do what one thinks one ought to do." But this clearly will not do as it stands. (Of course, in giving this assessment of the case, one is presumably discounting the possibility of negligence being a factor—and let us continue to assume that it is not a factor.) The assessment relies on the claim that what one ought to do is what one thinks one ought to do, a claim which, without refinement, is incoherent. Many philosophers have recognized this incoherence and have tried to provide refinement.

A first step toward such refinement, and one that several philosophers have taken, is to distinguish (i) doing what is best from (ii) doing what one thinks is best. Clearly, Jones did not do what was best, although he did what he thought (at the time) was, or would prove to be, best. Some claim that both (i) and (ii) capture a sense of "doing what one ought to do"; (i) captures the "objective," and (ii) the "subjective," sense. And then they say that "one ought to do what one thinks one ought to do" may be understood as true, in the sense that what one "ought" subjectively to do is what one thinks one ought "objectively" to do.[7]

This seems to me to be roughly correct and, in particular, I would endorse this (roughly worded) corollary: what one ought "subjectively" *not* to do is what one thinks one ought "objectively" *not* to do—or, as I would much prefer to put it: what one is to be blamed for is doing that which one thinks one ought not to do. Thus, while some philosophers talk of "subjective" and "objective" obligation, and analyze the former in terms of the latter, I would prefer to talk of "culpability" and "obligation" (with its concomitant, "wrongdoing") and, again, analyze the former in terms of the latter.[8] But, having said this, I should immediately stress that further refinement is necessary. For, while I believe that "ought (objectively)" is indeed to be understood in terms of doing what is best (although I shall not try here to fill in this account, nor even to say what type of "best" is at issue), I agree that this is controversial. It is certainly arguable, for instance, that what one ought to do is not what *is* best but what it is *most reasonable to think* best.[9] If this is the case, Jones, far from having done wrong (as I believe), will quite possibly have done right in dragging the driver from the wreck. Or it might be that doing wrong (failing to do what one ought to do) requires some sort of defective intention and that Jones, not having had such an intention, did no wrong.[10] And it must be admitted that, on both these latter interpretations of "ought" and "wrong," there is something about obligation (and failing in one's obligation) which can legitimately be called "subjective." But, even if this is so, and even if one of these accounts (or yet some other account) of obligation and wrongdoing is correct, *still* there is a distinction to be drawn between doing what one ought (or ought not) to do (according to the account of obligation at issue) and doing what one *thinks* one ought (or ought not) to do. For example, even if wrongdoing requires a defective intention, such that, say, not all harming is wrong but only intentional harming is, still one must distinguish, on the one hand, doing wrong by intentionally harming someone and, on the other, intentionally doing wrong. The latter, in my view, confers culpability, but the former does not. Or again, even if wrongdoing consists in not doing what it is most reasonable to think best, still one must distinguish, on the one hand, doing wrong by not doing what is most reasonable in this respect and, on the other, doing what one thinks is wrong. Again, it is only the latter which, on my view, confers culpability. (Thus, while I am persuaded that many of those who insist that there is something "subjective" about obligation are simply failing to distinguish what I call culpability from what I call wrongdoing,[11] I agree that this is not true for all who insist on this.)

Moreover, while I have said that I subscribe to the (only roughly worded) view that ("objective") wrongdoing consists in not doing what is best, this in fact does *not* mean that I subscribe to the view that culpability is incurred when one does what one thinks is not best. Rather,

I subscribe to the view that culpability is incurred when someone does what *he* thinks (and not what *I* think) is wrong. The point is, someone may not subscribe to my view as to what constitutes ("objective") wrongdoing, and such a peson therefore may well not believe that he is doing wrong when he does what he thinks is not best. If so, this person does *not* incur çulpability by virtue of doing what he thinks is not best. Thus, it is in fact misleading to say, as some have said (and as I initially said), that (ii) in the next-to-last paragraph captures a ("subjective") sense of "ought." Rather, what captures this sense is this: (ii') doing what one thinks one ought ("objectively") to do. (ii) is distinct from (ii'), a fact which was glossed over in the initial presentation of (i) and (ii).

Thus I would urge that we distinguish culpability from wrongdoing and analyze the former in terms of the latter. I am persuaded that this accords with how many of us on reflection do—and with how all of us on reflection ought to—understand the relation between these concepts. Indeed, without such a distinction, I am at a loss to account for the common phenomena of a person's justifiably seeking advice lest he do wrong and of a person's justifiably ruing the fact that he unwittingly did wrong. And if we do distinguish them as recommended in (P3.1), the following very important possibilities emerge: that one do wrong and not be culpable (as in the Jones case); and that one be culpable and not do wrong. (As we shall see, the former possibility renders my account of responsibility *"deflationary,"* and the latter possibility renders my account *"inflationary."* (See Section 1.3 concerning my present use of these terms.)

Third, what it is to "do wrong by virtue of willing *e*" needs clarification. If *S* wills *e* and, by virtue of this volition, brings about *f* (see (P2.1)) and if, by bringing about *f*, he does wrong, then *S* will have done wrong by virtue of willing *e*. For example, if *S* wills his right index finger's retraction of the trigger, and if, as a consequence of this volition, *S'* dies, and if, by killing *S'*, *S* does wrong, then *S* will have done wrong by virtue of willing his finger's retraction of the trigger. (There is a certain awkwardness of locution lurking here. It was noted in the last chapter that one does not in general will to raise one's hand but rather wills its rising. So, too, one does not in general will to retract the trigger but rather wills its retraction.) We should beware of English here. "Doing wrong" sounds like "doing good" or "doing harm," but, while doing good and doing harm are actions, doing wrong is *not*. One brings about good, or brings about harm, and the good and the harm are the issues internal to the actions. But one does not (in general) bring about wrong; rather one "does wrong" *in* bringing about something. There is no issue internal to wrongdoing, for wrongdoing is not an action; on the contrary, *wrongness* is a *property* of actions. One *does wrong* by virtue of the fact that one *does something* and the doing something *is wrong*.[12]

We may yet talk of believing that one will (or may) do wrong, being willing to do wrong, intending to do wrong, willing to do wrong, and willing to do wrong for wrong's sake. What these amount to, roughly, are as follows. One believes that one will (or may) do wrong just in case one believes that one will (or may) do something the doing of which is or will be (or may be) wrong. (An alternative phrase for "believing that one will (or may) do wrong": "*foreseeing* that one will (or may) do wrong.") One is willing to do wrong just in case one does something the doing of which one believes is or may be wrong and one believes that the risk of doing wrong would have been less had one done something else instead (see (P2.8)).[13] (In this connection, it should be mentioned that the phrase "*to will e in the belief that* one will do wrong," as used in (P3.1), is intended to convey, not simply contemporaneity of the volition and the belief in question, but rather a grounding of the volition in the belief. I shall forgo trying to give a precise account of the nature of this grounding, but it is common enough. It is that sort of grounding expressed in such phrases as "he decided to do this *in light of the fact* that . . ." and "she chose to do that *on the basis of* . . .") One intends to do wrong just in case one intends to act wrongly, where the "wrongly" is of course part of the object of the intention.[14] (That is, one does not intend to do wrong simply by intending to perform some action, an action that happens to be wrong. (Compare intending to act flamboyantly, or annoyingly, or recklessly, and so on.) And this is so even if one believes that one's action will or may be wrong. For this would simply constitute intentionally doing something which one foresees to be wrong, and thus would simply be a matter of foreseeing doing wrong; it would still fall short of intending to do wrong.) One wills to do wrong just in case one wills to do something and intends to act wrongly thereby. And, finally, one wills to do wrong for wrong's sake just in case one wills to do something and intends to act wrongly thereby and intends this for the purpose of nothing further.

Fourth, I am of course still working under the assumption that events are abstract and finely grained. This especially simplifies matters in the present context. For one may talk of intending to bring about an event *e*, willing to bring about *e*, and so on, without qualification. One need not talk of intending to perform some as yet nonexistent act-token *a* that falls under some presumably eternally existent act-type *A*. For example, suppose that Smith intends to annoy Jones. On the present assumption, we may simply put this (roughly) as follows: Smith intends his annoying Jones, that is, Smith intends that his annoying Jones occur. We need not say this: Smith intends that some act-token of the type *Smith annoying Jones* occur. Nor need we talk of intending to perform some act *a* under some description *d* but not under another description *d'*, or of being blameworthy for some volition *v* under some description *d* but not under another description *d'*. Some such talk is required where events are coarsely individuated. For example, on the present assumption, even if, in annoying Jones, Smith inadvertently pleases Brown, Smith's annoying Jones and his pleasing Brown are distinct actions. But, on the assumption that actions are to be coarsely individuated, they might well not be distinct, and so we would have to say something like: Smith intended to do *a* under the description *Smith annoying Jones* but not under the description *Smith pleasing Brown*. Similarly, on the present assumption, even if, in deciding to annoy Jones, Smith inadvertently disappoints Green, these are distinct events. But, on the assumption that events are to be coarsely individuated, they might not be distinct, and so we would have to say something like: Smith is to be blamed for *v* under the description *Smith deciding to annoy Jones* but not under the description *Smith disappointing Green*. This is a very cumbersome way of talking, and it is partly with a view to avoiding such talk that I here treat events as abstract and finely grained.

Still, a concomitant complication must be acknowledged. If, on some occasion, *S* wills *e* in order that *f* may occur, in the belief that, by virtue of so willing, he will do wrong, just what event is it for which *S* is culpable? Is it: his willing *e*; his willing *e* in order that *f* may occur; his willing *e* in order that *f* may occur, in the belief that . . . ; or what? The answer is: all of these (and more). But henceforth I shall mention only the simplest of these, namely, his willing *e*. This is merely for the sake of convenience. It is especially important to note in this context that the fact that *S* is really directly culpable for an indefinite number of events does *not* imply that the blemish on his record is indefinitely large or that there is an indefinite number of such blemishes. One must individuate blemishes coarsely, even if one individuates events finely. Consider this closely related case: it would have been a travesty of justice if Lee Harvey Oswald had been accused of an indefinite, perhaps infinite, number of murders simply because the prosecutor subscribed to a theory of events according to which events are finely-grained. For purposes of such prosecution, one must be able to individuate murders coarsely. So, too, for purposes of counting and sizing up blemishes, one must individuate the volitions which ground them coarsely. I have shown elsewhere how this might be done.[15]

Finally, where the "right-hand side" of (P3.1)—namely, that segment which follows the "if and only if"—is called (P3.1r), we may note that (P3.1r) implies, with one important exception to be noted later:

(P3.2)   *S* was willing to do wrong.

(Here "was willing" is used to express the state of *being* willing, as in (P2.8), and not the event of willing.) But (P3.1r) does *not* imply:

(P3.3)   *S* intended to do wrong,

and so it does *not* imply:

(P3.4)   *S* willed to do wrong,

and so it does *not* imply:

(P3.5)   *S* willed to do wrong for wrong's sake.

But (P3.1r) is consistent with each of (P3.3), (P3.4), and (P3.5).

The distinctions between (P3.2), (P3.4), and (P3.5) are important. It is the belief with respect to wrongdoing in (P3.1r) that accounts for (P3.1r)'s implication of (P3.2); it is the lack of the necessity of intention with respect to wrongdoing in (P3.1r) that accounts for (P3.1r)'s failure to imply (P3.4) and hence (P3.5). English is tricky here; (P3.2), (P3.4), and (P3.5) look pretty much the same, but, as we have seen, they emphatically are not.

In semistipulative fashion, we may say that (P3.2) expresses *S*'s manifestation of *callousness,* (P3.3) and (P3.4) his manifestation of *malice,* and (P3.5) his manifestation of *satanic wickedness.*[16] These terms are clearly used here much as they are ordinarily used, and so their use here is not wholly stipulative; but I say that it is semistipulative because, although I recognize that the terms can be properly used somewhat differently, I am stipulating that they are not to be otherwise understood in the present context.[17] I use the awkward phrase "manifestation of" because it would be misleading to say that *S* in (P3.2) *is* callous, or in (P3.3) and (P3.4) *is* malicious, or in (P3.5) *is* satanically wicked. Normally, to say that someone *is* any of these things is to imply that he has certain *long-term dispositions* to act in certain ways; and I mean *not* to imply this here. *S* in (P3.2) *manifests* callousness, but perhaps he has no long-term disposition to act callously; perhaps, indeed, he has a long-term disposition to act benevolently and this disposition is simply idle, or overridden, on this occasion.

Some philosophers doubt that it is possible for (P3.2)–(P3.5) (or some subset thereof) to be instantiated.[18] A full discussion of this issue would require mention not just of (P3.2)–(P3.5) but also of the matters of willingness, intention, and so on with respect to what is *prima facie* wrong and what is nonmorally wrong (*e.g.,* imprudent); and it would require mention not just of willingness, intention, and so on but of other so-called pro-attitudes. This is a discussion into which I shall not enter here; pursuing it would take us far too far afield. But as for (P3.2)–(P3.5) themselves, I must say that each of them seems to me such that it is perfectly logically possible that it be instantiated.[19] Indeed, (P3.2)–(P3.4) seem to me not only possibly, but all too frequently actually, instantiated. Whether or not (3.5) is ever in fact instantiated, I am not sure.[20] Anyway, even if none of (P3.2)–(P3.5) were possibly instantiated, this would imply only that it is not possible for anyone to be directly culpable for any volition; it would not imply that (P3.1) is false. (So let me reiterate something that I said in Chapter 1. I am not strictly presupposing that anyone ever is morally responsible for anything; I am merely inquiring into the condition that would have to be satisfied if anyone were to be morally responsible for something.)

Degrees of direct culpability. However, (P3.1) is not sufficiently precisely formulated, for it does not explicitly account for degrees of direct culpability. There are several dimensions along which such culpability may vary in degree.[21] The following suggest themselves. The degree of culpability varies according to: (i) whether the agent manifests satanic wickedness, or only malice, or only callousness; (ii) the seriousness of wrongness at issue; (iii) the likelihood of wrongdoing; and (iv) the degree of freedom that the agent enjoys in relation to his willingness to do wrong. I believe that (i)–(iii) are correct, and I shall discuss them shortly. I believe, however, that (iv) is false; I shall discuss it first.

Our discussion of (iv) can be brief. With respect to strict freedom, it is vacuous, since, intrinsically, strict freedom does not vary in degree.[22] With respect to broad freedom, (iv) is not vacuous; nevertheless, it is, I believe, false. I shall postpone discussion of this issue, however, to Section 4.6.

As for (i): satanic wickedness seems to represent the epitome of evil (or at least, of that sort of evil for which one may be appraisable[23]). Someone who manifests satanic wickedness wills to do wrong for wrong's sake; someone who manifests malice or callousness is certainly no rose either (at least on the occasion in question), but at least wrongdoing is not the focus of his volition. For this reason, I would say (along with many others, I believe[24]), that one is more culpable, *ceteris paribus*, for a volition which constitutes the manifestation of satanic wickedness than for a volition which constitutes the manifestation of malice or callousness. May we also say that the manifestation of malice likewise contributes to culpability to a greater degree than that of callousness? This seems initially attractive, and perhaps it is correct; but I am not sure. For, when malice does not amount to satanic wickedness, wrongdoing is not the focus of the agent's volition. To be sure, the agent wills to do wrong, but only for the sake of something else. The wrong is seen to be a means to some further end—but does this confer more culpability on the agent than if the wrong were foreseen by him "merely" to be a side-effect of, rather than a means to, his achieving his end?[25] Why should this be? If this is so, then perhaps some principle of double effect is correct; but I am unclear why we should think it to be so.[26]

As for (ii): if the agent does not believe that wrongness may vary in seriousness, then of course no variation of degree of culpability is forthcoming here. But if the agent does believe that some acts are (as it is often put) "more seriously wrong" than others—we might just say: more wrong than others—then such belief can affect the degree to which the agent is culpable. To use numerals in a wholly *ad hoc* fashion: if S believes that in bringing about e he would do wrong to degree 10, whereas in bringing about f he would do wrong to degree 50, and if he chooses to bring about e rather than f, then he, while culpable, would seem not to be as culpable *(ceteris paribus)* as he would be if he were to choose to bring about f. (After all, S may balk at bringing about f, even though not at bringing about e, and here we should give him credit—or, at least, reduce his discredit—for this. Of course, it might be that S does not balk, for *moral* reasons, at bringing about f but chooses to bring about e anyway, and it might seem that in this case he is no less culpable than he would be if he were to choose to bring about f. This may or may not be so—it is a difficult matter. At the moment I shall assume that it is not so; it is a matter of what he would have done had he found himself in different circumstances, which is an issue that I shall discuss in Section 4.11.) Degree of wrongdoing constitutes one element of *risk* in wrongdoing.

As for (iii): we must take care to distinguish between the likelihood of doing wrong and the likelihood, for example, of doing harm. S may believe that there is a probability of .5 that, in bringing about e, he will do harm; but this does not imply that he believes that there is a probability of .5 that, in bringing about e, he will do wrong. He may believe that it is quite wrong to risk the harm; that is, he may believe that, if he brings about e, he will certainly do wrong (whether or not he in fact does harm). Or he may believe that it is quite all right to risk the harm; that is, he may believe that, if he brings about e, he will certainly do no wrong (whether or not he in fact does harm). Here I am concerned with an agent's belief concerning the likelihood of his doing *wrong*.[27] I suppose that one of the most common cases in which an agent believes it possible, or probable, but not certain that, in bringing about e, he will do wrong, is where he is just unsure as to whether bringing about e constitutes wrongdoing. (An important variation on this case is this: the agent has an inadequate grasp of the very concept of wrongdoing.[28]) At any rate, it seems that we may say the following (where again the use of numerals is *ad hoc*): if S believes that in bringing about e there is a probability of .1 that he would do wrong, whereas in bringing about f there is a probability of .5 that he would do wrong, and if he chooses to bring about e rather than f, then he, while culpable, is not as culpable *(ceteris paribus)* as he would be if he were to choose to bring about f.

I have just mentioned the matter of risk. When one chances doing wrong, one *risks* it. It is perhaps more in keeping with current English usage of "chance" and "risk" to confine one's use of these terms in this context to *likelihood* of wrongdoing, so as to exclude reference to *seriousness* of wrongdoing. But there is some precedent, I think, for including the latter as one of the elements of risk, and it is certainly economical to do this. At any rate, however one puts it, one must, I think, recognize degree of culpability to be in part determined by some function of likelihood and seriousness of wrongdoing *combined*. Thus, I propose that we say that there are these two elements of risk in wrongdoing; that the more serious the wrongness that one attributes to an action, the greater the risk of wrongdoing that one attributes to the volition involved; and also that the greater the likelihood of being wrong that one attributes to an action, the greater the risk of wrongdoing that one attributes to the volition involved.[29] And then I propose that in general we say that, the greater the risk of wrongdoing that one attributes to a volition, the more culpable one is for one's volition. But there are two important exceptions to this. First, if S believes that, in bringing about e rather than f, he would *minimize the risk* of wrongdoing, then it seems that he deserves no blame at all for his choice to bring about e. The reason for this is that he thereby demonstrates no callousness, no willingness to do wrong. In other words, (P3.1r), as indicated earlier, does *not* in fact imply (P3.2) without qualification; the implication fails when S believes that he would minimize the risk of wrongdoing.[30] Secondly, if S wills to do wrong for wrong's sake, then, while the seriousness of the wrong seems pertinent to the degree to which he deserves blame, the likelihood of wrongdoing does not. After all, he is "going for it," no matter what the odds; the *likelihood* of wrongdoing is not a factor in his volition.

Of course, there is a real roughness in all of the foregoing; but this is unavoidable. Degrees of culpability are simply not necessarily open to exact computation; there can be, and often is, a genuine objective indeterminacy concerning a person's moral worth. Nevertheless, what has been said suggests the following revision of (P3.1):

(P3.1') S is directly culpable to degree x for willing e if and only if
(a) S strictly freely willed e, in the belief[31] that it was likely to degree y that, by virtue of so willing, he would do wrong to degree z, and
(b) S did not believe that his bringing about e would minimize the risk of his doing wrong.

In this statement: x is a function of z; x is a function of y if and only if S did not strictly freely will to do wrong to degree z for the sake of wrong to degree z;[32] and the risk at issue in clause (b) is seen by S to be some function of both the seriousness and the likelihood of the wrongdoing that he believes may occur by virtue of his willing e. It is impossible to specify these functions further; only in particular cases where S's beliefs happen to be specific in this regard can a more specific account of x be given. Still, it is instructive, or at least suggestive, to think of the functions as multiplicative (where we indulge the fiction that the degrees at issue may be assigned precise numerical values). In such a case, where y is pertinent, x approaches zero when y does and, where z is pertinent, x also approaches zero when z does. Moreover, the degree of risk of wrongdoing may be thought of as (or as analogous to) a multiplicative function of the degree of seriousness of wrongdoing and the degree of likelihood of wrongdoing. Of course, all of this holds only as long as S attributes some degree y to the likelihood of his doing wrong and some degree z to the seriousness of the wrongness at issue. If this is not so, then S will be directly culpable and yet not directly culpable to any specific degree. And even if this is so, if the degrees x and y in question are not fully determinate, then the degree to which S is directly culpable will also not be fully determinate. It is for this reason that I said that there might be a genuine objective indeterminacy concerning a person's moral worth.

No doubt many may find (P3.1') dubious, for a variety of reasons. I shall discuss what I take to be the major reasons for such doubts in the next chapter.

3.2 Direct Laudability

Doing right. There is an important asymmetry to be noted between direct culpability and direct laudability. It rests on the fact, roughly put, that what is perceived as obligatory or as one's duty demands its pursuit, what is perceived as right invites its pursuit, and what is perceived as wrong demands its eschewal. Thus one deserves praise only if one pursues the right, while (as we have seen) it is *not* the case that one deserves blame only if one pursues the wrong; rather, one deserves blame only if one does not eschew the wrong.[33]

Thus the conditions of direct laudability do not parallel those for direct culpability. A first approximation of what I take the former to be may be put as follows:

(P3.6) S is directly laudable for willing e if and only if
(a) S strictly freely willed e for right's sake, and
(b) S believed that he would thereby avoid merely doing his duty.

As with (P3.1) and its use of "wrong," by "right" I here mean that which is *morally* right *all things considered* and by "duty" that which is *morally* obligatory *all things considered*. And again, I emphasize the strict independence of rightness and obligatoriness, on the one hand, from laudability, on the other. Also, as with (P3.1), the right-hand side of (P3.6)—specifically, its clause (a)—has certain important implications, among which are not only:

(P3.7)   *S* was willing to do right

(compare (P3.2)), but *also* each of the following (compare (P3.3), (P3.4), and (P3.5) respectively):

(P3.8)   *S* intended to do right,

(P3.9)   *S* willed to do right,

(P3.10)   *S* willed to do right for right's sake.

(P3.10) is crucial. *S* earns no luster on his record if he wills *e*, merely believing that he will thereby do right; nor if he wills *e*, merely intending that right thereby occur. To deserve praise he must will *e* for the sake of right; rightness must be the focus of a volition of his.

This is strong stuff; in particular, the "only if" of (P3.6) may appear much too restrictive. What makes (P3.6) especially restrictive is that its right-hand side implies (P3.10). This implication is pretty much in line with what Kant says in the *Groundwork*. There he clearly draws a distinction between acting in accordance with duty and acting for the sake of duty, and he is adamant that only the latter confers moral worth on one's action.[34] Some have criticized Kant on this score, claiming this to be too rigid an ethic.[35] What, after all, if an action is motivated by compassion rather than duty? Is there not, surely, some moral worth to be seen in such action? But I think that Kant is quite right to resist this, for reasons that I shall present in Section 4.9.

There are of course differences between Kant's position and mine. First, he talks of the moral worth of actions; I would rather talk of the moral worth of persons (measured by the credits and debits in their ledgers) as constituted by their actions or, more precisely, their volitions. In so doing, I do not mean to downplay the role of volitions or actions; they form part of the "praise-basis" or "blame-basis."[36] But it is after all the *agent* whose credit or discredit is at issue, in the manner indicated at the outset of this chapter. Secondly, Kant talks of acting for *duty's* sake; I would rather talk of acting for *right's* sake. I shall discuss this shortly when discussing clause (b) of (P3.6). Thirdly, there is reason to think that Kant believes that, if one acts for the sake of duty, then one acts in accordance with duty.[37] But I believe that one can aim for the right without doing right; and, as I shall argue later, failing to do what is right does not detract from one's laudability.

Kant is sometimes interpreted as saying not only that an action has moral worth only if its agent performs it for the sake of duty, but that it has such worth only if it is performed *solely* for the sake of duty.[38] This seems to me an erroneous interpretation, as it does to many others.[39] Even if it is a correct interpretation, I certainly do not intend for (3.6) to have the implication that one is laudable only if one is motivated to bring about *e* solely by the thought that one will thereby be doing right. Surely a concurrent inclination, based on self-interest or whatever, to bring about *e* does not detract from one's moral worth in willing *e* for right's sake. On the other hand, in order for this volition to be a willing of *e for right's sake,* one's motivation to do right must, I think, be in and of itself not just a *sufficient* but also a dominant or *primary* (or at least nonsecondary) motivation for bringing about *e*. Thus, any concurrent differing purpose that one has in willing *e* must be superfluous. I do not deny that there are conceptual difficulties involved in the notion of such motivational superfluity, but I shall not discuss them here.[40]

Kant is sometimes charged with embracing an incoherent view of moral worth. He is sometimes interpreted as claiming that it is our duty to act for the sake of duty, and this is taken by some to be an incoherent doctrine. Whether or not the interpretation is correct[41]—I think that some passages in the *Groundwork* warrant such an interpretation while others do not—and whether or not such a doctrine is incoherent[42]—I suspect that it is—is of no concern to me here. For I am certainly not advocating any such view. In Kantian terms, all that I am advocating (and all that Kant is himself advocating, according to some) is that an action is morally worthy only if it is done for the sake of duty, and not that an action fulfills one's moral duty only if it is done for the sake of duty.

Finally, the rationale for clause (b) of (P3.6) is this: freely willing not to do what one perceives to be one's duty occasions culpability; if freely willing not to do something occasions culpability, then freely willing to do that thing does not (in and of itself) occasion laudability (but merely the absence of culpability); hence, freely willing to do what one perceives to be one's duty does not (in and of itself) occasion laudability (but merely the absence of culpability). Of course, this conclusion may well appear too harsh to some, and its alleged objectionability might perhaps be traced to the second premise. What argument do I have for this premise in turn? None. It just seems to me that an enhancement of one's moral standing cannot be attributable solely to the avoidance of a diminution of that standing—but this is to repeat the point in different terms, and not to argue for it. And I do acknowledge the apparent austerity of the conclusion. For instance, it requires that we say that someone who does what is in fact supererogatory, but which he regards as merely obligatory, deserves no praise. But do we really want to say that a famine relief worker, who laboriously saves hundreds from starving and insists (sincerely) that he is merely doing his duty, deserves no praise? I shall return to this issue in Section 4.9.

Degrees of direct laudability. Just as (P3.1) required refinement in terms of the introduction of degrees, so too does (P3.6). And, as before, we may distinguish four initially attractive dimensions. The degree of laudability might be thought to vary according to: (i) whether the agent willed to do right for right's sake, willed to do right, or merely foresaw doing it;[43] (ii) the "seriousness" of rightness at issue; (iii) the likelihood of doing right; and (iv) the degree of freedom that the agent enjoys in relation to his willingness to do right.

Again, despite its attractiveness, I believe that (iv) is false. With respect to strict freedom, it is vacuous; with respect to broad freedom, it is false for reasons that I shall give in Section 4.6.

But, in addition, I believe that (i) is false. (This reflects the asymmetry between laudability and culpability.) It is false because, according to (P3.6), laudability requires willing to do right for right's sake, so that the analogues to malice and callousness are nonstarters.

What of (ii) and (iii)? As with wrongdoing, we may talk of "risking" or "chancing" doing right, where such "chance" is seen to be a function both of the "seriousness" and of the likelihood of doing right. (In my opinion, there are no degrees of rightness—that is, there is no variation in the "seriousness" of rightness—while there are degrees of wrongness.[44] But the question here is not what the correct value-system *is,* but what the agent *believes* to be correct.) It might be thought that, while there can be variation in the degree of chance of doing right which the agent attributes to some volition, this has no interesting bearing on degree of laudability. For laudability requires willing to do right for right's sake, and if one does not aim to maximize the chance of doing right, then one is not aiming to do right for right's sake. But I am not sure that this is so; indeed, I am inclined to think that it is not so. For I can conceive of an agent who, while aiming to do right for right's sake, also aims to avoid being thought of as holier-than-thou. He believes that he can achieve the latter goal only by consciously steering clear of the best alternatives, and so he aims only at second- or third-best alternatives. But he still regards these inferior alternatives as cases of doing right, and he chooses them because of this rightness. Such behavior might be odd, I suppose, but I do not think that it is incoherent. Thus I would claim that degree of laudability varies directly with the degree of chance of doing right which the agent attributes to his volition—subject to these two qualifications. First, the agent must of course genuinely will to do right. If he thinks that it is so unlikely that he would succeed in doing right that he cannot summon up the intention, and thus the will, to do it, but can only wish that he could do it, then no praise is earned; for he has not, through the free exercise of his will, committed himself to what is right.[45] Secondly, if S believes that he is maximizing the chance of doing right and S' believes that *he* is maximizing the chance of doing right, but the chance of doing right which S attributes to his volition is smaller than that which S' attributes to *his* volition, S nonetheless deserves, *ceteris paribus,* the same praise as S'.[46]

The modification that I think is called for in (P3.6) is therefore as follows:

(P3.6')   S is directly laudable to degree x for willing e if and only if
(a) S strictly freely willed e for right's sake, in the belief[47] that it was likely to degree y that, by virtue of so willing, he would do right to degree z, and
(b) S believed that it was likely to degree w that, if he did right by virtue of willing e, he would avoid merely doing his duty.

As with (P3.1'), we may say that in (P3.6') x is a function of z (a complicated function, given the matter of maximization of chance just mentioned). We may also say, without qualification, that x is a function of y. (Of course, *this* qualification remains: "as long as S attributes some degree y to the likelihood of his doing right and some degree z to the seriousness of the rightness at issue.") And we may also say that x is a function of w. Finally, as with (P3.1'), many may entertain doubts about the truth of (P3.6'); but, again, I shall postpone discussion of such doubts until the next chapter.

3.3 Indirect and Conjoint Laudability and Culpability

Laudability and culpability may, of course, be indirect, just as freedom may be. One may, that is, deserve praise or blame for the consequences of volitions as well as for volitions themselves. Indeed, the bulk of actual praising and blaming surely concerns such consequences.

Yet there is something empty about such appraisability. Recall the diagram and commentary from Section 2.2 (see p. 30). Just as indirect freedom is wholly parasitic on direct freedom, so indirect laudability and culpability are wholly parasitic on direct laudability and culpability. Just as indirect freedom is wholly contained in direct freedom, so indirect laudability and culpability correspond with no entries in a person's ledger above and beyond those already entered as a matter of direct laudability and culpability. The point might be put this way: one is *substantially* laudable for an event if, but only if, one is directly laudable for it; similarly one is *substantially* culpable for an event if, but only if, one is directly culpable for it. This point has rarely been fully appreciated by philosophers.[48] The temptation to deny it is, I believe, often attributable, first, to the confusion of appraisability with liability and, second, to the confusion of liability with the overall justifiability of commending or censuring (especially, punishing) someone—matters to be discussed in Chapter 5. The temptation may also often be due to a failure to distinguish appraisability from causal responsibility (or from a hybrid personal-*cum-*

of the sort mentioned in Section 1.1.) For an agent can be causally responsible (or personally-*cum*-causally responsible) *only* for an event which occurs as a causal consequence of some event in which he is involved; clearly, then, there could be no such responsibility in the absence of the former event. Finally, the temptation may often be due to a failure to distinguish decisions from desires. I grant that there can be a morally important difference between a person who desires to do something that he recognizes as wrong and a person who acts on this desire; for the former may successfully resist the desire whereas the latter does not. But my point concerns a distinction *within* the category of acting on the desire, namely, that between the decision so to act and the consequence(s) of so deciding. The point does not (presently) concern the desire at all (I shall take up the issue of appraisability for desires in Section 4.9).

That indirect appraisability is essentially empty or insubstantial is a point whose importance, in the present context, cannot be overestimated. It is a point that seems often to be at variance with our common practice of ascribing responsibility, as I shall have occasion to note and discuss in some detail in the next chapter. (In the terminology that I have already used, the claim that indirect appraisability is essentially empty renders my account of responsibility deflationary.) In view of this, it is desirable that some proof of it be furnished. I offer the following: one is substantially (*i.e.,* nonemptily, *i.e.,* nonparasitically, *i.e.,* in a manner which is the occasion of a fresh entry in one's ledger) appraisable for an event only if one was substantially (*i.e.,* nonparasitically) free with respect to that event; one is substantially free with respect to an event only if one is directly free with respect to it; one is indirectly free with respect to an event only if one is not directly free with respect to it;[49] one is indirectly appraisable for an event only if one was indirectly free with respect to it; hence, one is indirectly appraisable for an event only if one is not substantially appraisable for it. Two points should be noted concerning this argument. First, the argument is overly simple, in that it ignores the possibility that one be both directly and indirectly appraisable for the same event; but this is a complication that need not be discussed here (although I shall mention it again shortly). Second, and more importantly, the argument is *not* grounded in any special theory of action or of freedom. On the contrary, its premises concern *only* the two basic assumptions that appraisability requires freedom and that direct freedom is to be distinguished from indirect freedom.

Just as indirect freedom, while empty in a sense, is freedom nonetheless, so too indirect laudability and culpability, while empty in a sense, are not to be discounted. Still, given this emptiness, we do have a certain leeway here. There are several positions that one might adopt with respect to indirect laudability and culpability, and none of them does violence to the underlying facts concerning direct laudability and culpability. I shall discuss four such positions.

When we attribute indirect laudability or culpability to someone for some event, we are saying that this event, with respect to which he had indirect freedom, is to his credit or discredit. (In the latter case, we more commonly say that the event is *his fault*.) In saying this, we are saying that, in bringing about (or helping to bring about, or contributing to—see (P2.1)–(P2.3)) the event in question, he was directly laudable or culpable. (In the latter case, we more commonly say that he was *at fault* in bringing about (or helping to bring about, or contributing to) the event.) Given the essential emptiness of indirect appraisability, we are at liberty to adopt a variety of positions concerning what we take to be its defining character-istics, these positions being dictated by extraneous considerations.[50]

One position is simply this: S is indirectly appraisable for e just in case e is a consequence of some volition for which S is directly appraisable. I shall call this the *Externalist Position*. Somewhat more precisely, the position is this:

(P3.11) S is indirectly laudable [culpable] to degree x for e if and only if, for some volition v of S,
           (a) S is directly laudable [culpable] to degree x for v, and
           (b) e is or was a consequence of v.

Clearly, this is a very liberal position; it is not one which we often adopt. I call it "externalist" since it does not impose any "internalist" require-ments for indirect appraisability beyond those which pertain to direct appraisability.

It will have been noted that in (P3.11) the degree to which S is said to be indirectly appraisable for e matches the degree to which S is directly appraisable for that volition of which e is or was a consequence. This is a stipulation on my part; insofar as one is at liberty to adopt a variety of positions on the conditions of indirect appraisability, one is also at liberty to adopt a variety of positions on the degree to which a person may be said to be indirectly appraisable for some event. Nevertheless, the stipu-lation that the degrees match is a healthy one; it serves to remind us that nothing substantial is added to (or subtracted from) a person's ledger when he becomes indirectly appraisable for some event. Henceforth, I shall stick with this stipulation. At any rate, it is extremely important to note that the *number* of events for which S is appraisable has no bearing on the *degree* to which he is appraisable. In particular, if S is directly appraisable to degree x for v, then the degree to which he is *substantially* appraisable remains constant *whether or not* v has any consequences for which he is also appraisable. The luster or blemish on S's record becomes no greater simply because his volition bears fruit and he is also appraisa-ble for this fruit. If his volition bears fruit, then he is *appraisable for more,* but he is no *more appraisable* than if it had been barren. This is simply a reflection of the essential emptiness of indirect appraisability.

A second, somewhat less liberal position that seems to me at least close to one which we often adopt is one that I shall call the *Externalist Right/Wrong Position.* It is this:

(P3.12)   *S* is indirectly laudable [culpable] to degree *x* for *e* if and only if, for some volition *v* of *S*,
  (a) *S* is directly laudable [culpable] to degree *x* for *v*,
  (b) *e* is or was a consequence of *v*, and
  (c) in bringing about (or helping to bring about, or contributing to) *e* by virtue of *v*, *S* did right [wrong].

A third position, which I shall call the *Internalist Position,* requires an understanding of what it is for an event to enter into a volition. Let us say this:

(P3.13)   *e* enters into *S*'s volition *v* if and only if, for some event *f*,
  (a) *S* wills *f*, in the belief that it is likely that he will thereby bring about (or help to bring about, or contribute to) *e*, and
  (b) *v* is *S*'s willing *f*.

We may then put the Internalist Position as follows:

(P3.14)   *S* is indirectly laudable [culpable] to degree *x* for *e* if and only if, for some volition *v* of S,
  (a) *S* is directly laudable [culpable] to degree *x* for *v*,
  (b) *e* is or was a consequence of *v*, and
  (c) *e* entered into *v*.

Clause (c) of this position establishes its "internalist" credentials.

A fourth position is one that I shall call the *Internalist Right/Wrong Position.* As might be expected, it is this:

(P3.15)   *S* is indirectly laudable [culpable] to degree *x* for *e* if and only if, for some volition *v* of *S*,
  (a) *S* is directly laudable [culpable] to degree *x* for *v*,
  (b) *e* is or was a consequence of *v*,
  (c) *e* entered into *v*, and
  (d) in bringing about (or helping to bring about, or contributing to) *e* by virtue of *v*, *S* did right [wrong].

Clearly, other positions on indirect appraisability are open for adoption. It is tempting to ask: but what is the *correct* position? My answer is, of course, that there is none; that, due to the essential emptiness of indirect appraisability, none of the four foregoing (or any other) positions on indirect appraisability has a claim to being "the correct" position. Again, which position one adopts is to be dictated by extraneous considerations.

However, having said this, I shall add that the Internalist Position seems to me, in general, to be the least misleading. The great merit of this position is that the internal source of S's appraisability for e is revealed. When we employ this account of indirect appraisability and say that S is indirectly appraisable for e, we give an indication as to what it is that gives rise to such appraisability, what that volition is for which S is directly appraisable.[51] Let us say the following:

(P3.16) S is substantially laudable [culpable] to degree x concerning e if and only if either
(a) S is substantially laudable [culpable] to degree x for e, or
(b) S is substantially laudable [culpable] to degree x for some volition which concerned e.

What is it for a volition to concern an event? For present purposes we may say simply this: if e enters into a volition v, then v concerns e. It follows that, if we adopt the Internalist Position on indirect appraisability, we shall ascribe indirect appraisability for an event e only where the agent is in fact substantially appraisable concerning e. In thus restricting our ascriptions of appraisability, we effectively resist the temptation (as we may well not on the Externalist Position) to see *substantial* appraisability where there is none. For this reason, I believe that the Internalist Position is often the most advisable position to adopt. What is more, it seems clear to me that, in ascribing indirect appraisability, we often in fact cleave to something like the Internalist Position. For example, I may quite willfully fail to keep a promise by not turning up at the library at noon, and I may well be culpable for my volition. But if, as a consequence, I fail to rescue a child from drowning in the river next to the library—a rescue which I would easily have performed had I kept my promise—most people, I think, would not blame me for the child's death. Why? Because I am clearly not substantially culpable concerning the child's death; I was quite unaware of the child and his plight and thus did not willingly let him drown. (Notice what a good, but clearly not infallible, indicator of unwillingness with respect to e is the absence of transparent freedom with respect to e. The child's death was beyond my transparent freedom and thus, in an important sense, beyond my control.[52]) Of course, even if we commonly adopt the Internalist Position in a case such as this, it may yet be that we commonly adopt a different position in a different sort of case. And I think that this may be so in cases of ignorance, negligence, and other matters. But whether it is advisable to discard the Internalist Position in such cases is another matter. I shall address this issue in Chapter 4.

Is it common or advisable to adopt the Right/Wrong Position (whether Externalist or Internalist)? I think that it is quite common to do this but, again, whether or not it is advisable to do so is another matter. Perhaps there is good reason to do so when one refers to appraisability merely as a preliminary to punishment; I shall discuss this in Section 5.4. And it must be acknowledged that it can seem odd to praise someone for some event e, the bringing about of which was wrong, or to blame someone for some event e, the bringing about of which was right. But the fact remains that laudable volitions can be involved in doing wrong and culpable volitions in doing right, and one must beware overlooking this fact through an unquestioning adherence to the Right/Wrong Position (whether Externalist or Internalist); for where the Internalist Position serves to reveal the source of an agent's appraisability, the Right/Wrong Position can serve to conceal it.

Whichever of the foregoing positions is adopted, it should be noted that someone may be indirectly appraisable to several differing degees all at once for the same event. This is usually because one and the same event can be a consequence of *several* volitions, as when a bank is successfully robbed after months of preliminary work. (Several events may also be a consequence of one and the same volition, but this is beside the point.) Thus, if one is appraisable to degree 10 for v' and to degree 20 for v', and if e is a consequence of each (and enters into each, if we are adopting the Internalist Position, and constitutes doing right or wrong, if we are adopting the Right/Wrong Position), then S is appraisable *both* to degree 10 *and* to degree 20 for e.

It is possible to be both laudable and culpable for the same event. This can happen in several ways. S may be directly laudable for e but indirectly culpable for it (as could be true of Jones in the original car-accident case—see p. 41); S may be indirectly laudable for e but directly culpable for it (a case of this sort is more difficult to imagine, but here is a possible one: Jones is laudably about to rescue the driver, an enemy of his, when he has a change of heart and attempts to paralyze him by pulling him from the wreck; he may well be directly culpable for attempting to pull the driver from the wreck while being indirectly laudable for this, in that the attempt is, in part, a consequence of a laudable volition); and S may be indirectly laudable for e and indirectly culpable for it. This is important. We often have conflicting reactions to a certain episode of behavior—for instance, to someone meaning well but acting negligently; and we are often at a loss as to how to evaluate this episode. The answer is: we should both praise and blame the agent for it; we need not, indeed should not, settle on just one or the other.

Is it possible for someone to be both *directly* laudable and *directly* culpable for the same event? This is unclear to me, although I think that it is possible. Consider the following case. S strictly freely wills e for the sake of nonobligatory right; but he also believes that, in so willing, he is running a less-than-minimal risk of doing wrong. For example, e may be a charitable act of some kind, and the wrong risked that of not repaying a loan. It might be retorted that this case is incoherent, that if S really had his sights set on doing right, he would attempt to minimize the risk of doing wrong. But, as before, while I agree that S's behavior may be odd, I am reluctant to say that it is incoherent.

In Section 3.1 of this chapter, it was noted that perhaps it is appropriate on occasion to ascribe "retrospective" responsibility for some *future* event. Whether or not it is appropriate was said to rest on whether or not there can be true propositions about the free volitions and actions of persons in the future. But we may note here that, if there can be true propositions about any future events (and not necessarily about free volitions and actions), then there would seem to be no logical barrier to ascribing *indirect* appraisability to someone for some future event. (If so, then "or will be" should be added to clause (b) of each of (P3.11), (P3.12), (P3.14), and (P3.15).) For, if S has willed e, and if it is true that f will be a consequence of this volition, and if S is directly appraisable for his volition (and if whatever a non-Externalist Position requires to be satisfied is satisfied), then it is true *now* that S is indirectly appraisable for f.

It is very important to note that indirect appraisability of course requires only indirect freedom. It is perfectly possible to be appraisable for an unfree action by virtue of being indirectly appraisable for an unfree volition. For example, I may freely take a pill now that I expect will make it impossible for me an hour from now to resist choosing to run amok, thereby causing considerable damage.[53] If in an hour I do so run amok and cause damage, then (given certain assumptions) I am to be blamed for the damage I cause, even though, *at the time I cause the damage*, my action is beyond my control. For I could have prevented the damage; there was an *earlier* time at which my *later* causing of the damage *was* in my control. That is, at that earlier time, I was in indirect, remote control of the damage.

So far I have talked of (direct) appraisability for volitions and of (indirect) appraisability for the consequences of volitions, but I have not talked of appraisability for actions, which are complexes of volitions and their consequences. And yet it is often for their actions that people are primarily held responsible. Here I suggest that we simply say that appraisability for actions involves a "conjunction" of direct and indirect appraisability. More precisely:

(P3.17) S is conjointly laudable [culpable] to degree x for bringing about e if and only if, for some volition v of S,
(a) S brings about e by virtue of v,
(b) S is directly laudable [culpable] to degree x for v, and
(c) S is indirectly laudable [culpable] to degree x for e.[54]

We may treat in exactly analogous fashion those episodes of acting which are not bringings about but rather helpings to bring about or merely contributings.[55] Notice that there are a variety of positions that one may adopt with respect to conjoint appraisability, just as there are with respect to indirect appraisability. If one adopts the Externalist Position with respect to indirect appraisability then, by virtue of clause (c) of (P3.17), one is committed to adopting it also with respect to conjoint appraisability. So too with the Internalist Position, and so on. As before, I find the Internalist Position least misleading here. In this regard we may note that, while one may not talk of substantial appraisability for actions, one may talk of substantial appraisability *concerning* actions. Here, however, we must refine our understanding of what it is for a volition v to *concern* an event, in particular an *action*, e. Let us say that, if f is what I have called the issue internal to e and f enters into v, then v concerns e. In this way we may talk of substantial appraisability concerning, not just volitions and their consequences, but also those actions of which these events are parts.

Finally, in light of the foregoing, we may of course say the following:

(P3.18) S is laudable to degree x for e if and only if either
(a) S is directly laudable to degree x for e, or
(b) S is indirectly laudable to degree x for e, or
(c) S is conjointly laudable to degree x for e.

(P3.19) S is culpable to degree x for e if and only if either
(a) S is directly culpable to degree x for e, or
(b) S is indirectly culpable to degree x for e, or
(c) S is conjointly culpable to degree x for e.

As mentioned before, doubts concerning the truth of (P3.18) and (P3.19) will be addressed in the next chapter.

3.4 Indifference-Worthiness

While inward praise- and blameworthiness are the main forms of appraisability, they are not the only forms. There is also what I shall call *indifference-worthiness* or, for short, *i-worthiness*.

There is a difference to be noted between (i) having no entry in one's ledger with respect to e, (ii) having both a credit and a debit of the same "amount" entered into one's ledger with respect to e, and (iii) having an entry of "neither credit nor debit"—a moral "zero"—entered into one's ledger with respect to e. All three possibilities concern a sort of neutrality, but only the last expresses the possibility of one's being i-worthy for e.

As for (i): this can arise in a number of ways. One may have no ledger, as when, for example, one is a stone, an animal, an infant, an idiot; this is due to the lack of a capacity to will freely or to have appropriate beliefs and intentions concerning doing right and doing wrong. Or one may have a ledger but simply lack this freedom or these beliefs or intentions on the occasion in question.

As for (ii): this has in essence been discussed in the preceding sections of this chapter.

As for (iii): this arises on those occasions where the agent manifests both appropriate freedom and appropriate moral beliefs but nonetheless incurs neither laudability nor culpability. (An extreme case of this is that of the 'moral nihilist,' as he may be called, whose ledger consists of a series of zeros due to the continual belief that he is not doing wrong and also not going beyond duty.) I-worthiness may be understood somewhat roughly as follows:

(P3.20) S is directly i-worthy for willing e if and only if S strictly freely willed e
(a) in the belief that thereby he was risking no wrong or at least was minimizing the risk thereof, but
(b) not for the sake of thereby doing nonobligatory right to any degree.

An account of indirect and conjoint i-worthiness may be given that parallels those given for indirect and conjoint laudability and culpability; again, there are an Externalist, an Internalist, and also Right/Wrong Positions between which one must distinguish and choose. And one may be said to be i-worthy just in case one is directly, indirectly, or conjointly i-worthy.

There are no degrees of i-worthiness.

3.5 Appraisability Analyzed

The analysis of moral appraisability is now to hand. I shall spell it out in somewhat tedious detail; none of it is difficult or surprising.

(P3.21) S is directly appraisable to degree x for willing e if and only if either
(a) S is directly laudable to degree x for willing e, or
(b) S is directly i-worthy to degree x for willing e, or
(c) S is directly culpable to degree x for willing e.

(P3.22) S is indirectly appraisable to degree x for e if and only if either

(a) S is indirectly laudable to degree x for e, or
(b) S is indirectly i-worthy to degree x for e, or
(c) S is indirectly culpable to degree x for e.

(P3.23) S is conjointly appraisable to degree x for e if and only if either
(a) S is conjointly laudable to degree x for e, or
(b) S is conjointly i-worthy to degree x for e, or
(c) S is conjointly culpable to degree x for e.

(P3.24) S is appraisable to degree x for e if and only if either
(a) S is directly appraisable to degree x for e, or
(b) S is indirectly appraisable to degree x for e, or
(c) S is conjointly appraisable to degree x for e.

An equivalent alternative to (P3.24), relying on (P3.18) and (P3.19) and the closing remarks in Section 3.4, is this:

(P3.24′) S is appraisable to degree x for e if and only if either
(a) S is laudable to degree x for e, or
(b) S is i-worthy to degree x for e, or
(c) S is culpable to degree x for e.

Given that one may be appraisable in several ways for or concerning one and the same event, one may bear several degrees of appraisability for or concerning one and the same event. (In the case of i-worthiness, talk of degree of appraisability is of course, redundant.)

Finally, and perhaps most importantly, we may say:

(P3.25) S is substantially appraisable to degree x *for* e if and only if S is directly appraisable to degree x for e.

(P3.26) S is substantially appraisable to degree x *concerning* e if and only if either
(a) S is substantially appraisable to degree x for e, or
(b) S is substantially appraisable to degree x for some volition which concerned e.

(P3.25) is crucial. To put the matter in terms of our initial metaphor about "ledgers of life," what (P3.25) tells us is this. First, a person has a credit in his ledger just in case he satisfies the analysans[56] of (P3.6′) (let us call this his having the property F). Second, a person has a discredit or debit in his ledger just in case he satisfies the analysans of (P3.1′) (let us call this his having the property G). Third, a person has a zero in his ledger just in case he satisfies the analysans of (P3.20) (let us call this having the property H). Fourth, a person has an entry in his ledger just in case he has either F, or G, or H. And, fifth, a person is worthy of being judged to have an entry in his ledger—is, in short, substantially appraisable—just in case he has an entry in his ledger. This fifth step is, in a sense, redundant, but it is worth making explicit note of it; for there is a difference between having an entry in one's ledger and being worthy of being judged to have such an entry, even if the two are necessarily coextensive.

Appraisability is a type of responsibility which is broad in one sense but narrow in another. It is broad in that it encompasses each of (inward) praise-, i-, and blameworthiness and, in particular, is not restricted to blameworthiness.[57] It is narrow in that it is to be distinguished from liability.

It is perhaps worth recapitulating here two salient features of the foregoing analysis of appraisability. First, one may do right without being laudable, do neither right nor wrong (if this is possible) without being i-worthy, and do wrong without being culpable. Second, one may be laudable without doing right, i-worthy without doing neither right nor wrong, and culpable without doing wrong;[58] indeed, one may be laudable and yet do wrong, culpable and yet do right.[59] For it is the thought—in particular, the volition—that counts where appraisability is concerned. Indeed, it is *only* the volition that counts, insofar as indirect appraisability is essentially empty—hence my claim that the present analysis of appraisability is appropriately termed "internalist."

3.6 Justification and Excuse

To exculpate someone is to defend him successfully; more particularly, it is to clear him of a charge; more particularly still, it is to prove him blameless. It is common to distinguish two types of exculpation—justification and excuse—where one has a justification just in case the means by which one would be exculpated, if charged, would be that of justifying, and one has an excuse just in case the means by which one would be exculpated, if charged, would be that of excusing.[60] In the law, the distinction is perhaps clear enough; if, in bringing about *e*, *S* commits no offense, then and only then is it the case that he is justified in—that is, he has a justification for—bringing about *e;* if he commits an offense but is not liable to penalty or punishment for so doing, then and only then is it the case that he has an excuse for bringing about *e*.[61] There are just three possibilities here, and they may be tabulated as follows:

Table I

		O	&	Li	iff	J	&	E
Case	1	yes		yes		no		no
	2	yes		no		no	←	yes
	3	no	→	no		yes	→	no

The table is to be read as follows. Case 1: in bringing about *e, S* commits an *offense (O)* and is *liable (Li)* to penalty or punishment, if, and only if, being charged with bringing about *e,* he has neither a *justification (J)* nor an *excuse (E)* for bringing about *e;* similarly for cases 2 and 3. The arrows indicate implications; for example, case 2 tells us that, if *S* has an excuse for bringing about *e,* then he does not have a justification for this.

Many philosophers appear to think that this way of accounting for justification and excuse may be carried over wholesale from the legal to the moral arena.[62] This is a mistake; there is both a barrier to doing so and a problem in doing so. First the barrier; moral blame may be directed on to volitions as well as actions, and we cannot simply assume that an action is morally wrong just in case it contains a volition that is morally wrong; for one volition may feature in many actions, and many volitions in one action. Still, I suppose that it may be true that, whatever criterion we should adopt in determining the rightness or wrongness of actions may also be used (perhaps in somewhat modified form) for determining the rightness or wrongness of volitions, so that the tables that follow may be seen to apply equally well to volitions as to actions.[63] But, even so, there is a problem, and that is that we cannot simply apply Table I to the moral arena; and this is because (i) one can be morally blameworthy, that is, culpable without having done moral wrong, and *vice versa,* and (ii) one can be morally responsible, that is, appraisable without being culpable. In this context, (i) serves to emphasize a very important point, namely, that *to justify is not to exculpate.* The failure to appreciate this point can be very damaging. Too often, our moral inquiries are prematurely terminated when it is determined that no wrong has been done. It is thought that, where there is justification, there is nothing further to look into—that "of course" no question of an excuse arises, because there is "nothing (left)" to excuse. But this just is not so. Given the total independence of culpability and wrongdoing, we must recognize the total independence of justification and excuse. Indeed, the truth of the matter seems to be captured in the following table:

Table II

		W	&	A	&	C	iff	J	&	RadE	&	RegE
Case	1	yes		yes		yes		no		no		no
	2	yes		yes		no		no		no		yes
	3	yes		no	→	no		no		yes	→	yes
	4	no		yes		yes		yes		no		no
	5	no		yes		no		yes		no		yes
	6	no		no	→	no		yes		yes	→	yes

This needs some clarification.

Case 1 of Table II tells us that, in bringing about *e, S* does *wrong (W),* and is *appraisable (A)* for so doing, and is *culpable (C)* for so doing, if, and only if, being charged with bringing about *e*, he has neither a *justification* (*J*), nor a *radical excuse* (*RadE*), nor a *regular excuse* (*RegE*) for so doing. (The arrows in Table II, as in Table I, signify implication.) What is the distinction between a "radical" and a "regular" excuse? Simply this: if *S* is not appraisable at all (and hence, of course, not culpable) for *e,* then *S* has what I call a radical excuse for *e;* while, if *S* is appraisable for *e* but not culpable for it (that is, he is either laudable or i-worthy for *e*), then he has a regular excuse for *e*.[64] Of course, if *S* has done no wrong and is not culpable for what he has done, then it might seem a little odd to say that he has an excuse (whether radical or regular) for what he has done; but the point is that an excuse is in practice tendered only when a charge has been made, and it can of course happen that *S* is charged with culpable wrongdoing even when in fact he is not culpable and has not done wrong. Also, one might think it less odd to say that one has a regular excuse only if one does *not* have a radical excuse (that is, that only those who are appraisable can have regular excuses); but, for simplicity's sake, I think that we should say that whoever has a radical excuse *ipso facto* has a regular excuse.[65] Table II may thus be summarized as follows. (i) I have a justification for what I have done if and only if I have not done wrong[66]—and this is quite independent of any question of appraisability for what I have done. (ii) I have a radical excuse for what I have done if and only if I am not appraisable (and hence not culpable) for what I have done—and this is quite independent of any question of actual wrongdoing. (iii) I have a regular excuse for what I have done if and only if I am not culpable for what I have done—and, again, this is quite independent of any question of actual wrongdoing.

Notice that Table II allows, as Table I does not, for the possibility that an agent have both a justification and an excuse for bringing about *e*.[67] This arises in case 6, due to the fact that an agent may be appraisable for doing something which is not wrong but in this case is not so appraisable. It arises in case 5 also, due to the fact that an agent may be culpable for doing something that is not wrong but in this case is not, even though he is appraisable.

It is a commonplace in legal theory that the distinction between a justification and an excuse, while easy to state, is often difficult to apply.[68] This is true; for it often happens that, while it is clear that a defendant should not be found guilty, it is unclear whether this is because he has committed no offense or because he has done so but excusably. This is a matter of interpreting the law. Similar difficulties of course beset one who wishes to apply Table II to moral matters; it is often difficult to decide what is right or wrong, let alone what an agent has willed with respect to what he regards as right or wrong. But these practical difficulties do not affect the theoretical accuracy of the table.

Still, it may be pointed out that the common difficulty in determining whether, for example, in cases of necessity or duress, the agent has a justification or an excuse for acting as he does may be alleviated somewhat by taking note of certain distinctions. These are: the distinction between what is wrong under normal circumstances and what is wrong under actual circumstances; the distinction between what is *prima facie* wrong and what is wrong all things considered; and the distinction between what is legally wrong and what is morally wrong. It may be that someone who, for example, has eaten a human corpse in order to survive a blizzard in the Andes has done something that is morally wrong all things considered under normal circumstances, *prima facie* morally wrong, and legally wrong; it does not follow that what he did was morally wrong all things considered under actual circumstances. Under the actual circumstances, then, where the agent's broad freedom is severely compromises, it may be that he has a justification for acting as he was compelled. Whether or not this is so depends on which theory of "objective" obligation is correct. (See the discussion of this issue on pp. 41–43 above.) In my opinion, this is in fact not so, if he would have done better not to eat the corpse, whereas it is so, if he could have done no better than to eat it. Of course, whichever is the case, it may well be that it was perfectly *reasonable* for the agent to have thought he was doing what was, or would prove to be, best; and if this fact prompted him to believe that he was not, or was not likely to be doing wrong, then he has an excuse, regardless of whether or not he has a justification, for acting as he did. On the other hand, if he believed that he was doing wrong and if he strictly could have done otherwise, then, in my view, regardless of whether he has a justification for acting as he did, he has no excuse.

In concentrating on justification and excuse, I have overlooked a third main category of defense, that of denial.[69] But I have been working under the assumption that *S* has willed *e* or brought *e* about; thus denial of this is irrelevant here.[70]

It is clear that excuses (often) come in degrees; for culpability (often) does. (It may be that justification comes in degrees also, although this is not so commonly noted; it depends on whether wrongness does.[71]) One may thus distinguish between total and partial exculpation; in the former all blame is eliminated, while in the latter blame is merely diminished. I think that radical excuses are always totally exculpatory except in one instance, although I am not sure about this; for they apply where either strict freedom is absent (which, I noted earlier, appears not to be, intrinsically, a matter of degree) or relevant beliefs are absent (which again appears not to be a matter of degree—except in one instance). The one instance that I have in mind is that where the agent has an inadequate grasp of the very concept of wrongdoing. This was mentioned briefly in Section 3.1 as being one factor that might affect degree of culpability. It does this, I think, by affecting appraisability as its "roots," so to speak, in that, if one has an inadequate grasp of the concept of wrongness, then one must also have an inadequate grasp of the concepts of obligation, rightness, and of any sort of neutrality that mediates rightness and wrongness. Thus any diminution of culpability for e due to an inadequate grasp of the concept of wrongness occasions a diminution of *any* type of appraisability for e.

Otherwise, it seems to me, only regular excuses come in degrees. These reflect the degrees of culpability already accommodated by (P3.1'): the stronger the excuse, the weaker the culpability, and *vice versa*. But a complication arises here. It is this: if there is no upper limit (as there seems not to be) to the degree to which someone may be culpable for e, there would seem to be serious problems with any talk of "full" responsibility.[72] But is there then no occasion on which someone who is culpable cannot be said to have some (regular) excuse for e? Surely this seems a silly thing to say. And in a way it is. Again, we should not lose sight of the fact that having an excuse is always relative to some charge; thus, whether or not there is an excuse, and to what degree, is likewise so relative. If the charge is perfectly accurate, then, relative to it, there is no excuse whatsoever—to any degree—despite the fact that the agent cannot be infinitely culpable; and if there is no charge, no ac-cusation, there is again no ex-cuse.

A variation on diminution of blame for e without total exculpation is this: total exculpation for e but culpability for some related event f. In the law, for example, a defendant may be found not guilty of "murder one" but guilty of "murder two."[73] Similarly, in the moral arena, one may initially be thought culpable to degree x for e but then found to be culpable to a lesser degree y, not for e, but for some related event f.

Finally, we should note that exculpation is just one side of the moral coin; there is what may be called "exlaudation" also. If we talk of "dejustification" as the counterpart to justification and of "disentitlement" as the counterpart to excuse[74], we get a table that matches Table II:

Table III

		R	&	A	&	La	iff	Dej	&	RadD	&	RegD
Case	1	yes		yes		yes		no		no		no
	2	yes		yes		no		no		no		yes
	3	yes		no	→	no		no		yes	→	yes
	4	no		yes		yes		yes		no		no
	5	no		yes		no		yes		no		yes
	6	no		no	→	no		yes		yes	→	yes

Case 1 of Table III is exactly analogous to Case 1 of Table II, in that it tells us that, in bringing about e, S does *right* (R), and is *appraisable* (A) for so doing, and is *laudable* (*La*) for so doing, if, and only if, being "charged" with bringing about *e,* he has neither a *dejustification (Dej),* nor a *radical disentitlement (RadD)* nor a *regular disentitlement (RegD)* for so doing. So too with the other cases; thus a summary of Table III may be given which is exactly analogous to that given earlier for Table II.

With this my account of the basic structure of appraisability is completed. I turn now to a defense and amplification of this picture of appraisability.

NOTES

1. See Squires (1968), especially p. 211, for extended treatment of inward blaming. There it is unjustifiably denied that blame is, or can be, overt. Contrast Donagan (1977), p. 55, where it appears to be unjustifiably denied that blame is, or can be, inward.

2. *Cf.* Feinberg (1970), pp. 30–31, 124–25; Glover (1970), p. 64; Morris (1976), p. 124.

3. What I have said here should forestall the charge of "moral escalation" made in Beardsley (1979), pp. 579–80. (*Cf.* Milo (1984), p. 221.) I do not pretend that it is easy to characterize the relation that obtains between individual entries in one's ledger and one's overall moral worth. Indeed, I do not know what this relation is. I certainly do *not* think that it is simply a matter of totting up the individual entries (even if one had the requisite information to do so, which in practice one surely never does). For consider these troubling questions. Can one slough off one's past—*e.g.,* by repentance? Can one accumulate credit in advance? (*Cf.* Feinberg (1970), pp. 23–24.) In this work, it is *only* with the individual entries that I shall be concerned, and not with their relation to one's overall moral worth. (Still, the questions of casting off discredit and of building up credit will be briefly addressed in Section 5.3.)

4. In Dennett (1984), p. 165, it is claimed that there is nothing in this world that constitutes "total, before-the-eyes-of-God Guilt." So far as I understand what Dennett means by this, I am about to try to spell out the conditions for just this sort of guilt, this sort of culpability. As just mentioned, I do not presuppose that there is some God before whose eyes one is (or is not) guilty; but I do think it possible, indeed frequently actual, that people are just plain culpable.

5. *Cf.* Feinberg's use of "forever" in Feinberg (1970), p. 30.

6. See, *e.g.,* Dahl (1967), pp. 420–21.

7. See, *e.g.,* Russell (1910), p. 16ff.; Broad (1946), pp. 108–11; Brandt (1959), pp. 358–66.

8. In spirit, then, I take myself to be in agreement with the three philosophers mentioned in the last note, and also with the following: Abelard, "Desire and Sin," p. 251; Moore (1912), pp. 79–80; Beardsley (1969), p. 34; Feinberg (1970), p. 13; Fried (1978), p. 21; Lemos (1980), pp. 309–10; Smith (1983), p. 543; and, in the legal arena, Fletcher (1978), p. 455.

9. Indeed, all three philosophers mentioned in note 7 explicitly allow for this as a legitimate sense of "ought."

10. *Cf.* (perhaps) Kant (1785), p. 68, on the "third proposition of duty"; *cf.* (definitely) Fried (1978), p. 21.

11. See, *e.g.:* Prichard (1949), pp. 30–31, 37–38; Ross (1960), pp. 147–56; Milo (1984), p. 21ff.

12. One must distinguish modification of the issue of an action from modification of the action itself. Only in the former case is a new *action* created; in the latter case there is only a new *event* created. Consider, for example, my raising my arm quickly.

On the fine-grained ontology of events that I advocate, this is clearly a different event from my raising my arm. But is it a different *action?* The answer, I think, is that it *is*. For, on analysis, we find that the "quickly" modifies the issue, and hence a new issue is created, and *hence* a new action is created. That is, my raising my arm is the same as my bringing about *my arm's rising,* and my raising my arm quickly is the same as my bringing about *my arm's rising quickly*. But it is different with my raising my arm wrongly. This is not a matter of my bringing about *my arm's rising wrongly,* but rather a matter of *my wrongly bringing about* my arm's rising. No new *issue* is created, and hence no new action is created either.

In fact, I believe that wrongness is not even a property of actions, but rather a *relation* that binds actions and times. See Zimmerman (1986b) and (1987b). But this is a subtlety that need not be discussed here. (Note, however, that I do not say that it is a relation which binds *persons,* actions, and times, since—on the account of action I favor, presented in Zimmerman (1984)—persons are constituent parts of their actions in a way which precludes the possibility of personless actions to which persons may be related.)

13. In fact, risk here is not *just* a matter of the likelihood of doing wrong. I shall discuss this shortly.

14. On "intend to do," see notes 10 and 12 to Chapter 2.

15. Zimmerman (1984), pp. 33–34. Briefly, and roughly, the trick is to pick out the simplest, most general event in the group of events comprising, say, someone being murdered, someone being murdered by gunfire, Kennedy being murdered, Kennedy being murdered by gunfire while riding in a limousine, . . .—namely, the first event in this list—and to identify a murder with *it*. A corresponding coarse-grained counting of volitions which ground blemishes will produce an appropriately coarse-grained counting of blemishes.

16. I borrow the last term from Milo (1984), pp. 7–8. Note that the attitude toward wrongdoing (namely, intention) does not vary from (P3.3) to (P3.4); what varies is whether *S* actually wills some event *e* or merely intends that it occur.

17. Such treatment has already been given to the terms "laudable" and "culpable," and it will be given to "negligence," "recklessness," and other such terms. See the preamble to (P2.8).

18. This issue stems from Plato, if not before, in his discussion of prudence in *Meno,* 77b–78b, *Protagoras,* 358c, and *Gorgias,* 468c. Kant seems to deny that (P3.5) is possible, and perhaps (P3.3) and (P3.4) also (see Kant, "Jealousy, Envy, and Spite," p. 276; Silber (1960), p. cxx ff.); in fact, it is unclear how his metaphysics even allows him to accept the possibility of (P3.2) (see Silber (1960), pp. lxxxii, xcviii ff.; Wolff (1973), pp. 122, 172–73). A prominent modern doubter of (P3.2)–(P3.5)—or something like them—is Hare, both in Hare (1952), Part II, and elsewhere. For a strongly contrary view, see Augustine (400), p. 242.

19. For what I regard as a successful refutation of the opposite view, see Milo (1984), Chapter 6, especially pp. 170 and 178–80. *Cf.* Gardiner (1955), pp. 105, 112; Lukes (1965), p. 152; Ayer (1984), p. 26.

20. *Cf.* Ross (1930), p. 163; Milo (1984), pp. 7–8.

21. Most philosophers who write on the subject appear to accept that culpability may come in degrees, although this is sometimes denied, as in Thorp (1980), p. 8.

22. The extrinsic mode is irrelevant here, since we have to do with variations in degree of freedom with respect to one and the same event.

23. See Section 4.9.

24. See, *e.g.*, Beardsley (1979), p. 575; Milo (1984), p. 244

25. It is in fact quite hard to come up with an example of willing to do wrong for the sake of something else—surely, merely foreseeing doing wrong is far more straightforward and common—but perhaps the following will do. Smith is normally a morally upright person, but he has developed a perverse love for Jones, perverse in that Jones is most pleased when Smith does something that he (Smith) regards as wrong. On

occasion Smith's love for Jones overrides his moral scruples, and so he tries to please Jones as best he can—which, of course, means doing something which he (Smith) regards as wrong. Here the wrong is intended by Smith as a means to pleasing Jones.

26. I say "*some* principle of double effect," because there are many principles that may go by this title and because those usually discussed in the literature do not directly concern what the agent is to be blamed for but rather what it would be wrong for the agent to do.

27. See the discussion on p. 43 above concerning the distinction between (ii) and (ii').

28. Of course, the question arises: what constitutes an adequate grasp of the concept of wrongdoing? I am not sure how this very important question is to be answered. On the one hand, one is inclined to think that we all have an inadequate grasp of the concept—we are unsure of its analysis, we are puzzled about questions of consequentialism *versus* deontology, and so on—but, on the other hand, one recognizes that most of us can employ the concept perfectly well in many cases. (Indeed, if we could not do this, we could not undertake its analysis.) Now, this notion of "employing the concept perfectly well" is decidedly rough, and I do not know how to explicate it further (beyond saying that the psychopath, whose behavior betrays a lack of "inner" understanding of the concept, does *not* employ the concept of wrongdoing "perfectly well," even though he can apparently make use of it in an "externally" adequate fashion), but it is this which I take to constitute an adequate grasp of the concept. *Cf.* Fingarette (1972), p. 142ff., on the difficulties in interpreting the "knowledge-of-wrong test" proposed in the M'Naghten Rules.

29. *Cf.* Rescher (1983), pp. 18, 33, 36, 49. In the legal arena, *cf.* Terry (1915), p. 244; Prosser (1971), p. 147.

30. See note 13. There can be a twist to this. Suppose that S believes that, in bringing about e rather than f, he is minimizing the risk of wrongdoing but the risk is still be pretty high, and that if he had believed the risk to be pretty low, he would then have brought about f instead (for he likes to run some appreciable risk of doing wrong). Should we *then* say that he deserves no blame at all? With respect to *direct* culpability, the answer is, I believe, that we should. This leaves open the possibility of S's being "*situationally* culpable" (a matter that I discuss in Section 4.11) and of his being otherwise "*reprehensible*" (a matter that I discuss in Section 4.9).

31. See the remarks on Audi (1982) in note 15 to Chapter 2.

32. If malice contributes more, *ceteris paribus*, to culpability than does callousness, further refinement of (P3.1') is called for.

33. See D'Arcy (1963), p. 129, for a similar point.

34. Kant (1785), pp. 65–66.

35. See, *e.g.*, Aune (1979), p. 10.

36. See Beardsley (1979), p. 579.

37. See Kant (1785), p. 65, ll. 6–10.

38. See, *e.g.*, Henson (1979).

39. See, *e.g.*, Greene (1934), p. lvi; Silber (1960), p. cxi f.; Beck (1960), p. 228; Paton, in Kant (1785), p. 19; Wolff (1973), p. 66.

40. *Cf.* Henson (1979), p. 43f.

41. *Cf.* Ross (1930), p. 5, and Aune (1979), p. 173; contrast Wolff (1973), pp. 80–81, and Nell (1975), p. 99ff.

42. See Ross (1930), p. 5; Wolff (1973), pp. 80–81; Nell (1975), p. 99ff.

43. I find no obvious correlates of the terms "satanic wickedness," "malice," and "callousness."

44. More precisely, I believe that: (i) there are degrees of a certain type of value of which rightness and wrongness are functions; (ii) rightness is a matter of maximization of such value, and hence itself admits of no degrees; and (iii) wrongness is a matter of nonmaximization, of "departing from" maximization, of such value, and hence itself does admit of degrees (the greater the "departure," the greater—that is, the more

serious—the wrong). One may superimpose upon this picture of "degrees" of wrongness an account of "levels" of wrongness, which is a matter of ranking wrongs in terms of their seriousness. See Zimmerman (1986b) for further details; these details help explain the detachment of "absolute" from "conditional" obligation.

45. But he may yet be "situationally laudable." See Section 4.11; and see note 30, this chapter. Also, see Section 2.1 where it was said that S's willing e for the purpose of f implies that S believes that he has strict standard control over both e and f. It was not said that this implies that S believes that both e and f will occur, or even that he believes it likely that they will occur; nor do I think that this is implied. This is a difficult and controversial matter, however. See note 15 to Chapter 2. For further discussion, see Zimmerman (1984), pp. 69 and 137–38.

46. Indeed, it might even be that S is *more* laudable than S'—not directly, but situationally—in that S' would not have willed as he did had he perceived the chance of doing right to be as small as S perceived *his* chance of doing right. See note 30, this chapter.

47. As with note 31, this chapter, see the remarks on Audi (1982) in note 15 to Chapter 2.

48. But see Abelard, "Desire and Sin," p. 251: "[N]o one who sets out to assert that all fleshly desire is sin may say that the sin itself is increased by the doing of it. For this would mean extending the consent of the soul into the exercise of the action. In short, one would be stained not only by consent to baseness, but also by the mire of the deed, as if what happens externally in the body could possibly soil the soul. Sin is not, therefore, increased by the doing of an action: and nothing mars the soul except what is of its own nature, namely consent." See also Smith (1983), pp. 559 and 566–68, on what she calls the "Liberal View," to which she admits being inclined. A possible exception to the claim will be discussed in Section 4.11.

49. While it can happen that one *was* indirectly free with respect to an event with respect to which one is *now* directly free, it cannot be that one is now both indirectly and directly free with respect to the same event.

50. Feinberg claims that there is just one acceptable analysis in this context, but this view seems to be founded on the failure to note the essential emptiness of indirect appraisability. See Feinberg (1970), p. 195ff.

51. *Cf.* Smith (1983), where on pp. 547–48 there is talk of a "benighting act" (which corresponds fairly closely with what I say here about S's original volition v), and where on pp. 550–51 there is talk of some event "falling within the risk" of this act (which corresponds fairly closely with what I say here about the event e which enters into S's volition v). Note that, while S's volition is indicated, it is not pinpointed; even on the Internalist Position we are not told just *how* e enters or entered into v—whether as willed for its own sake, willed, or merely foreseen.

52. That e enter into one's volition is, I would say, a necessary but (clearly) not sufficient condition both for enjoying transparent freedom with respect to e and for being willing that e occur. One can, however, be willing that e occur without enjoying transparent freedom with respect to e, and one can enjoy such freedom without being willing that e occur.

53. Of course, I cannot be aware of the irresistibility of the choice at the time of the choice, for otherwise no choice would be possible at all. See Section 2.2.

54. While S may also contribute to e by virtue of some other volition v' for which he is appraisable to some degree y (where y is distinct from x), and so also be appraisable to degree y for e, the degree to which he is appraisable for e *by way of v* must be x.

55. In Section 2.1, it was noted that the phenomena of unthinking and habitual action are problematic. Their problematic nature also raises problems with respect to just how appraisability for them is to be accounted for. There seem to me to be three main options. (i) Such action is genuine action; the volition involved is conscious (that is, in willing e, S considers e). In this case, there is nothing special about appraisability

for such action. (ii) Such action is genuine action; the volition involved is not conscious. Here I am somewhat puzzled: may *S* be directly appraisable for willing *e* even if he was oblivious of *e*? I am not sure. If so, then there is nothing special about appraisability for such action; if not, then all appraisability for such action, including the volitions involved, is indirect. (iii) Such action is not genuine action; it is rote behavior, devoid of volition. If this is the case, then appraisability for such action is special in that it cannot be even in part direct. However, as noted in Chapter 2, I am inclined to reject this option.

56. That part that follows "if and only if."

57. *Cf.* Feinberg (1970), p. 30; Davis (1979), pp. 109 and 134.

58. Contrast Beardsley (1969), p. 36.

59. On both counts, *cf.* Donagan (1977), p. 112.

60. I am using "have" broadly here, in that one *has* a justification or excuse just in case there in principle *is* one—whether or not one is aware of its existence.

61. *Cf.* Fletcher (1978), pp. 458–59, 577. While this seems to be the usual way in which matters are put, it is questionable that this is how they should be put. In particular, the claim that, in the law, a justification precludes an excuse, is dubious; in addition, the claim that, in the law, a justification implies that no offense has been committed, is also dubious (see Husak (1987), Chapter 7).

62. See Austin (1956–57), p. 12; Brandt (1959), p. 471; D'Arcy (1963), pp. 79–80; Brandt (1969), pp. 339–40; Cummins (1980), pp. 209–10; Heintz (1981), p. 243.

63. *Cf.* Prichard (1949), pp. 34–35.

64. Quite different senses of "excuse" will be discussed in Section 5.4.

65. It should be noted that, while English clearly sanctions the use of "excuse" to express what I have called a regular excuse, it also appears at times to sanction the use of "justification" to express this same concept. If we were so to use "justification"—which I would not recommend—we should distinguish the concept so expressed from what I have already called justification. Perhaps we could talk of "objective" justification for what I have already called justification, and of "subjective" justification for what I have called regular excuse.

66. See note 60, this chapter.

67. It is arguable that Table I should allow this also. See note 61, this chapter.

68. *Cf.* Hart (1968), p. 16.

69. *Cf.* Glover (1970), pp. 57–60; Husak (1987), p. 189.

70. But denial is relevant to whether having a legal justification implies not having committed a legal offense. See note 61, this chapter.

71. See note 44, this chapter.

72. Contrast: Mellema (1984); Zimmerman (1985b).

73. *Cf.* Hart (1968), p. 15, on Mitigation; also Blatz (1973), p. 1, on the distinction between what he calls vindication and mitigation.

74. I borrow the term "disentitlement" from D'Arcy (1963), p. 93. *Cf.* Brandt's use of "debunking" in Brandt (1959), p. 471, n. 9.

4

OBJECTIONS AND AMPLIFICATION

WHILE THE ACCOUNT of moral appraisability offered in the last chapter no doubt has its attractive features, it may yet appear to be objectionable in several respects. In this chapter, I shall endeavor to address and refute what I take to be certain major objections to the account. In the course of so doing, I shall be trying also to round out the account by pointing up certain relations between the concept of appraisability and other important moral concepts. (I shall in fact not concern myself further with i-worthiness (see Section 3.4), which is a relatively unimportant concept, and shall confine myself to a discussion of laudability and culpability, the latter especially.)

There are three basic ways in which an account of the sort that I have given can be criticized. It can be claimed that the account is unduly inflationary (implying that a person is substantially appraisable to a certain degree, when, according to the conventional wisdom embodied in our common practice, he is appraisable to a lesser degree, if at all); or it can be claimed that the account is unduly deflationary (implying that a person is substantially appraisable to a certain degree, or perhaps not appraisable at all, when, according to conventional wisdom, he is appraisable to a greater degree); or it can be claimed that the account is insufficiently precise, in that, even if the exact degree to which they are substantially appraisable cannot be determined, it implies that two persons are appraisable to the same degree when conventional wisdom decrees that they are not. In what follows we shall meet with objections of all three sorts—that my account is unduly inflationary (Sections 4.5, 4.6, 4.7, and 4.11), that it is unduly deflationary (Sections 4.1, 4.2, 4.3, 4.9, and 4.11), and that it is otherwise insufficiently precise (Sections 4.3 and 4.4).[1]

4.1 Ignorance

Given (P3.1′) (the analysis of direct culpability) and (P3.6′) (the analysis of direct laudability) and also the claim that indirect appraisability is essentially empty, it might seem that (P3.25) (the analysis of substantial appraisability) implies that (i) lack of ignorance and (ii) advertence are both necessary conditions of substantial appraisability. Yet it is a commonplace that, while ignorance sometimes excuses, sometimes it does not; and it is a commonplace also that negligence, which essentially involves inadvertence, can be (indeed, on some understandings, necessarily is) culpable. In this section, I shall discuss the relation between ignorance and substantial appraisability, concentrating for the most part on the relation between ignorance and culpability. I shall discuss negligence in the next section.

(P3.25) clearly implies that an agent can be culpable for some event without doing wrong, so long as he was willing to do wrong, and this emphasis on the agent's mental state is surely to be welcomed. But, as emphasized in Section 3.5, (P3.25) also implies that whether or not an agent in fact does wrong is strictly irrelevant to his culpability. Is *this* to be welcomed also? What if an agent does wrong without realizing it? Is there not room for blame here, and does this not show that the foregoing account of appraisability is unduly deflationary? The answer is: yes, there is room for blame here, but no, no modification to the account is required to allow for it. Let us see why.

Ignorance is lack of knowledge. I shall take it that knowledge consists in justified true belief.[2] Ignorance, then, may consist in lack of justification, lack of truth, or lack of belief. The most important variable here is the last—lack of belief. I shall consider it first, and first with respect to direct culpability.

Direct culpability and lack of belief. According to (P3.1′), S is directly culpable to degree x for willing e *only if* he willed e, in the belief that it was likely to degree y that, by virtue of so willing, he would do wrong to degree z. Now one cannot, I believe, will something and not believe (at least dispositionally) (i) that one is willing that thing; hence there is no occasion for ignorance in this regard.[3] But even if one could fail to believe, and thus fail to know, that one was willing something, *this,* according to (P3.1′), would afford no excuse for willing it.

On the other hand, it is clearly possible for S to will e, but not in the belief (ii) that it was likely to degree y that, by virtue of so willing, he would do wrong to degree z; and, according to (P3.1′), if he does so will in this state of disbelief, he is not to be blamed for so willing, *even if he in fact does wrong by virtue of his volition.*[4] Is this reasonable? Well, surely it is in those cases where S is not to be blamed *for his disbelief.*

After all, such disbelief indicates that there is a lack of willingness on his part to do wrong, and it is the presence of such willingness for which an agent is to blame. This lack of willingness may be either *specific* or *general*. It is specific if the agent has a grasp of the concept of wrongness but simply fails to believe on this occasion that, by virtue of a certain volition, he might do wrong; in this case he may even be praiseworthy for his volition and, if so, his excuse will be a regular one. It is general if it is not specific. Two important cases of this sort are that where the agent is a moral nihilist and that where the agent has no grasp of the concept of wrongness. In the former case, his excuse will be regular but he will not be praiseworthy for his volition; in the latter case, he cannot be praiseworthy for his volition and his excuse will be radical.

Sometimes much is made of the distinction between ignorance about moral matters and ignorance about non-moral matters.[5] (Certainly, the analogous distinction between "ignorance of the law" and "ignorance of fact" is often thought to be significant.) But in the present context the distinction seems to me irrelevant. Suppose that S has a specific lack of willingness to do wrong and yet does wrong owing to the disbelief (obviously tantamount to ignorance) that, by willing e, he would do wrong. This ignorance is *itself*, clearly, ignorance about a moral matter. It may be *rooted*, however, either in moral ignorance or in nonmoral ignorance (or in both). (For example, S may fail to believe that his punching S' is wrong. This may be due to his failing to believe that persons have a right not to be assaulted (moral ignorance) or to his believing erroneously that S' is about to attack him (nonmoral ignorance).) But *how* it is rooted seems to me irrelevant—unless, of course, S is to be blamed for that ignorance in which his current ignorance is rooted, and this is possible whether the former ignorance is moral or nonmoral.

General unwillingness to do wrong, where this is due to a failure to grasp the very concept of wrongdoing, is an interesting phenomenon. It constitutes a sort of amorality *different* from that of the moral nihilist. If one is amoral in this way, one has no "ledger of life." It was said in Section 3.4 of the last chapter that stones, animals, infants, and idiots exemplify this sort of amorality. This is because they lack the requisite conceptual apparatus to grasp the concepts of rightness and wrongness. This is a difficult matter, of course. No stones, but perhaps some animals, infants, and idiots have a very rough grasp of these concepts—I doubt this but am not sufficiently expert to rule it out entirely. And clearly some children have a rough grasp of these concepts. The question of *degree* of comprehension of these concepts is one which I find very difficult to discuss, for two reasons. While it is clear that, in some sense, one's grasp of a concept may be more or less adequate, it is far from clear (to me, at least) (i) what this really amounts to and (ii) how this affects the question of laudability and culpability. I suppose that, the more adequate one's grasp of the concepts of rightness and wrongness, the more, *ceteris paribus,* one is to be praised or blamed (as mentioned in Section 3.1); but beyond that I am not sure what to say.[6]

Presumably, there will be little quarrel with the claim that someone who wills something, but not in the belief that he might thereby do wrong, is not to be blamed for so willing, unless he is to be blamed for his state of disbelief. So far, then, (P3.1') and thus those formulae which incorporate it—in particular, (P3.19), (P3.21), (P3.25), and (P3.26)—are vindicated. Of course the question still remains: but what if he *is* to be blamed for his state of disbelief? Do we not find an exception to (P3.1'), and thus (P3.19), *etc.,* here? I think not; but I shall return to this later in this section.

Indirect culpability, conjoint culpability, and lack of belief. I wish at this point to discuss the issue of indirect culpability for an event and the relevance of lack of belief to such culpability. Suppose that S willed e, is culpable for so doing, and that f was a consequence of this volition. But suppose that S failed at the time of his volition to believe that f would or might be a consequence of his volition (a matter of non-moral ignorance). Is he to be blamed for f, or does he have an excuse? Suppose, for example, that S culpably wills his punching S' in the stomach and that, as a result and quite unexpectedly, S' dies. Is S to be blamed for S''s death?

The answer that one gives to this question of course depends on whether one adopts the Externalist or the Internalist Position with regard to indirect appraisability (see (P3.11) and (P3.14)). (I shall not discuss the Right/Wrong Position on this issue.) On the Externalist Position, S has no excuse. On the Internalist Position, which I favor, he has an excuse; that is, on this position, since f (S''s death) did not enter into his volition, S is not indirectly culpable for it, even though it occurred as a consequence of his volition, a volition for which he is culpable. Anyway, whichever position one adopts, there is no denying that S is not *substantially culpable concerning f* (see (P3.26))—unless, perhaps, S, as before, is culpable for his disbelief. Of course, even on the Internalist Position, S has no excuse for f if his lack of belief occurs not at the time of his volition but at some other time (*e.g.,* at the time of f's occurrence); that is, in such a case, S *would* (or might well) be substantially culpable concerning f.

Similar remarks pertain to conjoint culpability and disbelief. If S brought about f by virtue of willing e, but not in the belief that f would or might be a consequence of this volition, then S is not substantially culpable concerning his *bringing about f*—unless, perhaps, S, as before, is culpable for his disbelief.

Here I should like to digress for a moment to discuss certain famous remarks made by Aristotle, for the *locus classicus* for discussion of the present issue is to be found in Aristotle's *Nicomachean Ethics*. There,[7] Aristotle, while not distinguishing between indirect and conjoint appraisability, does take care to distinguish several modes of ignorance, all of which may of course also be modes of disbelief. He says that one can be ignorant with respect to (i) what one's action is, (ii) what or whom one's action affects, (iii) what the instrument of one's action is, (iv) what the consequences of one's action are, and (v) what the manner of one's action is; and we could add: one can be ignorant of (vi) the place of one's action, and (vii) the time of one's action; and still other factors could be added (*e.g.,* the motive of one's action, and so on). On the present fine-grained approach to the individuation of actions, all of these various categories may in fact be subsumed under the first category. Let me illustrate. Aristotle furnishes the following examples: (i) betraying a secret unwittingly, (ii) mistakenly treating one's son as an enemy, (iii) using an unsafe spear, thinking it had a button on it, (iv) killing a man with a medicine that one expected would cure him, and (v) wounding someone, but meaning only to touch him; and we could add: (vi) disembarking from a train in New York, thinking one was in New Haven, and (vii) getting out of bed at 8:00 A.M., thinking that it was 7:00 A.M. Now, how might all this be subsumed under ignorance of one's action? Thus: one is ignorant of (i) one's betraying-a-secret, (ii) one's dealing-with-one's-son, (iii) one's using-an-unsafe-spear, (iv) one's killing-a-man-with-medicine, (v) one's wounding-someone, (vi) one's disembarking-from-a-train-in-New-York, and (vii) one's getting-out-of-bed-at-8:00-A.M. On the fine-grained approach, all of these are actions of which one is ignorant: and one may be ignorant of them all the while *not* being ignorant of the following, distinct actions that one is also performing: (i) one's talking-to-someone, (ii) one's dealing-with-someone, (iii) one's using-a-spear, (iv) one's treating-a-man-with-medicine, (v) one's coming-into-contact-with-someone, (vi) one's disembarking-from-a-train, and (vii) one's getting-out-of-bed. Now, in saying that all of (i)–(vii) can be subsumed under the rubric "ignorance of one's action," I do not mean that there are not interesting distinctions between these categories. All that I mean is that they are all treatable by means of the formula "not in the belief that it is likely that he will thereby bring about *e,*" and thus fall within the bounds of what was said in the last three paragraphs.

Aristotle is also well known for distinguishing between acting in ignorance and acting by reason of (or owing to, or as the result of) ignorance.[8] But the distinction is not clear to me. It is supposed, I think, to reside in this: one acts by reason of ignorance if one is unaware of what it is that one is bringing about and if the cause of one's action is this very lack of awareness as to what would be brought about; one acts in ignorance if one is similarly unaware but where the cause of one's action lies else-where. Aristotle gives an example of acting in ignorance: acting when drunk or in a rage; he gives no example of acting by reason of ignorance. The distinction is not clear to me because I do not understand what it means to attribute the cause of one's action to ignorance or lack of awareness. *One* way of trying to understand this is as follows: the cause of one's action is ignorance of such-and-such if one would not have so acted had one not been so ignorant.[9] But this seems *not* to be how Aristotle understands what it is to act by reason of ignorance. For he explicitly allows for the possibility of an agent, who acts by reason of ignorance, finding out later what he has done and being quite unrepentant concerning what he has done; and such lack of repentance would appear to belie the aforementioned counterfactual. Aristotle says that such an agent acted "not voluntarily" (as opposed to "involuntarily," which would have been the case had he been repentant), but he still says that the agent acted by reason of ignorance. At any rate, when it comes to ascribing culpability, Aristotle seems to commit himself only to the following: he who acts involuntarily and by reason of ignorance is to be excused; as for an agent who acts not voluntarily and by reason of ignorance, or in ignorance, Aristotle does not commit himself, although there is a suggestion that he believes such an agent to be culpable.

In my opinion, the distinctions that Aristotle has drawn, however they are to be understood, are irrelevant here. Ignorance—that is, for present purposes, disbelief—excuses just when (P3.1′) and, thereby, (P3.19) imply that it does. In saying this, I can agree with Aristotle that there is, or at least can be, something blameworthy about an unrepentant, though at the time ignorant, wrongdoer. But it seems that such a person, if he is to be blamed, is to be blamed not for what he has ignorantly done or brought about but for his failure to repent.[10] And this is so only if the agent believes it wrong not to repent for that which he now believes was wrong. At least, this is so unless the agent is to be blamed *for his ignorance*. Similarly, if his ignorance is due to drunkenness or rage, then he is not to be blamed for what he has ignorantly done or brought about, unless he is to be blamed *for being drunk* or *enraged*. Is he to be blamed *even then?* I shall argue that he may well *not* be—but, again, I shall take this up later in this section.

Culpability and lack of justification or truth. Where ignorance is due, not to lack of belief, but to lack of justification or truth, there is little to discuss.

First, with respect to direct culpability: I believe that it is not possible that S will e and that (i) he not be justified in believing this.[11] Anyway, even if this is possible, no excuse is forthcoming because of it. (And clearly it is not possible that S will e, that he believe this, and that (ii) this belief not be true.) On the other hand, it is possible that S will e in the belief that he will do wrong by virtue of this volition, and that either (i) this belief not be justified or (ii) this belief not be true. But even so, no excuse is forthcoming because of ignorance constituted by such lack of justification or truth.

Similarly with indirect culpability: even on the Internalist Position, no excuse is forthcoming where S is culpable for some volition into which e entered and of which it is a consequence but where S's belief that e would or might be a consequence of his volition was (i) unjustified. (Clearly this belief cannot be (ii) untrue, since e occurs.)

Laudability and ignorance. Much of what has been said about excuses grounded in ignorance may be said, *mutatis mutandis,* about disentitlements grounded in ignorance. The asymmetry between (P3.6′) and (P3.1′) is immaterial here, since willingness to do right is necessary for laudability just as willingness to do wrong is for culpability, and this is all that is at issue with regard to ignorance constituted by disbelief. And, just as ignorance constituted by lack of justification or truth fails to excuse, so too it fails to disentitle. Thus, as mentioned in Sections 3.2 and 3.5, whether or not one in fact does right is irrelevant to laudability, just as whether or not one in fact does wrong is irrelevant to culpability.

Culpable ignorance. But let us now turn to that one area where there may well be lingering doubts as to the power of ignorance to excuse. (What follows could also be put in terms of disentitlement, but I shall stick to the issue of excuses for ignorance.) This has to do with those occasions where someone does something in ignorance, but where he is to be blamed for his ignorance—that is, as it is often put, where his ignorance is culpable.

Again, we may narrow the focus of our discussion to disbelief, since only that type of ignorance, which is constituted by disbelief, serves to excuse even when the ignorance is not culpable. And here my contention, to put it somewhat roughly, is simply this: where ignorance is culpable, it still excuses just as if it were not culpable, although *it* is inexcusable. Suppose that S wills e, in the culpable disbelief that, by virtue of this volition, he will or might do wrong; and suppose, in addition, that he brings about e, thereby doing wrong. For example (to use an illustration given in Chapter 3, but now with the stipulation that the ignorance is culpable), suppose that Jones drags the driver from the wreck, in an attempt (grounded in culpable ignorance) to improve the driver's well-being, but succeeding only in paralyzing the driver. How is Jones to be appraised in this case? We are ambivalent; he seems at once both praise- and blameworthy. I urge that we not try to resolve this ambivalence, for it seems to me that Jones indeed is (given certain conditions) both praise-

and blameworthy. He is to be praised for his attempt; he is to be blamed for his ignorance. Jones is surely to be commended for his choice to help the driver, insofar as it reflects the will to do right for right's sake, even though he is to blame for the beliefs and, especially, disbeliefs in light of which he makes his choice.

All of this is of course in keeping with the account given in Chapter 3, but that account goes further than this; for (P3.1') implies that Jones is not *directly* culpable for his ignorance, since the only sort of thing for which one may be directly culpable is a volition. Now, whether or not one accepts that volitions play the role in action that I have ascribed to them, it seems to me that one must accept that culpability for ignorance (as constituted by disbelief) must be indirect and thus *empty*. For I cannot see any plausibility in the claim that one can be directly free with respect to being or not being in a state of disbelief. My argument, in brief, is this: no one can be directly free with respect to being or not being in a state of disbelief; one can be substantially appraisable for an event only if one was directly free with respect to it; hence, no one can be substantially appraisable for being or not being in a state of disbelief.

This is a strong conclusion. Note, however, that it does *not* imply that no one can be substantially appraisable *concerning* disbelief. (On the distinction between being substantially appraisable *for* something and being substantially appraisable *concerning* something, see (P3.25) and (P3.26).) On the contrary, such appraisability is perfectly possible, as long as the disbelief is willing—as long, that is, as there is a sort of belief-*cum*-disbelief, *i.e.,* an earlier belief that a later disbelief will or may occur, followed by such disbelief. But if there is no such prior belief, there can be no substantial appraisability concerning the disbelief in question.[12]

It is obvious that this unfamiliar picture of substantial appraisability concerning ignorance is deflationary with respect to our common practice of ascribing responsibility for ignorance. But it seems to me forced upon us by the observation that culpability for ignorance cannot be direct. It might be countered that, even if it is accepted that culpability for ignorance must be indirect, still we are not constrained to accept the belief-*cum*-disbelief picture; on the contrary, it may be urged, this picture is forced upon us only if we also subscribe to the claim that substantial appraisability concerning an event *e,* where the appraisability for *e* is indirect, can arise only if *e* enters into the agent's volition. But I would ask in return: how could such substantial appraisability be thought to arise but in some such way as this? Even if volitions are rejected, surely, if there is to be substantial appraisability concerning an event *e* for which an agent is only indirectly appraisable, then *e* must somehow "enter" into some event *f* for which the agent is directly appraisable. The only plausible way in which I know how to interpret this metaphor of "entering" is in terms of belief. Once again, then, the conclusion that I have reached, while naturally finding detailed expression in terms of the account of action that I espouse, seems to me not to be tied down to this account.

Several further points are to be noted here. First, in saying that Jones is not directly culpable for his attempt to save the driver, I leave open the possibility (as noted in Section 3.3) that he is indirectly culpable for this; for, just as he is indirectly culpable (I am assuming) for his ignorance, he may be indirectly culpable for what he wills in light of it and, indeed, for what he thereby brings about (namely, the paralysis).

Second, we may handle culpable inadvertence, culpable drunkenness, culpable rage, and so on, in a manner analogous to that in which culpable ignorance has just been handled.[13] (I shall discuss culpable inadvertence more fully in the next section.) For their very nature renders such phenomena beyond one's direct control, and thus any control that an agent has with respect to them, and so too any culpability for them, must be indirect. Thus, one can never be substantially culpable *for* them, although one can be substantially culpable *concerning* them. Again, this leaves entirely open the question of direct culpability for volitions made when ignorant, inadvertent, drunk, enraged, and so on.

Finally, a note on a particular form of culpable ignorance is in order here—that of a culpably erroneous conscience, which I take to consist in beliefs concerning right and wrong that are mistaken and for which one is indirectly culpable. Alan Donagan claims that the position of someone with a culpably erroneous conscience is a terrible one; for, if he acts according to his conscience, he must do a wrong for which he is culpable, while, if he acts against his conscience, he must also be culpable. [14] This is essentially accurate, but one should not make too much of it; in particular, one should resist any suggestion of paradox or dilemma (which there appears to be in Donagan's use of the word "terrible"). If one has a culpably erroneous conscience, then one is indirectly culpable for one's conscience. If one acts according to this conscience, one may also, therefore, be indirectly culpable for what one thereby brings about; if one acts against it, then one will be directly culpable for one's volition and, given that the attempt is successful, indirectly culpable for the consequence of this volition. Whatever one brings about, then, is something for which one is likely to be indirectly culpable. But there is nothing extraordinary, or even particularly noteworthy, about this. After all, the agent is already culpable anyway—for his erroneous conscience; such culpability is irrevocable, but it was not inevitable, and so also none of the culpability for other events which arises *via* the agent's culpability for his conscience was inevitable.

Foresight and foreseeability. It may seem that, despite whatever plausibility that the arguments just given may have, something must have gone wrong somewhere in the foregoing account of culpable ignorance. After all, it is a commonplace that substantial culpability concerning an event merely requires that the event be *foreseeable* by the agent, while the account that I have given implies that such appraisability requires that the event actually be *foreseen* by the agent. Surely, it may be objected, this requirement is too strong.

The short reply to this objection is that I stand by my arguments. But a longer reply may be more illuminating. In the course of this reply I hope to make it clear that foreseeability in fact requires foresight and hence that common practice, in ascribing responsibility in the absence of foresight, in this instance appears to be false to its own presuppositions.

Hitherto I have not talked much of foresight, but I agree that my account stipulates that culpable ignorance involves foresight. For I think we may say, for at least one respectable sense of "foresee":

(P4.1) S foresees (to some degree or extent) e's occurrence if and only if S believes that there is some likelihood that e is occurring or will occur.

(By including "is occurring" in this statement, I am deliberately blunting the force of "fore" in "foresees." The reason for this will become apparent shortly.) Now, in order to assess whether or not I am correct in insisting that culpable ignorance involves foresight rather than mere foreseeability without foresight, we must ask what foreseeability is. Several different answers suggest themselves. I shall consider three.

The first sense of "foreseeability" that I shall consider is that which the law invokes. It is this:

(P4.2) e's occurrence is foreseeable by S if and only if the reasonable man would foresee e's occurrence.

While there may be good reason to adopt this definition for purposes of the law,[15] it is apparent that there are many problems with it from the point of view of moral appraisability. One problem, of course, is that of understanding who and what the "reasonable man" is. Another problem consists in determining what the reasonable man would foresee, even when we have determined who he is and what general characteristics he has. But by far the biggest problem, it seems to me, is that of justifying this approach to foreseeability when it is moral, and not legal, responsibility that is at issue. How is it relevant, when trying to determine whether or not a particular person is substantially culpable concerning a particular event, whether or not the "reasonable man" would have foreseen it? If the person in question falls short of this criterion of reasonability, then how is it justifiable to judge him by it (unless, of course, he is substantially culpable concerning his falling short of it)?[16] On the other hand, if the person in question surpasses this criterion, it may be that to judge him by it (and it alone) is to judge him too leniently. In either case, it is surely to the person in question that we must look, and not to some criterion which may bear no relevance to him and to his capacities, when trying to determine moral responsibility.

It is noteworthy that (P4.2) does not give us a straightforward interpretation of the term "foreseeable," in that an event may be foreseeable by a person, according to this definition, without *that person* being *able,* in any standard sense, to *foresee* it. A more obvious way to construct interpretations of the term is, first, to devise the following schema:

(P4.3)   *e*'s occurrence is foreseeable by *S* if and only if it is possible that *S* foresee *e*'s occurrence.

One may then provide instantiations of this schema by making precise the sense of "possible" that is at issue. Here are two such instantiations that I shall discuss:

(P4.4)   [just as in (P4.3), except that it reads "logically possible" instead of "possible"]

(P4.5)   [just as in (P4.3), except that it reads "personally possible" instead of "possible"], *i.e.,*
     e's occurrence is foreseeable by *S* if and only if *S* is free to foresee *e*'s occurrence.

I include (P4.4) here for illustrative purposes only. I know of no one who accepts the definition in the present context, and this is just as well; for it is clearly far too liberal. Suppose that we keep an open mind as to what conditions are necessary for someone's being substantially culpable concerning something; and suppose that, whatever the conditions are, they are satisfied, save for the fact that the person in question does not foresee the event in question and that it is foreseeable by him only in the sense of (P4.4). Would this suffice for the person's being substantially culpable concerning it? Surely not. Any number of "chain reactions" of events may serve to illustrate this. For instance, suppose that I want to know the time, that my turning my wrist to consult my watch causes the sun to be reflected into the eyes of a distant pedestrian, that this pedestrian is temporarily blinded and bumps into a street vendor's cart, that the cart is thereby caused to capsize, its contents of apples and oranges spilling on to the street, that the horse attached to a passing horse-drawn carriage is frightened by this turn of events, shies from the fruit, and thereby causes extensive damage to the carriage and its occupants. Am I substantially culpable concerning the damage to the carriage and its occupants? Surely not. Was it foreseeable, in the sense of (P4.4)? Yes.

Of course, there are many ways to furnish more restrictive senses of "possible" so as to come up with less liberal instantiations of (P4.3) then

(P4.4). However, there is only one which seems to me of merit, namely, (P4.5). Indeed, it is (P4.5) to which, I believe, very many subscribe. I think that foreseeability is so often taken to be an element of culpable ignorance (and of culpable inadvertence) because, first, it is so often said that someone *ought* to have foreseen something that he did not foresee and, second, it is assumed that this implies that he *could* have foreseen what he in fact did not foresee; and it is thought that, all else being equal, this suffices for the person to be substantially culpable concerning the event in question. (P4.5) is tailor-made for such talk.

But is this popular picture of foreseeability as an element of culpable ignorance acceptable? The answer, I think, is this: yes, but it does *not* contradict the claim that all culpable ignorance involves foresight. It must be remembered that the "can," which expresses the sort of possibility presently at issue, and the "ought," which rides on this "can," standardly modify verbs of *action*. Now, foreseeing is not an action; to say "he ought to foresee *e*" and "he can foresee *e*" is therefore puzzling. It seems to me, however, that sense can be made of these phrases if they are understood to be elliptical for "he ought to *make himself* foresee *e*" and "he can *make himself* foresee *e*"; for here the "ought" and the "can" explicitly modify a verb of action. If this is correct, then the more common "he ought to have foreseen *e*" and "he could have foreseen *e*" are to be understood, respectively, as elliptical for "he ought to have made himself foresee *e*" and "he could have made himself foresee *e*." And it does seem appropriate to utter such sentences in many cases of culpable ignorance. Consider again the case of Jones and the wrecked car, where, we are now assuming, Jones's ignorance concerning how to handle an accident victim is culpable. Just *how* might this culpability have arisen? Well, suppose that Jones is a student nurse; he once had a class in how to handle accident victims, but at that class he declined to take notes, choosing to rely on his memory, although he was aware that his memory was not all that reliable and that he might well relapse into his former ignorance concerning the proper handling of accident victims. Here it is perfectly appropriate to say all of the following: Jones did not, at the time of his tending to the driver, foresee his mishandling of the driver (here the "fore" of "foresee" is mute; hence the use of "is occurring" in (P4.1)); this mishandling was foreseeable by him then—in the sense of "foreseeable" presently at issue, *i.e.,* that of (P4.5); Jones ought to have foreseen it at that time; and (given some further assumptions) Jones is culpable for not foreseeing it at that time. But all of this may be accepted because, at an earlier time (the time of the class), Jones did foresee his mishandling accident victims and this very foresight made it possible for him to make himself (by taking notes) foresee it later, *viz.,* at the time of the accident.

It might be objected that all that this illustration shows is that the foreseeability of *e can* be afforded by the foresight of *e,* and not that the former *requires* the latter. In a sense, this is correct; but in another sense, it is not. The "free to foresee" of (P4.5) admits of two interpretations: it may express either *opaque* freedom (the freedom to bring something about unintentionally) or *transparent* freedom (the freedom to bring something about intentionally). In Section 2.2 and again in Section 3.3, it was noted that, even if one is opaquely free with respect to some event, if one is also transparently unfree with respect to it then it is, in a significant sense, beyond one's control. This sense is important, in that it is *this* sort of control that appraisability apparently requires; the failure to do what one is merely opaquely free to do can never suffice for appraisability, for it reveals nothing commendable or defective about the agent. Thus I would urge that the sort of foreseeability that can indicate the presence of appraisability is *transparent* foreseeability. I would also point out that transparent foreseeability indeed requires foresight; for one cannot, I believe, be free at one time to *intentionally* make oneself forsee *e* at a later time without, at the earlier time, foreseeing *e.*

4.2 Negligence, Rashness, and Recklessness

Negligence. Culpable inadvertence constitutes an important species of culpable behavior. As just indicated, all culpability for inadvertence, for inadvertent action, and for the consequences of such must be indirect.

Inadvertence is the failure to advert to something, to consider or entertain it consciously. Culpable inadvertence—that is, inadvertence for which one is culpable—is an interesting phenomenon in that, insofar as one is culpable for the inadvertence, and inasmuch as such culpability must be indirect, and insofar as one presupposes the Internalist Position on indirect appraisability, much (if not all[17]) such inadvertence will be preceded by advertence. In particular, if an agent is culpable for some event *e,* by virtue of its being a consequence of his failure to advert to it at some time, then in many (if not all) such instances he will have adverted to it at some earlier time. In general, then, when, on the Internalist Position, there is culpable inadvertence, there is advertence-*cum*-inadvertence, just as, when there is culpable ignorance, there is belief-*cum*-disbelief. Thus *substantial* culpability concerning inadvertence generally requires advertence to that inadvertence.[18]

Perhaps all and only culpable inadvertence may be said to constitute negligence. Or perhaps negligence is to be thought of more broadly as inadvertence which is either culpable or wrong. Or perhaps it is to be thought of more narrowly as culpably inadvertent action that has arisen due to a failure to take care and precaution to avert such inadvertence. This last species of inadvertent behavior is a common one and is often referred to as negligence; henceforth, I shall call it and it alone negligence.[19]

I propose in this section to give a fairly precise account of negligence. My purpose is twofold. First, negligence, even more than culpable ignorance, is *very* frequently ascribed to agents, and it is therefore desirable that an accurate and detailed account of it be given. Secondly, I wish to demonstrate that, even given my claim that foreseeability requires foresight, my account of appraisability accommodates talk of negligence; for the cry of "he ought to have foreseen that" is as common to ascriptions of negligence as it is to ascriptions of culpable ignorance.

Sometimes the failure to take care and precaution to avert inadvertence is not culpable, as I shall shortly illustrate. Let us say that in general such failure, whether culpable or not, constitutes *neglect*.[20] Inasmuch as this failure must fit our advertence-*cum*-inadvertence model, it must be preceded or accompanied by advertence; the inadvertence must enter into a volition. A precise account of neglect, so construed, is really quite complex.[21] We need not enter into all the details here; even so, what follows is fairly complicated:

(P4.6) S neglects to some degree to (try to) prevent e if and only if, for some event f_i among events $f_1 \ldots f_n$, S wills that neither f_i, nor f_{i+1}, nor . . . , nor f_n occur, in the belief that
(a) there is some likelihood that he can prevent e,
(b) he can bring about each of $f_1 \ldots f_n$,
(c) if he brings about none of $f_1 \ldots f_n$, there is some likelihood that he will inadvertently omit to (try to) prevent e and, thereby, some likelihood that e will occur,
(d) $f_1 \ldots f_n$ constitute precautionary measures, in ascending order of probable efficacy, against his inadvertently omitting to (try to) prevent e and, thereby, against the occurrence of e itself, and
(e) there are no events other than $f_1 \ldots f_n$ that he can bring about and that constitute precautionary measures against his inadvertently omitting to (try to) prevent e and, thereby, against the occurrence of e itself.[22]

And, where "f_1," etc., function as in (P4.6) and "v" refers to the volition in (P4.6):

(P4.7) S acts neglectfully to some degree with respect to e if and only if, for some event g, S brings about g
(a) thereby inadvertently omitting to (try to) prevent e by bringing about either f_i, or f_{i+1}, or . . . , or f_n, and
(b) as a consequence of v.

Several points about (P4.6) and (P4.7) should be noted explicitly.

First, in both (P4.6) and (P4.7), I restrict my attention to bringing about (see (P2.1)), but there is nothing in principle that rules out in this context talking instead of helping to bring about (see (P2.2)), or contribution (see (P2.3)), or omission (see (P2.10)). Some writers, indeed, say that only omissions can be negligent, and that actions which manifest the same characteristics are to be called heedless.[23] I shall not enter into this terminological dispute here, although it is pertinent to note that even actions which are neglectful do, according to clause (a) of (P4.7), involve omissions.

Second, (P4.6) stipulates that S is neglectful only if he decides not to take *both* a precautionary measure *and* any probably more effective precautionary measure. The second point is important. It would not do to say that S is neglectful if he decides not to take the precautionary measure of bringing about f_i when he *does* decide to take (what seems to him) the probably more effective precautionary measure of bringing about f_j. Clause (e) of (P4.6) is included for a similar reason; for it would not do to say that S is neglectful if he decides not to take any of the precautionary measures involved in bringing about $f_i \ldots f_n$ when he *does* decide to take some other probably more effective precautionary measure.

Third, neither (P4.6) nor (P4.7) implies that S really could have prevented e's occurrence. (Hence the use of "(try to).") All that is required is that S believed that he could, or might be able to, prevent it but nevertheless undertook not to prevent it.

Fourth, neither (P4.6) nor (P4.7) requires that e occur. S may be mistaken as to the likelihood of e's occurring; or he may not be mistaken but, as long as the likelihood is not equivalent to a probability of 1, e may yet not occur. However, if e does occur as a consequence of S's volition, it may be said to be a consequence of S's neglect.

Fifth, (P4.6) is compatible with the theoretical possibility that there be "chains" of neglect. It might be that the belief involved, or the volition made in light of the belief, is itself a consequence of S's neglect.

Sixth, (P4.6) and (P4.7) mention *degrees* of neglect. I shall return to this shortly.

Finally, the neglect in (P4.6) is conscious,[24] but the neglectful action in (P4.7) is inadvertent. Thus the model of advertence-*cum*-inadvertence is preserved in these statements. But even so, these statements characterize neglect only, and not negligence; for an agent may well not be culpable for acting neglectfully. Suppose that it occurs to me on Friday that there is some likelihood that I will inadvertently break a routine appointment in my office Monday morning, and that, if I were to go there immediately, place a large notice "STAY UNTIL NOON MONDAY" on the inside of the door, and spend the weekend there, that would probably be an effective precautionary measure against inadvertently breaking the appointment; but suppose that I believe (quite reasonably, it seems to me) that I risk doing no wrong if I fail to do this; then, if I neglect to do this and, as a consequence, act neglectfully with respect to my keeping my appointment, no negligence is involved in this regard. On the other hand, another precautionary measure may also occur to me—probably less effective than the first, but probably effective nonetheless, and certainly better than nothing—and that is to write myself a note as a reminder and leave it in a place where I am likely to see and read it before Monday's appointment; and I may believe (again quite reasonably, it seems to me) that this is something I really ought to do; and if I neglect to do this and, as a consequence, act neglectfully with respect to my keeping my appointment, there *is* negligence involved.

Given (P4.7), it is easy to account for negligent action:

(P4.8) S acts negligently to some degree with respect to e if and only if
              (a) S acts neglectfully to some degree with respect to e, and
              (b) S is culpable to some degree for doing so.

Of course, (P4.8) constitutes a semistipulative definition, in keeping with my practice in this book,[25] and, of course, the culpability must be indirect.[26] If there is no "chain" of negligence involved, then the roots of the culpability will be found in S's being directly culpable for the volition involved in (P4.6); if there is a chain of negligence, then S's culpability for this volition may be indirect, or perhaps he is indirectly culpable for the belief involved in (P4.6). Again, while negligent action is itself inadvertent, it is rooted in advertence.

What of *degrees* of negligence? (It has been said that the notion of degrees of negligence is nonsensical because inadvertence does not come in degrees.[27] This, of course, is a *non sequitur,* for negligence does not consist solely in inadvertence.) This is in fact a complicated matter, and I shall simply sketch the relevant data here. First, of course, just as culpability may in general come in degrees, so may it when it is tied up with negligence. But neglect, too, may come in degrees. I think that we may say, roughly, that (i) the degree of neglect varies directly with the probability, as perceived by S, of e's occurring were S to take no precautions, but also, consistently with this, that (ii) it correlates inversely with the size of the "gap" between the perceived probability of e's occurring were no precautions taken and the perceived probability of its occurring given the precautions that he in fact decides to take. For (i) the less the perceived likelihood of the event's occurring "in its original setting," the less neglectful the failure to prevent it would seem to be; but also (ii) the greater the gap mentioned, the better the precautions and thus the less the neglect, and the smaller the gap, the worse the precautions and thus the greater the neglect.[28]

Rashness and recklessness. To indulge further in the semistipulative definition of semitechnical terms, let us note that negligence is to be distinguished from rashness. While negligence essentially involves culpable
inadvertence, rashness essentially involves the culpable underestimation
of the likelihood of some event's occurring, as when Jones unwittingly,
but culpably, risks injuring the driver by dragging him from the wreck.
(Here I am of course concerned with what is *morally* rash, as opposed,
for example, to what is prudentially rash.) By "underestimation" I mean
roughly the following:

(P4.9) S underestimates the likelihood of e's occurring if and only
          if
          (a) S believes that it is likely to degree x that e will occur,
          (b) it is in fact likely to degree y that e will occur, and
          (c) x is less than y.

Of course, just what it means to say that "it is in fact likely to degree y
that e will occur" is problematic; but I shall not discuss this issue here.

Just as inadvertence need not be culpable, so too underestimation need
not be. But just as, where inadvertence is culpable, the agent's culpability
for it must be indirect, so too, where underestimation is culpable, the
agent's culpability for it must be indirect.

Rashness is to be distinguished from over-caution, which essentially
involves the culpable overestimation of the likelihood of some event's
occurring. Of course, rashness and over-caution go hand-in-hand, in that,
whenever there is underestimation there is very probably overestimation,
and *vice versa*. If I underestimate the likelihood of e's occurring, I will
very probably overestimate the likelihood of its not occurring. Nevertheless, it seems appropriate to define rashness in terms of underestimation
rather than overestimation; to define it in the latter way would seem to
constitute a more "indirect" way of viewing the matter.

Negligence is also to be distinguished from recklessness. (Again, I am
of course concerned with what is *morally* reckless, as opposed, for
example, to what is prudentially reckless.) Recklessness, insofar as it is
understood essentially to involve the culpability of an agent rather than
the wrongness of some action, just is callousness (as defined in Section
3.1), *i.e.*, the willingness, but not the intention, to do—or, better (given
the subsequent discussion of risk), to non-minimally risk doing—wrong,
as is manifested by a wittingly, culpably, careless driver. Such culpability
may of course be direct, while the culpability involved in negligence and
rashness must be indirect.

While negligence, rashness, and recklessness are, then, clearly distinct
from one another, certain connections between them may yet be noted.
First, I believe that much rashness involves negligence in the following
way. It has been said that all rashness involves a culpable underestimation

of probability. Now, I think that it is rare that underestimation is advertent; indeed, I am not sure that it is possible for it to be advertent. At any rate, it is clear that much inadvertent underestimation is negligent, that is, a consequence of culpable neglect. Secondly, some negligence may itself involve rashness. This may happen when there are chains of neglect and where the belief mentioned in (P4.6) is false, by virtue of there being an underestimation of the likelihood of *e*'s occurring. Thirdly, the volition not to take precautions that is operative in all negligence may well involve callousness and thus recklessness.

4.3 Attempts

Whether or not an attempt succeeds is often thought to be relevant to the degree to which someone is to be praised or blamed. Is it? And does this show that the foregoing account of appraisability is insufficiently precise, implying that a person who is successful in his attempt is appraisable to the same degree as one who is not? Indeed, is it not unduly deflationary, insofar as it asserts that success in one's attempts confers no additional degree of substantial appraisability?

In Section 2.1, it was noted that there are two main sorts of attempts. In the broad sense, an attempt is simply a volition. In this sense, appraisability for attempts has already been covered. If *S* wills *e* and *e* results, his attempt at *e* is successful; if he wills *e* but *e* does not result, his attempt at *e* is unsuccessful. In both cases, he may be appraisable to some degree for willing *e;* in the first case, he may also be appraisable for *e* itself; in the second case, of course, he is not appraisable for *e*. Does this point up a difference between the cases as to the degree to which *S* may be appraised? Not at all. In the first case, *S* is (let us assume) to be appraised for two things, namely, willing *e* and *e;* in the second case he is (let us assume) to be appraised for just one thing, namely, willing *e*.[29] But this difference in the *number* of things for which he is to be appraised does not indicate any difference in the *degree* to which he is to be appraised.[30] For in each case the degree to which he is *directly* appraisable is the same. It is true that in the first case, but not the second, he is *indirectly* appraisable for *e;* but, as we saw in Section 3.3, such appraisability does not occasion a fresh entry in his ledger. While *S*'s being successful in his attempt will render him *indirectly* appraisable *for e* and, moreover, *substantially* appraisable *concerning e,* he cannot thereby be rendered *substantially* appraisable *for e*. I shall have more to say on this topic in Section 4.11.

What of attempts in the narrow sense, that is, attempts that are at least partly successful and commonly involve effort? Again, no modification to the account is called for here. For, whatever results from the volition involved will be something for which the agent is, at best, only indirectly appraisable; hence there will be no change in the degree to which he is to be appraised, although the number of things for which he is to be appraised will increase.

Legal theorists have exercised themselves a good deal in grappling with the matter of legal responsibility for attempts. Traditionally, it has been thought that one ought to be punished more for successful than for unsuccessful attempts to commit a legal offense. Now, for all that has been said here, this may be true. But if it is, it is true *despite* the fact that degree of moral appraisability does not vary according to whether or not one's attempt is successful. (I shall return to the issue of punishment for attempts in Section 5.4.) A second issue is this: traditionally, it has been thought that it matters, when ascribing legal responsibility, whether or not the attempt to commit a legal offense could have succeeded and, if it could not, whether this is due to the impossibility's being "factual" or "legal." In the former case, legal responsibility has traditionally been thought to remain intact, while, in the latter case, it has traditionally been thought to be voided. This tradition has been challenged.[31] Again, however, we need concern ourselves with none of this here, for there is no analogy between legal responsibility and moral appraisability on this score. The disanalogy is highlighted by the distinction between Tables I and II of the previous chapter. While legal responsibility requires legal wrongdoing, moral appraisability does not require moral wrongdoing. Thus, while it may be relevant to the matter of legal responsibility for an attempt at e that it is "legally impossible" to commit an offense by bringing about e (*i.e.,* bringing about e would not constitute a legal offense), it is irrelevant to the matter of moral appraisability for an attempt at e that it is "morally impossible" to commit an offense by bringing about e (*i.e.,* bringing about e would not be morally wrong). Rather, what matters for appraisability is simply whether or not the agent *believed* it morally wrong to bring about e.

Thus, we find no reason, stemming from the matter of attempts, to modify our account of appraisability. The success of an attempt does not occasion an increase (or, for that matter, a decrease) in the degree to which the agent is substantially appraisable. The prudence of the practice, adopted in (P3.11) and ensuing formulae, of matching the degree of indirect and conjoint appraisability with the degree of direct appraisability, is confirmed.

4.4 Omissions

It may appear that the account of appraisability given in the last chapter simply ignores appraisability for omissions. After all, direct appraisability concerns volitions only; conjoint appraisability concerns actions, but I have claimed (Section 2.1) that omissions are not actions, for they do not necessarily involve volitions, let alone bringing about; and indirect appraisability concerns the consequences of volitions. Where do omissions fit into this account?

The answer is that they are accommodated by the discussion of indirect appraisability. The point is that the question of appraisability for an omission arises *only* where there is an initial volition of which the omission in question is itself a consequence.[32] There is, therefore, this asymmetry between actions and omissions with regard to appraisability: appraisability for the former may be either conjoint or indirect, but for the latter it can only be indirect. A possible exception to this claim is appraisability for *intentional* omissions, where we might wish to say that the volition is *part* of the omission, even though the negative event involved—the not-doing—of course remains a consequence of the volition. In such a case we may wish, therefore, to talk of conjoint appraisability. But this question of classification of course leaves unaffected the issue of *substantial* appraisability, which remains a matter only of *direct* appraisability.

Still, it is often thought that there is something special about the relation between responsibility and omissions. Sometimes it is said that ascriptions of responsibility are improper in certain contexts involving omissions; sometimes it is said that the degree of responsibility is diminished in certain contexts involving omissions. Is the foregoing account of appraisability insufficiently precise, and thus defective, in not taking this issue into account?

At times, it appears that writers advocate something like the following argument, which concerns the *consequences* of omissions[33]: (i) one is morally responsible for harm only if one caused it; (ii) one causes harm only if one's action is the cause of it; (iii) an omission to avert harm is not an action which is the cause of harm; hence, (iv) one is not morally responsible for harm which one has merely omitted to avert.[34] Opponents to this sort of argument commonly take exception to premise (iii),[35] but, as noted in Section 2.1, this seems to me a mistake. Of course, the argument could be toned down a bit by substituting "a cause" for "the cause" in premises (ii) and (iii), but even so premise (iii) seems to me plausible. Other opponents to the argument reject premise (ii),[36] but this move also seems questionable to me. The most vulnerable premise seems to me to be the first.[37] For, as emphasized in Section 1.1, personal responsibility is to be distinguished from causal responsibility (and, of course, from a hybrid personal-*cum*-causal responsibility). One argument *for* premise (i) is this: (ia) one is morally responsible for harm only if one was in control of it; (ib) one was in control of something which occurred only if one caused it; hence, (ic) premise (i) is true. But (ib) is surely problematic. Omissions seem to me to afford a counterexample; cannot one have been in control of something which occurred and just have let it occur (perhaps, just have let it *continue* to occur) without, thereby, having *caused* it to (continue to) occur? But this will seem to some like begging the question, which, I suppose, it is. So let us consider this possibility: I hold a gun to your head and order you to open the safe, which you proceed to do strictly freely; I am in control of your opening the safe, but I do not cause it, for (let us assume) strictly free actions are not caused by any events whatsoever.[38] While this assumption is *not* presupposed by any of the main arguments presented in this book, it is nonetheless one that I in fact accept.[39] If it is rejected, I am unable to come up with another non-question-begging counterexample to (ib).

Of course, the question as to whether (iv) is acceptable is in a way moot, since we are dealing with indirect appraisability here; but, if we can do wrong by failing to prevent harm—as surely we can—then, whether or not such harm is a causal consequence of our omission, it can be just as revealing an indication of culpability as a causal consequence of an action. As before, whether there is such culpability of course depends on whether the agent was willing to do wrong by failing to avert the harm in question; but if he was, why not accept the resulting harm as something for which he is indirectly appraisable?

It has been suggested that causation is relevant to the ascription of responsibility in this way. While (i) is false, still there is a presumption of culpability for harm if one has caused the harm, while there is a presumption of nonculpability for harm if one has not caused it. It has further been suggested that this asymmetry explains why it is, in general, worse to kill someone than to fail to prevent someone's death.[40] This strikes me as very odd. I see no reason to accept the claim concerning presumptions; moreover, I see no reason to think that, even if this claim is true, it has the explanatory power attributed to it. Of course, it might still be that killing is, in general, worse than failing to prevent death; but this, whatever it amounts to exactly, is a separate question to which I shall return shortly.

Another argument concerning the consequences of omissions which has been advocated is this: (i) one is morally responsible for harm only if it is uniquely ascribable to one; (ii) harm which one fails to avert is not (or is hardly ever) uniquely ascribable to one; thus (iii) one is not (or is hardly ever) morally responsible for harm which one fails to avert.[41] The second premise must be accepted, in the sense that, where I fail to avert harm and it occurs, its occurrence is not (or is hardly ever) uniquely ascribable to my omission; for had not others also omitted to avert it, then it would not have occurred despite my omission. But the first premise is clearly implausible. Again, the point is in a way moot; still, harm which is ascribable, but not uniquely ascribable, to me would seem to be equally as revealing of culpability on my part as harm which is uniquely ascribable to me.

On the other hand, uniqueness may appear to be relevant in this way: where harm is not uniquely ascribable to one, then one is *less* culpable for it than if it were uniquely ascribable to one. In different terminology: if the freedom which one has with respect to some event is merely *supplementary,* then any appraisability that one has for it is of a lesser degree than that which one would have for it if one had *primary* freedom with respect to it.[42] This contention concerning the so-called "sharing" of responsibility is one that I shall take up in the next section.

Suppose that it is in general worse (that is, for our purposes, more seriously wrong) to cause harm (*e.g.,* to kill someone) than to fail to prevent it (*e.g.,* to let someone die). Why one should believe this, I am not sure; but many appear to accept it. And suppose that an agent accepts this. Then, if this agent were willingly to let die rather than kill, his culpability would in so far forth be less than it would be if he were willingly to kill rather than let die. This is the *only* way (apart from the possibly relevant matter of the sharing of responsibility to be discussed next) in which, so far as I can see, responsibility is diminished when there is omission rather than action. And notice how insignificant this is. For if the agent were to believe that it is in general worse to fail to prevent harm than to cause it, and if he were willingly to cause it rather than to fail to prevent it, his culpability would in so far forth be likewise diminished.

4.5 Sharing Responsibility

While the matter of sharing responsibility arises frequently in cases of omission, it can also arise in cases of action. Here I am concerned with the issue of *personal* responsibility in multiagent contexts, and not with responsibility to be ascribed to groups or collectives as a whole. And my concern in particular is this: some philosophers appear to suggest that the degree to which someone is to be appraised for an event is a function of the number of persons who are also to be appraised for that same event; in particular, the more such persons, the less each person is to be praised or blamed for the event in question.[43] The suggestion seems to be that there is just so much responsibility to go around—the "pie" is just so large—and the more people involved, the smaller the share for each. Insofar as my account implies no diminution of responsibility in group situations, it may appear unduly inflationary. But I shall argue that there is nothing about the sharing of responsibility which requires a modification to the foregoing account of appraisability.

Direct appraisability. Direct appraisability is an essentially private matter; it cannot be shared. That is, it is not possible for more than one person to be directly appraisable for one and the same event. This is due to the nature of direct freedom. (I would urge that this must be accepted whether or not one also accepts that direct freedom is anchored in volitions.) While more than one person can be indirectly free with respect to some event and while one's indirect freedom with respect to some event may be merely supplementary, none of this is possible in the case of direct freedom, and hence direct appraisability *cannot* be shared. Of course it remains possible that S should be directly appraisable for an event while S' is indirectly appraisable for it; this could arise where S's volition is a consequence of a volition of S'. And of course it remains possible that two persons should each be indirectly appraisable for the same event. It is on such cases as these that we must focus here.

Control. When appraisability is shared in such cases, it is often said that the degree, to which one or more of the parties concerned is responsible, is diminished; in cases where there is intervention by another agent, it is sometimes said that there is a preemption of responsibility, such that one of the parties is not responsible at all. But why should we think that the sharing of responsibility involves such diminution or elimination?

Perhaps the thought is this: where there is group action or group omission an individual's control of the outcome is impaired or eliminated, and this brings with it a diminution or elimination of responsibility. Let us examine this claim.

There is no doubt that control can be affected in cases of group action and omission. In cases where the action or omission is overfull, standard control is often absent so that there is, at best, curtailed control; for if one's action, or the action that one omits, is not necessary for the occurrence of e, then one is often not free with respect to not-e. And even when the action or omission is brimming rather than overfull, control can be affected in that one's control with respect to the outcome may be merely supplementary rather than primary. But note that none of this *need* be the case. Consider what is perhaps an overfull group action—for instance, ten people lifting a heavy object when any five could do the job.[44] It may be that, under normal conditions, if one of the ten were to refuse to help, the object would be lifted anyway; and so his control with respect to the object's being raised would be at best curtailed, for he would not be free with respect to its not being raised. But of course conditions could be such that he is free with respect to its not being raised; for example, he might have a machine-gun and be free with respect to shooting the other nine in the legs. Again, while control in cases of group action is often merely supplementary, it need not be. Consider again the case where ten people lift the heavy object, and suppose now that all ten are needed for this. But suppose that nine of the ten are under the hypnotic influence of the tenth person. In such a case, this tenth person may well have primary control with respect to the object's being raised. Their cooperation is "guaranteed"; *they* are in *his* control.[45]

The real question to be asked here, however, is this: even in those cases where control is curtailed, rather than standard, or merely supplementary, rather than primary—so what? I shall address the issue of curtailed *vs.* standard control in Section 4.10; there I shall argue that whichever it is that one has with respect to an event does not affect the degree to which one is appraisable for that event. And as for having merely supplementary control with respect to an event: we must bear in mind here that we have to do with indirect appraisability and that, given its essential emptiness and the consequent leeway that we enjoy with respect to its ascription, what we must concern ourselves with is the revealingness of the ascriptions that we make. For my part, I see no reason why the events with respect to which we have or had merely supplementary, rather than primary, freedom should be any less revealing of direct laudability or culpability on our part than events with respect to which we have or had primary freedom. For example, if we are indirectly culpable for an event, then the event is our fault, regardless of whether it is also someone else's fault. Our fault is not diminished by another's; our requiring help to produce an outcome does not diminish the degree to which we are at fault, for, as noted earlier, direct culpability is an essentially private matter. Thus, the fact that others may be appraisable for the same event does not diminish our substantial appraisability concerning it, and so I see no reason to say that it diminishes our indirect appraisability for it.

There may be lingering doubts, however. Does it not matter just what one's contribution toward the final outcome is? Do not some people contribute to a greater extent than others, and should not the degree to which they are appraised for the outcome reflect this fact? This is a difficult issue. On the one hand, of course it matters just what one's contribution is, in the sense that it matters (i) whether or not this was by way of a volition, (ii) whether or not the outcome entered into the volition, and (iii) just how it entered into the volition, that is, just what the volition was. But none of this has been denied. On the other hand, it should be pointed out that talk of the "extent" of someone's contribution is unclear. Suppose that, in a brimming object-lifting case, it was wrong for each person to help lift the object, but that one of the participants was forced by the others to help. Some might say that the reluctant participant contributed to a lesser extent than the others to the outcome, but I am not sure what this would mean in this context. Perhaps he did less wrong, or perhaps he is less to blame, but his contribution seems just like the others' in terms of being necessary, but not sufficient, for the outcome. Still it might be that those who forced him to participate contributed to a greater extent to the outcome in that they did more things which so contributed, *viz.*, not only lifting, or helping to lift, the object but also forcing the reluctant participant to do the same. This is true but, again, has not been denied. In this case we have the outcome being not only such that more than one person is appraisable for it but also such that some persons are multiply appraisable for it, that is, appraisable for it in virtue of more than one volition. And, anyway, the key point here is simply this: even if some other clear sense can be given to the claim that someone S has contributed to a greater extent to e than someone else S', who has also contributed to e, this in and of itself is essentially irrelevant to the ascription to S and S' of substantial appraisability concerning e; for such contribution is perforce "after the fact," that is, subsequent to and separate from those volitions for which S and S' are directly, and thus substantially, appraisable. And so there appears to be no necessity to appraise someone to a lesser degree than someone else for an event with respect to which his contribution is smaller, nor any necessity to appraise someone to a lesser degree for an event with respect to which he enjoyed merely supplementary freedom.[46]

Intervening agents. While what has just been said may appear acceptable in general, there is a specific type of sequential group action which some believe to prove exceptional: that which involves intervention. Suppose that some bracken has caught fire because Smith has thrown a lighted cigarette into it and, just as the flames are about to flicker out, Jones deliberately pours petrol on them and a forest-fire ensues.[47] Some seem to think it improper to blame Smith for the forest-fire; it is Jones, the intervening agent, who is to blame for it. Or suppose that Smith refuses to divulge certain information that Jones wants and that Jones, as threatened, tortures an innocent child because of this refusal. Again, some would blame Jones but not Smith for the child's suffering. Is this defensible, and does it point up a problem with our account? Let us see.

  First, why do I categorize this as "sequential group action"? It is clearly sequential, in that in each case Jones's action succeeds Smith's. And it is group action in that there is a common outcome. In the first case, the outcome is the forest-fire; in the second, the child's suffering. In each case, in fact, the outcome is a simple consequence of the original agent's (Smith's) action and a causal consequence of the intervening agent's (Jones's) action. Let us concentrate on such cases of intervention. There could surely be other types of cases, both where the types of consequences differ and where there is omission rather than action; but I shall not delve into these.

  Now, what is supposed to be so significant about such intervention?

Why even think that it diminishes, let alone that it eliminates, the responsibility of the original agent for the event in question? The only argument that I have found to be suggested in the literature—but, I hasten to add, not explicitly endorsed—is one which, emphasizing the fact that intervening agents intervene, claims that such agents interrupt the natural flow of causes and thereby pre-empt normal attributions of moral responsibility. In short, the argument is the following:[48]

(P4.10)   The original agent was not causally responsible for the event in question.

(P4.11)   One is morally responsible for an event only if one was causally responsible for it.

Therefore:

(P4.12)   The original agent is not morally responsible for the event in question.

There are several problems with this argument. First, it is not clear that (P4.10) is true; this depends on how it is interpreted. There are two main interpretations: (i) no action of the original agent was *the* cause of the event; and (ii) no action of the original agent was *a* cause of the event. On the first interpretation, (P4.10) seems to me true for both cases given; it is Jones's action which is the cause of the event in question. On the second interpretation, however, (P4.10) is problematic. In the case of the forest-fire, indeed, it is false; for Smith's throwing the cigarette clearly contributed causally to the fire.[49] In the case of the torturing, it is unclear whether (P4.10) is true on the second interpretation; if Smith acts freely, and if free actions are such that no event causes them, then it is true.[50]

Second, (P4.11) seems implausible, on either interpretation of "causally responsible." Indeed, it is surely to be rejected on either interpretation unless it is specified that it is indirect appraisability that is at issue, for on neither interpretation is one causally responsible for one's volitions;[51] but since indirect appraisability is exactly what is at issue here, I shall not pursue this point. And it is surely to be rejected on the first interpretation anyway, at least if we want a useful notion of indirect appraisability. Clearly, it is not useful to restrict the ascription of indirect appraisability to those cases where the event in question is such that the agent's action was *the* cause of it; for one can surely be substantially appraisable concerning some events for which none of one's actions is *the* cause. Nor is it useful even when we relax this condition to one concerning being-*a*-cause rather than being-*the*-cause. The motivation for (P4.11), so understood, might well be this: (i) one cannot have been in control of something which occurred unless one was causally responsible for it; (ii) one cannot be morally responsible for something which occurred unless one was in control of it; therefore (iii) (P4.11) is true. But the first premise of this subargument is, as we saw with (ib) of the last subsection, quite problematic.[52]

Finally, while (P4.12) is perhaps true (although I do not think that it is true) in the cases we have considered, there is clearly no necessity that it be true in all structurally similar cases of intervention. Consider this case: a bankrobber is to blame for the bank's funds being depleted, even though a teller, acting at gunpoint, was (temporally) a more proximate cause of the depletion. The teller's intervention surely need not block ascription of indirect appraisability to the bankrobber for the depletion.[53] Why should we say that it does? There seems to me no reason to say this, for clearly the bankrobber can be substantially culpable concerning the depletion. (The bankrobber may also be said to be culpable for the teller's action—a matter of *vicarious* responsibility. In general, there is no theoretical problem with vicarious responsibility, with one person being indirectly appraisable for the actions of another. Of course, this is not a matter of one person's somehow *assuming* responsibility for another's action, of, *e.g.*, "taking the blame," which would otherwise devolve on the other person. One person can substitute himself for another in terms of opening himself up to punishment, perhaps,[54] but he cannot substitute himself for another in terms of appraisability. This would be a theoretical impossibility.)

But, if (P4.12) is false, perhaps some modification of it is true, and perhaps this can be argued along similar lines. Indeed, remarks made by H. L. A. Hart and A. M. Honoré suggest that, while (P4.10) is false, the following is true:

(P4.10′)   The original agent was not causally responsible for the event in question, if the intervening agent's action was voluntary.[55]

And this perhaps suggests that (P4.12) may be modified thus:

(P4.12′)   The original agent is not morally responsible for the event in question, if the intervening agent's action was voluntary.[56]

One problem in understanding this modification of the argument is that voluntariness comes in degrees, and yet degrees are not mentioned in the modification. But let us, for simplicity's sake, assume that it is "full" voluntariness that is at issue. Then the case of the bankrobber will have been circumvented, since the teller's action was clearly not fully voluntary.

Of course, there are problems with this modified argument also. Since it still relies on (P4.11), it is at best shaky—and, at best, causal responsibility must be understood in terms of being-*a*-cause. Even so, why think that (P4.10′) is true? One line of thinking is this: (i) voluntariness (whether full or not) requires strict freedom; (ii) if one acts strictly freely, *nothing* (or, at least, *no event*) causes one's volition;[57] hence (iii) voluntariness requires that *nothing* (or, at least, *no event)* causes the consequences of one's volition except one's volition itself. Many would regard premise (ii) of this argument as false; but I do not wish to go into this here—the issue concerns whether or not incompatibilism is true, and to discuss it would lead us too far astray.[58] What it is crucial to point out, though, is that (iii) does not follow from (i) and (ii). Perhaps nothing causes *e,* and perhaps *e* causes *f,* but it does not follow that nothing but *e* causes *f.* Consider again the case of Jones's petrol-pouring: perhaps no event caused this event, and this event did contribute causally to the fire, but so too did the original cigarette-throwing contribute causally to the fire.[59] Thus there is no reason to accept (P4.10′) simply because one subscribes to an incompatibilist view of strict freedom. Moreover, if this subargument had worked, it would have proven too strong. After all, the teller acted strictly freely, even if not with full voluntariness; and yet this must not preclude ascribing responsibility to the robber.

In addition, (P4.12′) is clearly unacceptable. Alan Donagan, himself a staunch supporter of the claim that there is *something* special about the moral status of intervening agents, gives a clear counterexample to (P4.12′):

Consider the following case. A poisoner orders that a chocolate cake be made. While it is being made, he distracts his cook's attention and adds powdered arsenic to the sugar the cook is about to use. He then engages a parcel service to box and deliver the cake to his victim: whereupon one person takes the order, another collects the cake, another boxes it, and yet another delivers it. After it has been delivered, the victim's servant, believing his master to have ordered it, serves it at supper. Pleased, the victim cuts a slice, eats it, and dies of arsenic poisoning. Obviously, it would be absurd for the poisoner to disclaim causing the victim's death by poison; and yet there can be no doubt that his own action in adding arsenic to his cook's sugar only led to his victim's death by way of a long series of intervening actions.[60]

Donagan's commentary on this case implies that he believes that the poisoner is to blame for his victim's death, and surely this is possible. That is, insofar as the poisoner can be substantially culpable concerning the victim's death, it can be reasonable to say that he is indirectly culpable for it. Hence (4.12′) is to be rejected.

Donagan himself proposes that we modify the conclusion of our main argument still further. He notes that, in his example, there is a special relationship between the poisoner and the intervening agents. The poisoner may be called the *principal* agent and the intervening agents his *secondary* agents. It is in virtue of this special relationship, Donagan contends, that the poisoner is to blame for the death of his victim.[61] (Indeed, this special relationship also explains how a coercer is to blame for the misdeeds of the one whom he coerces; for the coercee is the secondary agent of the coercer.) And it is clear that Donagan, while rejecting (P4.12′), wishes to accept this modification of (P4.12):

(P4.12″)   The original agent is not morally responsible for the event in question, unless the intervening agent was his secondary agent with respect to this event.

(And Donagan would thus modify (P4.10) to read as follows:

(P4.10″)   The original agent was not causally responsible for the event in question, unless the intervening agent was his secondary agent with respect to this event.[62])

Clearly, neither the case of the bankrobber nor the case of the cake undermines (P4.12″).

Still, this argument, even so modified, must be rejected. On the understanding of causal responsibility in terms of being-*a*-cause, (P4.10″) is false, for reasons implicit in remarks already made. More to the point, perhaps, (P4.12″) cannot be accepted. To appreciate this, we need only consider what it is to be a secondary agent. Donagan himself says the following in this regard:

A man becomes the voluntary and witting agent of another, either by agreeing to do something at his request or at the request of his accredited representative, or by acting as a functionary in an institution whose services the other engages. . . . [A] man acts as the unwitting agent of another when that other takes advantage of something he does by anticipating that he may do it and surreptitiously intervening in such a way that his doing it will subserve some purpose of the other's.[63]

While this account of the concept of a secondary agent is not fully explicit, I think it fair to say that, according to this account, the following is true (at least for those cases where the principal's association with the secondary agent is not by way of some "accredited representative" who has been accorded a certain degree of discretion by the principal in the way that he carries out the principal's wishes[64]):

(P4.13)   If S' was S's secondary agent with respect to e, then S intended that e occur.

Now, (P4.13) seems to me true; that is, it seems to me to be in keeping with the way we normally think of the relation between principals and their (secondary) agents. But (P4.13) and (P4.12″) conjoined yield the following:

(P4.14)   The original agent is not morally responsible for the event in question, unless he intended that it occur.

But this seems to me quite unacceptable; hence I reject (P4.12″). Consider this case of negligence. A father lets his young child run in the street, and an accident results. The father does not intend that the accident should occur; he may surely nevertheless be said to be indirectly culpable for it, in that he can surely be substantially culpable concerning it.[65]

But, it might be said, this case only shows that (P4.14) and (P4.12″) are not sufficiently carefully formulated. In the father-child case, *only* the father is responsible; the child is only a child, after all. But in the original cases of petrol-pouring and torturing the intervening agent *is* responsible for the undesirable event in question; *hence* the original agent is not responsible for this event. Thus, we may say:

(P4.12‴)   The original agent is not morally responsible for the event in question, if the intervening agent is morally responsible for it.

But now we have come full circle. Either (P4.12‴) simply begs the question, or it is tantamount to a full-scale denial that responsibility can be shared—a denial which, we have seen, is itself to be denied.

Doing wrong. It may be thought that, in all of the foregoing, I have missed the point, which is simply this: in group action the *wrongness* of the individuals' actions is diminished, and hence their culpability is also; and, in cases of intervention, the *wrongness* of the original agent's action is nullified, and hence his culpability is eliminated.

It may of course happen that the wrongness of an individual's action is diminished (if wrongness can come in degrees, as I believe it can[66]) or eliminated in cases of group action or omission. But two points need stressing here. First, the crucial question is whether or not wrongness *must* be diminished or eliminated, not whether it *may* be. Secondly, and more importantly, while this question is crucial to a theory of wrongdoing, it is quite irrelevant here. For actual wrongness, as has been repeatedly noted, has nothing to do with culpability; it is what the agent perceives as wrong that matters.

Am I being too high-handed here? I think not. There are cases (*e.g.*, of brimming group action and, I would say, of intervening agency) where I think that the fact that others participate does nothing in and of itself to diminish the wrongness of one's participation; there are cases (*e.g.*, of overfull group action) where I am not sure what to think in this regard; and there are cases (*e.g.*, of brimming group omission) where I think that the fact that others participate does everything to diminish the wrongness of one's participation. But none of this affects the matter of culpability.

For example, consider a case where I think that degree of wrongness clearly is affected, a case of brimming group omission. Suppose that a group of three swimmers *(A–C)* watch a large man drown: the efforts of all three are necessary (and, *ceteris paribus*, sufficient) to prevent the drowning, and *none* makes the required effort. Compare this with another case where B and C do make the necessary effort, but A does not, and so the man drowns. And let us now ask: is there anything to distinguish, with respect to degree of wrongness, A's omission to help save the man in the first case from A's omission to help save the man in the second case? The answer seems to me clearly to be that there *is*. In the second case, we may assume, A's omission was wrong. But in the first case we cannot say this, simply because A did *not* in fact omit to save the man. The *group (A–C)* omitted to save the man in both cases, and so the *group,* I would say, did wrong in both cases.[67] But in the first case A *could not* save the man; for he could not do it on his own, and the cooperation of B and C was not forthcoming (and, I am assuming, he could do nothing to make such cooperation forthcoming). Thus, in the first case, A (as an individual) did *not* do wrong in not saving the man.

But even if I am right in this, A's culpability is unaffected. What matters is what he thought was the case. Suppose that, in the first case, he thought that B and C would cooperate, that he thought that he ought to help them, but that he simply decided not to. Here I would diagnose culpability, even in the absence of wrongdoing. The actual lack of cooperation by B and C, while highly relevant to the question of A's wrongdoing, is wholly irrelevant to the question of A's culpability. Or suppose that, in the second case, A thought that B and C would not cooperate and that it would be wrong to try to save the man on his own, inasmuch as he would not be successful and would place his own life in danger. Here I would diagnose no culpability, even in the presence of wrongdoing—unless, of course, A is culpable for his mistaken belief.

4.6 Compulsion

I shall use the term "compulsion" semistipulatively to indicate the lack of broad freedom. More precisely, S is compelled to degree x to bring about e just in case S is broadly unfree to degree x not to bring about e. A common form of compulsion is coercion—as, for example, in the case, discussed in Section 2.2, of the bankrobber compelling the teller to hand over the money.

While there is perhaps an odd ring to saying that someone can be compelled to do something and yet not do it, I wish to allow for this possibility for two reasons. First, one may be broadly unfree not to bring about something and yet strictly free not to bring it about—indeed, this is so with the teller, who strictly could have refused to hand over the money.[68] Secondly, since compulsion comes in degrees, one may be both broadly free to some degree and broadly unfree to some degree with respect to the same event.[69]

Coercion is by no means the only form of compulsion. It requires a purposeful coercer, and yet its effects can be simulated in the absence of such. (Consider: a customer enters a bar, hears a menacing voice behind him say, "Don't turn around! Raise your hands! One false move and you're history!", and fearfully obeys—only to discover that the voice came from a television in the corner.) Moreover, fears, temptations, desires, obsessions, and so on, however aroused, may compel. In this context, it is common to talk of "irresistible impulses," and I know of no reason to deny that they sometimes occur. Still, one must be careful how one engages in such talk. First, one must distinguish between that which is broadly irresistible and that which is strictly irresistible. In the example, the teller's "impulse" to hand over the money—his desire to do this—was strictly resistible but broadly irresistible. (I put "impulse" in quotation marks here, because my concern is not so much with *impulsive* behavior as with behavior which occurs by dint of *irresistible conditions*.[70] In the present case, the condition is the teller's desire to save his skin by handing over the money.) Second, while some impulses may perhaps be strictly irresistible (perhaps, *e.g.*, fear or pain can be literally disabling on occasion, although I am not at all sure that this is so[71]), they cannot be *regarded* as such by agents who act on them, for reasons given when discussing (P2.7)—unless, of course, the agent acts on them in the belief that they will *become*, but are not yet, strictly irresistible (as may be the case, for example, in certain cases of drug addiction[72]). Third, it cannot be denied that there are epistemological difficulties involved in distinguishing between actions whose impulses were irresistible and actions whose impulses were resistible but just not resisted. But this does not imply that the notion of such irresistibility is in any way improper.[73] Finally, insofar as I am unable to provide an analysis of broad freedom, I am unable to say just what it is in which compulsion, and hence broad irresistibility of impulse, consists; as for strict irresistibility of impulse, this is to be understood in terms of the account of strict freedom alluded to earlier.[74]

My concern in this section is, of course, with the power of compulsion to excuse. Does it have such power and, if so, does this show that the account of culpability given in Chapter 3 is unduly inflationary, implying that some people are culpable when in fact they are not? Given what has just been said, we may confine our attention to cases of compulsion where the agent is both strictly free with respect to the event in question and believes that he is strictly free in this regard.[75]

Very roughly, when one is compelled to do something, it is difficult (in some sense that I myself find difficult to explicate) for one not to do that thing. The greater the difficulty, the greater the compulsion. Moreover, I think that we may say (barring some possible problems with sub- or unconscious motivation) that it is difficult for one to do something just in case one finds it difficult to do that thing. (Again, such difficulty is not tantamount to strict impossibility.) Now, it is perhaps true that difficulty in performing an action diminishes, *ceteris paribus,* the wrongness of not performing that action.[76] I tend to think that this is not so, although I would agree that such difficulty tends to *minimize the risk* of doing wrong in not performing the action, insofar as, the greater the difficulty, the more reasonable it is to believe that one is not doing wrong in not performing the action. (For example, if the teller handed over the money to the robber but the robber would *not* have carried out his threat if he had not been given the money, then, I am inclined to say, the teller did wrong although it was quite reasonable for him to believe that he was not doing wrong (insofar as it was quite reasonable for him to believe that the robber *would* carry out his threat if there were no compliance with it). Compare the discussion of "objective" obligation in Section 3.1.) It also seems to me likely to be true that, the greater the moral seriousness of not performing the action, the less, *ceteris paribus,* the difficulty in performing it diminishes the wrongness, or the risk of wrongness, of not performing it.[77] Perhaps there are limits here. Perhaps it matters just what *type* of difficulty one encounters. Perhaps it matters just *how* great the seriousness is relative to the difficulty encountered (such that sometimes difficulty serves to diminish the wrongness, or the risk of wrongness, not at all).[78] I am not sure.

Now, if difficulty diminishes wrongness, or the risk of wrongness, in this way, and if the agent has a correct moral belief about this, then difficulty diminishes culpability. (See (P3.1').) (Indeed, if the agent finds himself in a position where he believes that the right, but not obligatory, thing to do is what he is compelled to do, and if he does it for this reason, then, far from being culpable, he will be *laudable*.[79] (See (P3.6').) Or, if the difficulty somehow renders him belief-less concerning the wrongness of handing over the money ("driving" all thought of wrongdoing from his mind), then again the difficulty diminishes, indeed eliminates, culpability. But, as before, if the agent believes that such difficulty does *not* diminish the (risk of) wrongness of what he wills to do, then there is *no* diminution of culpability.[80] (See Section 3.6.) Suppose, for example, that the teller had believed that it was quite wrong of him to hand over the money but that he nevertheless gave into the temptation to save his skin—something it was strictly open to him to avoid doing. Then he is to be blamed for handing over the money, and the facts that it was not wrong for him to do this (if this is a fact) and that he was compelled to do this do not serve to diminish the degree to which he is to blame.

4.7 Mental Disorders

There is a widespread opinion that suffering from a mental disorder can be relevant to one's laudability or culpability, although there seems to be very little consensus as to just what the conditions are for such relevance. I do not pretend to any expertise concerning mental disorders but, with that understood, there is nevertheless much that may be said concerning the relation between them and moral appraisability.

I use the term "mental disorder" rather than "mental illness" or "mental disease" because the former seems to me marginally more neutral than the latter two with respect to its medical status; but I have no particular axe to grind here. Thomas Szasz is well known for arguing that a mental disorder is not an illness or a disease, on the basis that it constitutes a social rather than a medical phenomenon.[81] Perhaps he is right; I have no intention to try to rebut this. On the other hand, Szasz also seems to intimate that there is no such thing as a mental disorder and that there is no excuse for misconduct that is derivable from it.[82] This seems to me quite wrong.[83] Clearly, there are mental disorders, however difficult they may be to understand, categorize, or deal with, and however many borderline cases between order and disorder there may be. Of course, one must be wary about misdiagnosis of such disorder and misapplication of the term "disorder"; but these caveats are not unique to the phenomenon.[84]

As far as I can tell, mental disorder may be relevant to the ascription of moral appraisability in three ways. It may affect an agent's beliefs, or his strict freedom, or his broad freedom. I shall consider these in turn. It will become apparent that no modification to our account of appraisability is called for here; mental disorder does not furnish a distinct excuse, and our account is not unduly inflationary in implying that it does not.

Beliefs. A person's beliefs may be affected by mental disorder in three main ways that are relevant to the ascription of moral responsibility. He may have a false belief concerning certain non-moral facts; he may have a false belief concerning what is right or wrong; or he may have no beliefs concerning what is right or wrong. (See Section 4.1 concerning the distinction between moral and non-moral ignorance.)[85]

First, suppose that Smith believes that everyone is bent on harming him and that this is a false belief. Perhaps he believes this because he is paranoid. His belief may not be reasonable, and so the actions that he takes in light of it may not be reasonable; but these actions may well be reasonable-in-light-of-his-belief. Suppose, for instance, that he acts in a hostile manner to everyone who approaches him; this may be wrong, but he may well believe it right, and this belief may well be attributable to his false belief concerning his persecution by others. In such a case as this, then, there may well be an excuse in the offing, a regular excuse derivable from Smith's paranoia.[86] Perhaps Smith is culpable for his paranoia (this is possible, although frankly it strikes me as unlikely in any actual case), but, even if so, and even if he is therefore culpable for his paranoid actions, this does not imply that he is not also to be excused for his paranoid actions. As we saw in Chapter 3, it is possible to be both culpable and not culpable for one and the same event, and this is especially common in cases of indirect appraisability (such as the present case).

Or suppose that Jones believes that lying is not wrong. Perhaps this is a relatively fleeting belief, one that is attributable to the drug that he has recently ingested and that has rendered him intoxicated. Suppose that Jones then acts on this belief—with no compunction, naturally. He may thereby do wrong, but he believes otherwise, and his belief is attributable to the mental disorder induced by the drug. In such a case as this, Jones has a regular excuse for his action that is derivable from his mental disorder. Of course, he may well also be culpable for his action.

Finally, suppose that Brown fails to believe that lying is wrong. This failure to believe may be fleeting, perhaps attributable to intoxication, in which case Brown has an excuse for much the same reason as Jones. But it could be otherwise. It could be that Brown fails to believe that lying is wrong because he does not understand the concept of wrongdoing. This condition could be fleeting, too, but it is more likely to be chronic; in either case, it affords a radical excuse and may be attributable to a variety of causes. Brown may be an infant or an idiot, as mentioned in Section 4.1. (Idiocy, I suppose, is a mental disorder, while infancy is not; but they are alike with respect to the power to excuse.) Or Brown may be a psychopath. Now, I am not sure what psychopathy is supposed to be. Perhaps some people who are called psychopaths are simply chronically callous, or perhaps even wicked, agents. If so, their "condition" affords them *no* excuse. And, of course, we must guard against inferring otherwise *simply* from the fact that their condition is chronic.[87] On the other hand, chronic wrongdoing can be a sign of the failure to believe that what one is doing is wrong, and such a failure to believe may well characterize many psychopaths and surely does excuse.[88] There is evidence that psychopaths understand that certain actions are such that others disapprove of them and such that, if they perform them, they may be punished, but that they do not believe these actions to be wrong, and that this failure to believe is attributable to a failure to understand the concept of moral wrongness.[89] Many philosophers are impressed by the typical psychopath's lack of a caring attitude; he can fake remorse and shame but apparently does not feel them.[90] Some philosophers claim that having such a genuinely caring attitude is a necessary condition for understanding the concept of wrongness.[91] This seems to me false, where "necessary" expresses logical necessity; but it may be true, where "necessary" expresses some weaker concept.[92]

In a variety of ways, then, mental disorder can occasion a lack of appropriate beliefs and thereby serve to excuse an agent. In this sense, whether or not a person suffers from a mental disorder can indeed be relevant to the ascription of moral responsibility. But there is nothing *special* to be seen in such mental disorder; it calls for no modification to the account of appraisability given in the last chapter.

Strict freedom. So too with mental disorders that affect strict freedom. Clearly there are such; certain instances of so-called automatism, which is often categorized under the rubric "mental disorder," obviously affect strict freedom of action. For example, epileptic seizures strip one of one's strict freedom to do many things. But here it is worth noting three ways in which a condition may affect one's strict freedom of action. First, a condition may eliminate such freedom in such a way that one does not act at all; let us call this *undercutting* one's freedom. Presumably, an epileptic seizure undercuts strict freedom of action; when in the throes of such a seizure, one is not acting at all. Secondly, a condition may eliminate one's strict freedom in such a way that one acts (unfreely, of course); let us call this *confining* one's freedom. If the incompatibilist is right, then determinism is just such a condition on those occasions on which one acts. Thirdly, a condition may *decrease* one's strict freedom by rendering one strictly unfree to bring about some event e while leaving one strictly free to bring about some other event f.[93] This seems to be the case with respect to the physical condition of my body, on the one hand, and my running a four-minute-mile (bringing about e) and my running an eight-minute-mile (bringing about f), on the other.

Now, it is not clear to me that a mental disorder can affect one's strict freedom other than by undercutting it, as an epileptic seizure does; but perhaps it can. Perhaps, for example, hypnosis, or intoxication, or fear, or anger may on occasion function so as to decrease or confine, but not undercut, one's strict freedom of action. If so, then they can serve to excuse. At any rate, whenever a mental condition or disorder occasions the absence of strict freedom to bring about some event, one is not appraisable for not bringing it about; and this is so whether the condition decreases, confines, or undercuts one's freedom. But there is nothing new here and, again, nothing special to record about the relation between mental disorders and moral responsibility.

My hesitancy here to ascribe to mental disorders the power to diminish or confine, but not undercut, strict freedom might seem ill-advised. For it might seem *clear* that such disorders often have such power. Consider this passage by a noted writer on the subject, where it appears to be claimed that mental abnormality typically confines an agent's strict freedom of action:

The rationale of excusing for mental abnormality may be summarized in this way. Certain forms of mental incapacity deprive a person of his ability to act other than the way he does because resources for an effective choice are lacking. He is in this condition when he lacks the capacity to tell what he is doing, or what is likely to happen; or when he lacks the capacity to appreciate its significance as something wrong, or lacks the ability to restrain himself. A person incapacitated in any of these ways is unable, as a matter of choice, to do otherwise.[94]

But this seems to me to be an attempt to force too much into the category "unable to do otherwise." A person may lack the capacity to tell what is likely to happen, for example, or lack the capacity to appreciate the wrongness of his action, but neither of these facts implies that he is strictly unable to do otherwise, although both might make it likely that he will not do otherwise. On the contrary, these facts are matters of belief and disbelief and fall into the category just treated in the last subsection.[95] Moreover, the inability to do otherwise may simply be broad rather than strict, as might often be the case where someone is said to be "unable" to restrain himself. So, once again, it really is not so clear that mental disorders often affect an agent's strict freedom in a non-undercutting fashion.

Broad freedom. Presumably mental disorders can affect one's broad freedom of action, that is, can compel one to do things. Compulsions (so-called), obsessions, psychoses, neuroses, delusions, illusions, and so on can, it seems, all act in this way.[96] For this reason, there may be a tendency to excuse those who suffer from such disorders. But we should note four important points in this regard.

First, there seems to be no necessity that motivational deviancies be especially compelling. For example, pedophiliac desires, as far as I know, need be no stronger than normal sexual desires; one who acts on them, therefore, need not be any more compelled to do so than one who acts on normal sexual desires.[97] Of course, one must not be complacent here. Sexual desires, whether normal or not, will usually become stronger when frustrated. The normal person's desires would appear typically to be less often frustrated than the abnormal person's; thus there is probably a tendency *in fact,* even though there seems to be no *necessity,* for abnormal sexual desires typically to be more compelling than normal ones.[98]

Second, while the strength of certain compulsions can increase for the reason just given, there is again no necessity that chronic compulsions be any stronger than fleeting ones. Indeed, there is reason to think that, while they can become stronger, they can also become weaker, or at least more easily accommodated, in that the agent has time to adapt to his condition. Those who recognize this fact are sometimes moved to assert that, for this reason, those who act under compulsion, when the compulsion is fleeting, have an excuse where those who do so, when the compulsion is chronic, do not.[99] While this obviously may not apply on some occasions, nevertheless it may well apply on others.

Third, we should note that, if the compelling nature of certain mental disorders is to serve to excuse at all, there must be an identity between that which one is compelled to do and that for which one has an excuse. (A similar point applies also to excuses based in ignorance or the absence of strict freedom.) A pedophiliac has no excuse for robbery, a klepto-manic no excuse for child-molestation.[100]

Finally, and most importantly, there is, as we saw in the last section, no necessity that there be an excuse to *any* degree afforded by the absence of broad freedom. Thus compelling mental disorders may afford no excuse, as long as they leave strict freedom intact. It all depends on what the agent believes concerning the relation between his disorder and wrongdoing.

The non-special nature of mental disorder. I cannot think how mental disorder might be thought to excuse other than by way of affecting an agent's beliefs, strict freedom, or broad freedom; and if I am right that, insofar as it does affect these, it serves to excuse in the ordinary way, then we can say that there is nothing special about mental disorder and its power to excuse and that our account of appraisability requires no modification in this regard. This is a position which, though inflationary (but, I would of course urge, not unduly so) with respect to much common ascription of responsibility, has come recently to be accepted by several philosophers.[101]

Still, one may again feel a lingering doubt. Joel Feinberg, who feels such a doubt, notes that in our cooler moments we tend not to feel outrage at the misconduct of those with mental disorders but rather to feel pity for them. He believes that this reaction is attributable in part to our noting that their misconduct does not even benefit *them* and they appear not to have any insight into their own motives.[102] Perhaps this is so, although we should note that there are exceptions both ways. That is, surely some people with mental disorders do not satisfy both, or even one, of these conditions; and some people without mental disorders may sometimes satisfy one, or even both, of them. Perhaps we may agree that anyone who satisfies one or both of these conditions is unfortunate and to be pitied. But, again, pity may properly be felt for people who suffer not from these conditions but from others; and, also, there seems to be no necessity that, where it is proper to pity, it is not proper to blame. Of course, the real question to be asked here is this: how is the fact that some, perhaps many, of those with mental disorders satisfy these condi-tions relevant to their appraisability for their actions? And to this my answer is: as far as I can see, it is quite irrelevant. Of course, I suppose that it may well be true that someone who satisfies these conditions often fails to have any intention to do wrong, or belief that he will do wrong, by virtue of his action, inasmuch as he is not seeking to benefit himself at the expense of others; if so he will have an excuse for his action. But, again, nothing special emerges here about the relation between mental disorders and appraisability.

4.8 Character

What is the relation between appraisability and character? It might be thought that appraisability is best understood in terms of the evaluation of an agent's character. Certainly, moral responsibility is often seen in this light.[103] But this is *not* how appraisability is to be understood. Laudability and culpability attach primarily to an *agent,* to his "self," and not to his character. One *has* a character; one *is* not one's character. A character, in any standard sense of that term, is a set of properties; and a person is not a set of properties.[104]

Normally, and to put it very roughly, a character is to be thought of as a set of relatively long-term, relatively general dispositions that a person has to feel, think, and act in certain ways.[105] (I take dispositions to be genuine properties and not merely logical constructs supervenient upon an established pattern of behavior.) One may distinguish between an agent's *given* character, which comprises those dispositions to feel, think, and act, the existence of which owes nothing to the actions of the agent himself (and some of which may be innate), and his character *as so far formed,* which comprises both his given character and those dispositions to feel, think, and act (if any) to which he has contributed by virtue of his actions.[106] An agent's being to blame for some event implies no defect of character in either of these two senses of "character." Of course, his being to blame does imply that there is a "defect" in what may be called his *total* property-set, in that, if he is to blame for willing *e,* then he has the "defective" property of having willed *e.* But such a property is not one which goes to make up either his given character or his character as so far formed.

But if appraisability does not concern the evaluation of an agent's character, what does it concern? It concerns the agent himself. It concerns *his* ledger, not his character's; it is *he* who is evaluated, not his character.[107] Of course, it is not an evaluation of him *in toto* that is at issue—at least not directly—but merely "slices" of him at particular periods of his life. One blemish does not besmirch his entire record; it is just one blemish, which takes its place alongside all the other entries in the ledger. (See again the introduction to Chapter 3.)

Even if there is no essential connection between appraisability and character, there may be a contingent one. One can be indirectly appraisable for having a certain property, and there is no reason why the property in question should not form part of one's character. Thus there is no reason why one should not on occasion be substantially appraisable concerning part of one's character. (Of course, I am here talking of one's character as so far formed; by definition, one cannot be appraisable for one's given character, since one has not contributed to it in any way.[108]) Still, I think it not very likely that one should be appraisable for many of one's character-traits.[109] Those dispositions that it is easiest to affect are relatively short-term, relatively specific ones (such as my desire to write on this paper with my pen now), and these seem not to be properly classifiable as character traits. Long-term, general dispositions (such as my desire for companionship) are less easily affected. They are most easily affected when one is young and malleable, but at that point one is unlikely to grasp the concepts of right and wrong; still, they can be altered by oneself when one is older (one can submit oneself to brain surgery, for example, or one can diet, and so on), and so it is certainly possible for one to be appraisable for certain of one's character traits.

One can of course be appraisable also for actions which "stem from" one's character, that is, for acting "in character," and this is possible even if one is not appraisable for the trait or traits from which the action stems. For example, I may not be appraisable for my desire for companionship, but I may well be appraisable for a certain action that constitutes acting on that desire. As long as the desire does not render me strictly unfree not to act on it, it is open to me not to try to satisfy it; if I kidnap someone in order to satisfy it, I may well be culpable for doing so.[110]

It is possible also, I think, both to act "out of (that is, not in) character" and to be appraisable for one's action. But just what it is to act out of character is not clear to me. Certainly, doing something that it is unusual for one to do does not suffice for acting out of character; for circumstances may be extraordinary, in which case dispositions to act, which have long lain dormant, may be actualized. But it is unclear to me (i) just what dispositions are, or are supposed to be, and (ii) just what it is to have a disposition to bring about an event, to be strictly free to bring it about, to be aware of this, but not to bring it about. These are issues that I shall not try to tackle here. How we answer them will dictate how we account for acting out of character and, in particular, whether we accept the possibility that one retain one's character and yet act out of character or insist that, to act out of character, one's character must have changed (the change perhaps being only temporary).

4.9 Virtues and Vices

As often before, doubts may still linger. What character one has seems to be at least in part a moral matter and, if it is not a matter of moral appraisability, what type of moral matter is it? What about such com-

monly recognized virtues and vices as: compassion, pitilessness; kindness, cruelty; courage, cowardice; temperance, intemperance; generos-
ity, meanness; truthfulness, mendacity; and so on? Are these not traits
for which one is to be praised and blamed, respectively? Is my account
not unduly deflationary in implying that they are not?

I wish to deny neither the fact that these traits constitute excellences
and defects, nor the fact that they constitute moral excellences and
defects, nor the fact that they constitute moral virtues and vices. All of
this *could* be questioned, and it certainly deserves investigation. Just
what do these traits amount to? Just what types of excellence and
defectiveness do they exemplify? Why call such excellence and defectiveness *moral?*[111] Why call such excellences and defects *virtues* and *vices?*
These are all very important questions; but they are also very complicated and difficult to deal with, and I shall not try to deal with them here.
For doing so is not necessary for my purposes.[112]

I stress that I am concerned not to deny, but rather to affirm, that
virtues and vices of the sort listed constitute moral excellences and
defects. Indeed, I would admit that being virtuous in a certain respect
adds to a person's moral worth and being vicious in a certain respect
detracts from his moral worth. In fact, I would even go so far as to say
that a virtuous person is, in so far forth, to be praised and a vicious
person blamed. I would say the same, too, concerning certain related
phenomena, in particular emotions, desires, and beliefs. A display of
anger, for example, is something for which someone can sometimes be to
blame, whether or not this is a manifestation of the vice of irascibility,
and whether or not there is any indirect culpability for the display.[113] But
I would resist any modification to our account of appraisability that this
admission might seem to require.

The point is that there are (at least) two types of moral worth, only one
of which is the concern of our account in Chapter 3, but the other of
which is at issue when discussing the virtues and vices, emotions, desires,
and beliefs.[114] And there are two types of inward praise and blame which
correspond with these two types of worth. Cruelty, for example, is
something which is morally reprehensible, and one may blame a person
either for his cruelty or for the cruel acts which he performs. But the
reprehensibility at issue, and the blame which rides on it, are wholly
independent from what I have called culpability. It is very easy to confuse
the two types of moral worth and the two types of praise and blame
which attach to them. Indeed, this confusion has been perpetrated by
many philosophers.[115] But in what, exactly, does the confusion consist?

Clearly, the will may be "engaged" when virtues and vices are
manifested[116], for their manifestation often requires acting on some motivation, or at least the disposition so to act. (This is not always the case,
however. Certain virtues and vices involve the disposition to feel, desire,

or believe rather than, or in addition to, the disposition to act—witness irascibility, fetishism, or conceit[117]—and in such cases the will may have no role.) But even where the will is engaged, this does not imply that it is either free or directed on to the motivations at issue. And this is the key. Generally, one is not free to be motivated in a certain way (although one is often free as to whether or not one *acts on* one's motivations). And really it is as simple as that. If one is congenitally congenial and cannot help but be motivated by compassion, such compassion may constitute a virtue nonetheless and it (and oneself, *qua* possessor of it) may warrant some sort of admiration, but one does *not* deserve praise for it *in the sense that one is laudable for it* (where "laudability" is to be understood as in the analysandum of (P3.18)). (Compare Mark Twain's remark: "I am morally superior to George Washington. He couldn't tell a lie. I can and don't."[118]) Similarly, if one cannot help but be motivated by venge-fulness, such vengefulness may constitute a vice nonetheless and it (and oneself) may warrant some sort of reprehension, but one does *not* deserve blame for it *in the sense that one is culpable for it* (where "culpable" is to be understood as in the analysandum of (P3.19)). (Thus a vengeful but conscientious terrorist—one who sincerely believes that he is doing right in blowing people to bits in airports—may be *laudable,* rather than culpable, but still of course reprehensible.[119]) Of course, instead of "admiration" we may talk of "praise," and instead of "reprehension" "blame," but this does not alter the fact that there are two types of moral worth at stake here. Now, I have drawn the distinction between them only negatively, in that I have said that one sort of praise-and blamewor-thiness is that which is accounted for in (P3.18) and (P3.19), while the other sort is simply not that which is at issue in (P3.18) and (P3.19); but this suffices for my present purpose, which is simply to spell out the conditions of what I have called moral appraisability—one type of moral responsibility—and not also to give a detailed account of that type of moral worth inherent in the virtues and vices.[120] The distinction rests squarely in strict freedom.

The argument upon which I am relying here is a simple one. It may be formulated as follows: one is not free with respect to whether or not one is compassionate (or pitiless), kind (or cruel), courageous (or cowardly), *etc.;* if one is not free with respect to any such character trait, then one is not appraisable for it; hence, one is not appraisable for any such character trait. A similar argument pertains to emotions, desires, and beliefs. Of course, a critic may simply try to turn this argument on its head and state: (granted) one is not free with respect to whether or not one is compassionate, *etc.;* but one *is* (on occasion) appraisable for such character traits; hence, appraisability for such character traits does not require that one be (or have been) free with respect to them. Just such an argument has recently been proposed by Robert Adams, and it constitutes a challenge to what I have made one of the foundation stones of this book.[121] How is it to be rebutted? Well, I have admitted in Section 2.2 to knowing of no positive argument for my contention that appraisability requires strict freedom; but a somewhat less robust rebuttal is surely to be found in the fact that there is a plausible alternative to Adams's unqualified assertion that there can be appraisability for character traits (and emotions, desires, and beliefs) with respect to which one is not strictly free, and that is a denial that this is so *qualified* by the admission that a person may be admirable or reprehensible in some *other* way for such phenomena. In this way, I would seek both to have my cake and to eat it.

It is most important to note that this move is not purely *ad hoc*. On the contrary, it is grounded in the observation that there is surely something *very* different qualitatively in the judgments that we make concerning the admirability and reprehensibility of persons for phenomena (character traits, emotions, desires, beliefs) over which they have, and have always had, no control, and the judgments that we make concerning their appraisability for phenomena over which they have, or have had, control.[122] Consider, for example, this remark by Adams:

The beliefs ascribed to the graduate of the Hitler *Jugend* are heinous, and it is morally reprehensible to hold them (even if one has no opportunity to act on them). No matter how he came by them, his evil beliefs are a part of who he is, morally, and make him a fitting object of reproach.[123]

Surely, *if* we assume that the person in question could not help but come by the beliefs that he has, our moral evaluation of him, while decidedly "negative," is and must be quite different from that which we would have made if we had judged him appraisable for these beliefs. Or consider this claim by Richard Brandt:

There are some things no decent person will believe to be right . . . , and if we must defend our act by saying we believed what no decent person would believe, we may have condemned ourselves more than excused ourselves.[124]

It is surely reasonable to contend that, by virtue of the failure to draw the distinction that I urge between the two types of moral worth, the issue is obfuscated by such a claim. Of course, one may be condemning oneself by saying that one believes something (when no decent person would believe such a thing), in that one will be pointing up one's reprehensibility, but this should not be thought of as *taking the place of* (see the use of "more than") an excuse; for one may *also* excuse oneself by such a remark, in that one will be pointing up one's lack of culpability.

Thus I hold to the claim that one is not appraisable for one's virtues and vices (and related phenomena). It may be instructive to note that the distinction that I advocate between the two types of moral worth is closely allied (but is certainly not identical) with the distinction between two types of moral "ought" that some philosophers have proposed (and which I also would propose). Many philosophers have claimed that "ought" implies "can." Some have rejected this, pointing out that it is appropriate to say (for example) that one ought not to feel the anger which one does, and cannot help but, feel. The reply on the part of the former philosophers has often been: the sense of "ought" in which it is true that one ought not to feel the anger that one cannot help but feel is not that sense of "ought" according to which "ought" implies "can."[125] Some have dubbed the former sense of "ought" the "ought-to-be," while calling the latter sense of "ought" the "ought-to-do."[126] There has been much debate as to how to account for these different senses of "ought," including whether either one is analyzable in terms of the other. In my opinion, it is a mistake to think that either is analyzable in terms of the other, and I would similarly claim that neither of the two types of moral worth that I have mentioned is analyzable in terms of the other. But, again, this is strictly beside my present purpose, which is simply to point out that there are these two types of moral worth, and to present a detailed account of one of them, an account according to which one is not appraisable for one's virtues and vices and other phenomena (such as emotions, desires, and beliefs) over which one lacks strict control.

As always, there is a complication here; but it is one that has already been discussed in the last section. The complication concerns the fact that one may be indirectly appraisable for certain of one's character traits; and there seems to be no reason why some of the virtues and vices may not feature among these. So, too, for certain emotions, desires, and beliefs. Thus, while it may be that kindness, cruelty, and so on are not in our *direct* control, they may be in our *indirect* control.[127] Perhaps I cannot immediately summon up a kindly motive; but this leaves open the possibility of my indirectly instilling such a motive in myself (by self-education, say, or by submitting to hypnotism).[128] Indeed, Aristole thought that *all* our virtues and vices are thus in our control, and on this basis he thought us all responsible for all our virtues and vices.[129] This is surely a gross exaggeration. Still, it must be acknowledged that sometimes a virtue may indicate not only admirability but laudability; and a vice, not only reprehensibility but culpability. But this fact neither nullifies the distinction between the two spheres of moral worth just noted nor calls for a modification of the account of laudability and culpability given earlier. For, as argued earlier, all indirect appraisability is, in a sense, superfluous; it occasions no new entry in our ledgers.

It may still seem that something has gone seriously wrong with the foregoing distinction between laudability and admirability, culpability and reprehensibility. The objection may be put as follows. The foregoing argument establishes (or purports to establish) that one cannot be laudable for one's *virtues* and culpable for one's *vices* (except indirectly), but that leaves untouched the question of laudability for *acting virtuously* and culpability for *acting viciously*. After all, we commonly praise people for their kind *actions,* blame them for their cruel *actions*. It has already been conceded that, even if one is not free (except, perhaps, indirectly) with respect to *how* one is motivated, one may well be free with respect to whether or not one *acts* on one's motivations. Thus one may well be free with respect to whether or not one *acts* virtuously or viciously, and so what barrier can there be to ascribing laudability or culpability here?

This is an interesting objection, but it is flawed. The moral worth that attaches to a virtuous or vicious action derives directly from the virtue or vice involved.[130] There is no element that occasions appraisability with respect to the action when there is none with respect to the virtue or vice that motivates it. Consider, for example, the virtue of compassion. Compassion may prompt me to help someone in distress, and my so doing may well be free (even though I am not free with respect to being compassionate), but the moral worth that attaches to my action derives directly from the compassion that prompts it. After all, in indulging my compassion, I may be quite oblivious as to what it is right or wrong for me to do, and such oblivion surely indicates a lack of laudability. Or, worse, I may be quite mindful of the fact that it would be wrong in this case to indulge my compassion and yet indulge it anyway; in such a case, I am surely *culpable* for my action (even though its motive remains admirable).[131] Of course, it *can*—and, I am sure, often does—happen that an agent indulges his compassion *because he believes this to be the right thing to do*. In such a case, there is no barrier to ascribing laudability to the agent; but such laudability, of course, derives primarily from his aim to do that which is right and *not* from the promptings of compassion.

I believe, therefore, that the foregoing distinction between two types of moral worth must be maintained. This distinction may help to mitigate the appearance that, in Section 3.2 when I was discussing clause (b) of (P3.6), I was unduly harsh in claiming that an agent who does what is in fact supererogatory, but that he regards as merely obligatory, "deserves no praise." What I meant, of course, was that he is not *directly laudable* for his volition. This leaves open the possibility that there is occasion for *admiring* the agent, for praising him in a non-laudatory way. What might the occasion for this be? Well, perhaps we should admire his high standards, and thus admire him for having these standards. (Moreover, he might of course also be *indirectly* laudable for having these high standards—but that is another story.) At any rate, to say that he is not directly laudable for his volition is not to say that no praise of any sort should be directed towards him. Still, it must be reiterated that setting oneself unduly high standards carries with it a double risk. First, if, in doing what is in fact supererogatory, one is doing something that one regards (because of one's high standards) as merely obligatory, one forfeits the laudability that one would otherwise incur. Secondly, if, in failing to do what is in fact supererogatory or merely permissible, one is failing to do something that one regards (because of one's high standards) as obligatory, one incurs the culpability that one would otherwise avoid. In face of this, the admirability of one's high standards may seem small solace. And there is a flip side to this "paradox." Just as a person with overly high standards may incur culpability with greater ease and laudability with greater difficulty than a person with correct standards, so a person with unduly low standards may incur laudability with greater ease and culpability with greater difficulty than a person with correct standards. This result may be surprising, but I submit that it is important and must be accepted. The implication is that a terrorist may be laudable while a famine relief worker is culpable—a sobering thought. So let me reiterate one more time: someone who blows people to bits in airports does a very serious wrong and, even if inculpable, is quite reprehensible, while a famine relief worker who sleeps in an extra half-hour before tending to his laborious task is highly admirable, even if culpable; and such reprehensibility and admirability are also matters of moral worth.

4.10 Alternate Possibilities

A second challenge to the claim that appraisability requires strict freedom has recently emerged in the literature. An assumption that appears to have been a very common one in debates concerning moral responsibility throughout the history of such debates is this: a person is morally responsible for what he has done only if he could have done otherwise. Harry Frankfurt, who is himself responsible (causally, at least) for much of the recent attention that has been given to this assumption, calls it the principle of alternate possibilities.[132] He argues that the principle is false.

As it has just been formulated, the principle of alternate possibilities concerns actions exclusively. It may be put, somewhat more pedantically, as follows:

(P4.15)   S is morally responsible for bringing about e only if he could have brought about something other than e.[133]

This principle is to be distinguished from a closely related one:

(P4.16)   S is morally responsible for e (an event which he has brought about) only if he could have brought about something other than e.

Both (P4.15) and (P4.16) concern *indirect* appraisability, the former partially (by dint of conjoint appraisability), the latter exclusively. A similar principle concerning direct appraisability is this:

(P4.17) S is morally responsible for willing e only if he could have willed something other than e.

Each of these principles is a version of the following:

(P4.18) S is morally responsible for e only if S was free with respect to not-e.

Given the further assumption, which seems also to have been almost universally accepted and which I have herein accepted, that:

(P4.19) S is morally responsible for e only if S was free with respect to e,

what we in effect have is a common allegiance to these two principles:

(P4.20) S is morally responsible for e only if S was in standard control of e,

and (for indirect appraisability, at least):

(P4.21) S is morally responsible for e only if S was in primary control of e.

Now, (P4.21) was rejected in Section 4.5 where the issue of sharing responsibility in contexts of group action was discussed. In this section I shall concentrate on (P4.20) and argue that it is false.

In focusing his attention on (P4.15), Frankfurt in effect bridges two issues, although this is not something that he appears to recognize: the issues of direct and indirect appraisability. In addition, the cases that he cites in an effort to undermine (P4.15) bridge two further issues, and this *is* something that he recognizes: strict and broad freedom.[134] Because I have already ruled out broad freedom as a necessary condition of appraisability in Section 4.6, I shall here confine myself to the issue of whether *strict* standard control is such a necessary condition.[135] To begin, I shall focus exclusively on indirect appraisability, and thus on (P4.16), where this is understood to concern strict freedom.

Indirect appraisability: a first approach. John Locke asks us to consider a case of the following sort.[136] A man—call him Peter—is carried, while fast asleep, into a room where there is another man—call him Paul—who is fast asleep too. Peter is locked in the room and will not, upon awakening, be able to leave unless and until somebody else unlocks the door. Eventually, Peter wakes up and is surprised but delighted to find himself in Paul's room—delighted not because he likes Paul, but because he dislikes him and is glad of the opportunity to annoy him. So, instead of attempting to leave (something that he—falsely—believes that he can do), Peter stays where he is, patiently waiting for Paul to wake up, in the firm belief that Paul will be very annoyed to find him there, and in the firm belief that it is wrong of him to annoy Paul. And, soon, Paul does wake up and, as predicted, is enraged at Peter's presence (and would have been so, no matter how hard Peter might have tried to placate him). Peter finds this all richly rewarding.

I have, with philosophic license, embellished Locke's original case a little; but, so embellished, the case is instructive. Since we have supposed that Peter believed it wrong to annoy Paul, it might well seem that Peter is indirectly culpable for Paul's annoyance, indeed, that he is substantially culpable concerning Paul's annoyance.[137] (Of course, whoever carried Peter into the room in the first place may well be to blame for this also; but, as we saw in Section 4.5, this need not eliminate, or even diminish, Peter's culpability.) But it is also true, it seems, that Peter could not have brought about something other than Paul's annoyance.[138] If this is so, then (P4.16) would appear false. Is it and, if so, so what?

First, in order to scotch misunderstanding, I should note that I am taking it that Peter does *act*, he *does* something, both when he remains in the room and when he annoys Paul. By virtue of his decision to stay in the room, he *brings about* both his remaining and Paul's annoyance.[139] Some may desire a more "positive" action for the sake of illustration and this of course could be provided. It could have been stipulated, for example, that Peter annoyed Paul not merely by remaining in the room but by punching him in the nose. Of course, the strict *inevitability* of his punching Paul in the nose would require more than his just being locked in the room; in fact, it would require something quite fantastic (such as his brain's being monitored by an evil demon[140]), and for this reason I shall stick with the more mundane example just given. It might also be pointed out, however, that, while Peter's remaining in the room *is* an action of his (due to the volition involved—but there is an important issue lurking here, concerning causal overdetermination, to which I shall return shortly), had he tried to leave his remaining would *not* have been an action; for then he would have recognized the impossibility of leaving (see the discussion of (P2.7) in Section 2.1). This is true but does not affect the present issue, which concerns the fact that Peter *did* act in remaining in the room and in annoying Paul and that, apparently, he could not have *done* otherwise.[141]

We must ask why it is that (P4.16) has seemed so attractive to so many philosophers. I take it that the reason is that these philosophers have accepted the following two principles, to put them somewhat roughly:

(P4.22)   *S* is morally responsible for *e* (an event which he has brought about) only if he freely brought it about.

(P4.23)   *S* freely brought about *e* only if he could have brought about something other than *e*.

And, of course (P4.22) and (P4.23) jointly imply (P4.16). Indeed, the latter may be seen to be a "contraction" of the former two.

But to put matters thus is to put them too roughly. So stated, (P4.22) is false, and many recognize it to be false. It in effect stipulates that indirect appraisability requires direct freedom, whereas we have seen (in Section 3.3) that what it requires is indirect freedom. So let us reformulate matters as follows:

(P4.22') S is indirectly appraisable for e only if S was indirectly free with respect to e.

(P4.23') S was indirectly free with respect to e only if S was indirectly free with respect to not-e.

(P4.16') S is indirectly appraisable for e only if S was indirectly free with respect to not-e.

If we put matters thus, though, an interesting point emerges. The case of Peter, Paul, and the locked doors turns our clearly *not* to be a counterexample to (P4.16'). For, although it is true that, when he is in Paul's room, Peter cannot avoid Paul's annoyance, we are not told that there is *no* time at all at which Peter can avoid Paul's annoyance.[142] The point is that it may be true, for all we are told, that Peter could have avoided becoming locked in Paul's room in the first place and could thereby have avoided his annoyance; in fact, it would be very odd if this were not the case. For instance, we may safely assume that Peter could have left town the previous day, in which case he would not have been a candidate for clandestine transportation to Paul's room; and, of course, if Peter had not been transported to and locked in Paul's room, he would not then have annoyed Paul. So, although it is true that there was a time at which Peter was not free to do other than annoy Paul, it is not true that there was no time at which he was free to do other than annoy Paul. Hence (P4.16') has not been shown false.

One's immediate reaction to this observation might be to point out that, while the case of Peter, Paul, and the locked door admittedly is not a counterexample to (P4.16'), it *is* nonetheless a counterexample to the more complex claim that S is indirectly appraisable for e only if S was indirectly free with respect to not-e *while e was foreseeable by S*. After all, prior to his transportation to the room, Peter clearly could not foresee his annoying Paul (in the manner in which he did annoy Paul); and so the fact that he could, at this earlier time, have avoided Paul's annoyance is irrelevant. Now, I sympathize with this reaction. After all, in Section 4.1, I have argued that foreseeability (which, I claim, requires foresight) of e is required for substantial appraisability concerning e, and so concentrating only on those cases where there *is* foreseeability and asking whether, in *these* cases, S could have avoided e, is a procedure which I find congenial. Nonetheless, I shall not pursue this tactic here, for it would still leave open the more radical question whether appraisability requires avoidability *tout court* (that is, whether (P4.16′) is true); and since I believe that this more radical question can be given a definitive, negative answer, I wish now to look into this matter.

Indirect appraisability: a second approach. Consider this modification to our original case. Peter and Paul are twins placed in a room at birth from which they cannot escape. They grow up unaware of their being forcibly confined. After some years, the twins become "responsible" human beings, *i.e.,* persons to whom it is appropriate to ascribe moral appraisability for certain of their actions (and the issues thereof). In addition, Peter's very presence in the room has started to get on Paul's nerves, and Peter is aware of this; but, instead of deciding to leave the room (which is, it seems, something that he cannot and never could do, but something he nevertheless believes he can do), Peter decides to remain where he is, his express purpose being to annoy Paul thereby, in the belief that this is wrong. Now it seems that at no time could Peter do other than annoy Paul when he did,[143] and yet it also seems that Peter is indirectly culpable for, and substantially culpable concerning, Paul's annoyance. But, again *is* this correct; and if so, so what?

Doubtless some would wish to defend (P4.16′) against the present attack. There are basically two ways to do this. Either one can insist that Peter was free at some time to do other than annoy Paul. Or one can insist that Peter is not indirectly culpable for Paul's annoyance. The first tack, I think, has little to recommend it.[144] I acknowledge that no analysis has been offered here as to what renders a person strictly free to do something; nevertheless, it is surely plausible to say that, in the present modified case, at no time is Peter strictly free to do other than annoy Paul at the time at which he does annoy him.[145] The second tack, however, is more interesting and has been taken by some commentators on Frankfurt's paper.[146]

One might argue that, although Peter clearly is culpable for something in the modified case, it is not for annoying Paul, and that what he is culpable for is something he could have avoided. What might this "something" be? Perhaps annoying Paul intentionally; or annoying Paul "on his own" (whatever that comes to exactly).[147] Now, I do not wish to deny that Peter is culpable either for annoying Paul intentionally or for annoying Paul "on his own"; nor do I wish to deny that both these actions were avoidable by Paul—that is, that he enjoyed standard control with respect to them. But of course none of this implies that Peter was not culpable for annoying Paul (period). Perhaps this might be argued, but on what grounds I cannot say.[148] Indeed, any such argument seems doomed to failure; for surely it is possible that Peter should simply direct his thoughts on to Paul's annoyance (period) and thereby incur indirect culpability for and substantial culpability concerning it.

Of course, one might simply try to turn the counterexample on its head by insisting that the principle of alternate possibilities is true, that Peter was never free to do other than annoy Paul, and hence that Peter is not culpable for annoying Paul. The apparent hard-headedness of such a stance might be mitigated by noting that the modified case, like the original case, is set up so that Peter is unaware that his confinement is forced upon him. Why should this make a difference as to whether he is culpable for Paul's annoyance? The implication seems to be that, had he known of his confinement to the room—or even just believed that he was so confined—he would not have been culpable for Paul's annoyance, *even though* he desired it. But if the presence of a desire for Paul's annoyance is not, under the circumstances, sufficient to make Peter culpable for it, why should such a desire conjoined with a (false) belief that he can do otherwise be so sufficient? This is an important question. The answer, I think, is this. Desires are strictly irrelevant to questions of moral appraisability (no matter how admirable or reprehensible they may be in some other way—see the last section).[149] What counts is what Peter believes he can do and what he decides to do in light of this belief, and not what he desires to do (which may or may not be reflected in his decision). If he had been aware of his confinement, he could not have decided to remain; for a belief in strict standard control is necessary for *any* volition (see again (P2.7)). Had he not decided to remain, his remaining would not have been a consequence of any decision of his. Hence, his remaining would not have been something for which he would have been indirectly appraisable. But this shows only that a *belief* in strict standard control is required for appraisability, and not that such control really is so required.

But if the modified case is taken to show that (P4.16') is false, which of (P4.22') and (P4.23') should we then take to be false? One answer, of course, is that it is (P4.22') that we should reject. But I am convinced that this is the wrong answer. As noted in the last section, (P4.22') is something that I have made one of the foundation stones of this book; I have admitted to not being able to argue for it, but as long as there is a plausible alternative to its rejection this inability does not undermine my account of appraisability. And, of course, there is a plausible alternative, namely, the rejection of (P4.23'). Perhaps (P4.23') has been commonly accepted as true, but I take the present modified case to be proof that it is false. Freedom is not tantamount to standard control; control may be curtailed (see Section 2.3).

What might strict freedom be like in the absence of standard control? We need only look to the present case for an answer. While Peter strictly cannot do other than annoy Paul, he nevertheless annoys Paul strictly freely. He is the "source" of his action; his annoying Paul is an action which is "truly his." (See Section 2.2. Frankfurt himself talks in similar terms when he says that "there may be circumstances that . . . make it impossible for the person to do otherwise, but that do not impel the person to act."[150]) This, along with the other conditions that he satisfies, is sufficient to render Peter indirectly culpable for and substantially culpable concerning Paul's annoyance; Paul's annoyance reveals the source of Peter's culpability.[151]

Finally, it should be noted that this discussion of indirect appraisability and alternate possibilities is intended to accommodate the special case of indirect appraisability for omissions and their consequences. That is, while the following is of course trivially true:

(P4.24) S is morally responsible for omitting to bring about e only if he could have brought about e,

due to the fact that "omit" implies "can" (see (P2.10)), I take the following "negative counterpart" of (P4.15) to be *false:*

(P4.25) S is morally responsible for not bringing about e only if he could have brought about e.

And I take this to be false for essentially the reasons just given. Indeed, the case of Peter, Paul, and the locked door itself involves appraisability for a "not-doing," namely, Peter's remaining in, *i.e.,* his not-leaving, the room (where "remaining" now expresses the issue of his action, rather than the action itself)—hence my earlier characterization of the action itself as not being very "positive." Of course, there is also a "doing" involved—Peter brings about the not-doing by way of his volition—but this is exactly what we should expect, since it is only in this way that appraisability for a not-doing can arise at all. (See Section 4.4.)

But at this point an objection may be made. It may be claimed that the not-doing—*i.e.,* the remaining— is *not* a consequence of Peter's volition, and hence *not* something for which he may be indirectly appraisable, simply because there was already in existence a condition (*viz.,* the door's being locked) which, in the circumstances, sufficed for the occurrence of the not-doing. To borrow some useful terminology: there was a volition-independent, "actual-sequence" necessitation of the not-doing, and this robs the volition itself of any causal efficacy with respect to the not-doing. Such necessitation is to be contrasted with "alternate-sequence" necessitation, which would not have robbed the volition of causal efficacy with respect to the not-doing.[152] An example of the latter type of necessitation is this: Smith intentionally fails to signal Jones— *i.e.,* he chooses not to signal and this volition causes his not-signalling— but, had he chosen to signal, this volition would—somehow!—have resulted in a temporary paralysis, rendering him unable to signal.

In response to this objection, I shall say just this. First, while I am unable to make clear the distinction between actual- and alternate-sequence necessitation, I grant its intuitive plausibility and accept it. Secondly, however, I see no reason to retract the ascription of causal efficacy to the volition in the first, actual-sequence case; this seems to me to be a case where there is causal overdetermination, but in such cases each of the conditions involved seems to me to be causally efficacious. Notice, especially, that in the case of Peter and Paul, while there does seem to be volition-independent, actual-sequence necessitation of Peter's remaining in the room and of Paul's annoyance, there is *no* such necessitation of Peter's volition *itself*. *Hence* (I would say, but shall not argue), Peter enjoys direct freedom with respect to his volition and indirect freedom with respect to the consequent remaining (not-leaving) and annoyance. Thirdly, and perhaps most importantly, even if I were to retract my ascription of causal efficacy to the volition in the actual-sequence case of Peter and Paul, the alternate-sequence case of paralysis surely suffices to show (P4.25) false.[153] In this respect, the latter case resembles the more fanciful nose-punching case given earlier, which itself could have been used instead of the case of Peter and Paul as a counterexample to (P4.16) and (P4.16'); in the nose-punching case, too, the only necessitation that is operative is of the alternate-sequence variety.

Direct appraisability. It might still be thought, however, that standard control is necessary for moral responsibility; for it might still seem that (P4.17) is true. Even if we grant that Peter could not have done other than annoy Paul and that he is nevertheless culpable for Paul's annoyance, still he could have *willed* otherwise; freedom of *will* requires strict standard control, and this is what really matters in the ascription of appraisability (especially given the merely parasitic nature of indirect appraisability).

I grant the attractiveness of this reply. After all, it is standard control with respect to his volition that gives Peter standard control with respect to his annoying Paul intentionally, something that was already conceded. So, we must admit that, even in the modified case, Peter enjoys standard control with respect to his decision to annoy Paul. But the question is: *must* we grant this, or can another case be concocted in which Peter strictly freely decides to annoy Paul but (due to alternate-sequence necessitation) strictly could not have willed otherwise?

I do not see why in principle a case to this effect cannot be concocted. But it must be admitted that such a case would be quite outlandish and also problematic. Here is one such case (of the evil-demon variety). Peter has just become aware of Paul; he has never been free not to become so aware, due to the manipulations of an evil demon;[154] this demon can, and is prepared to, intervene if there are telltale signs that Peter will not decide to annoy Paul and, by such intervention, cause Peter to decide to annoy Paul; but Peter freely makes this decision "all on his own." There is no need to point out why this case is outlandish. But it is also problematic. Is the demon's foreknowledge of Peter's decision compatible with this decision's being free? I think so, but of course this is controversial. Still, at the very least we may note that, even if this case fails to establish that freedom of the will does not require strict standard control with respect to one's volitions, it surely raises the question: why think that freedom of the will *does* require such control? I can find no good answer to this question.

Compatibilism and incompatibilism. Finally, it is worth pointing out that the age-old debate between compatibilists and incompatibilists remains pretty much unaffected by the present findings. Frankfurt noted that this debate has traditionally relied on a common assumption by both parties that the principle of alternate possibilities is true. In arguing for the falsity of this principle, he took himself also to be undermining the debate to a large extent.[155] But, if we take it that (P4.18) is false because (P4.23′) (and its analogue for direct freedom) is false, and not because (P4.22′) (or its analogue for direct freedom) is false, the debate seems to be affected very little. Still concern with the possibility of anyone's being morally responsible for anything serves to fuel the debate, and still whether or not anyone can ever act freely lies at the heart of the debate. Of course, the traditional *approach* to these issues, by way of a discussion of alternate possibilities, needs to be changed, but the point is that these issues remain open.

It is interesting to note, however, that the incompatibilist who takes this tack, insofar as he believes that freedom of will or action is possible in the absence of alternate possibilities (as long as the volition or action in question is not event-caused), must accept the following principle:

(P4.26)   It is possible both that S be not strictly free with respect to *not* willing, or *not* bringing about, e and that S be not caused by some antecedent event *to* will, or bring about, e.[156]

For example, the incompatibilist, who rejects the principle of alternate possibilities but who regards Peter as the "source" of his own volition and action, is committed to saying that Peter was *not* caused by antecedent events to (decide to) annoy Paul even though he could not have done otherwise. (P4.26) might appear to be a difficult principle for which to argue, but I think that a successful argument can be made.[157] This argument would proceed by way of invoking the distinction between actual- and alternate-sequence necessitation and would rest on the claim that absence of causation is compatible with the latter, even though not with the former. However, I shall not pursue this point here, since it is not my intention to defend incompatibilism; nor, to repeat, am I sure just how to clarify the distinction at issue.

4.11 Luck

The final topic that I wish to discuss in this chapter concerns what has come to be called moral luck. Considerable attention has recently been given to this phenomenon by philosophers. It has been claimed that recognition of this phenomenon imperils the received conception of moral responsibility. The issue may be put in terms of a puzzle that revolves around the following argument:

(P4.27) S is morally responsible for e only if e's occurring was not a matter of luck.

(P4.28)   No event is such that its occurring is not a matter of luck.

Therefore

(P4.29)   No event is such that S is morally responsible for it.

The puzzle is supposed to reside in the fact that the premises seem true but the conclusion false. Reaction to the puzzle has been varied. Joel Feinberg, one of the first to pose the puzzle (though not exactly in these terms), seems prepared—at least provisionally—to accept the conclusion.[158] Thomas Nagel thinks that there is a genuine paradox here and seems prepared to accept both premises while denying the conclusion.[159] Bernard Williams, while arguing forcefully for the truth of the second premise, appears to deny the first, claiming that such denial runs counter to the received conception of moral responsibility.[160] Judith Andre likewise denies the first premise but rejects the claim that this runs counter to the received conception of moral responsibility, contending that this conception has Aristotelian as well as Kantian elements and that the former, if not the latter, countenance luck.[161]

In this section I shall critically evaluate the foregoing argument. I shall present two versions of it and argue that neither version is compelling. Nevertheless, it will be seen that one of the versions does carry some punch. Naturally, throughout this section I shall be concerned solely with moral *appraisability*. What the relation is between *liability* and luck is a matter that I shall not discuss here, although I shall take it up in Chapter 5; for it is a separate matter entirely.[162]

The two arguments. What is the issue here? Nagel puts it well:

Whether we succeed or fail in what we try to do nearly always depends to some extent on factors beyond our control. This is true of murder, altruism, revolution, the sacrifice of certain interests for the sake of others—almost any morally important act. What has been done, and what is morally judged, is partly determined by external factors. However jewel-like the good will may be in its own right, there is a morally significant difference between rescuing someone from a burning building and dropping him from a twelfth-storey window while trying to rescue him. Similarly, there is a morally significant difference between reckless driving and manslaughter. But whether a reckless driver hits a pedestrian depends on the presence of the pedestrian at the point where he recklessly passes a red light.[163]

Nagel goes on to distinguish a variety of types of luck. For present purposes, just two types may be distinguished. I shall call these *situational* and *resultant* luck. The former consists in luck with respect to the situations one faces, including the nature of one's character as so far formed. The latter consists in luck with respect to what results from one's decisions, actions, and omissions.[164]

Nagel explicitly ties the matter of luck in with the matter of control. Even so, it is not clear how we should interpret the crucial phrase "*e*'s occurring is a matter of luck." There seem to me to be two main interpretations, namely: (i) "*e* is not under anyone's control," and (ii) "*e* is not under anyone's complete control" (see (P2.18)).[165] We then have these two main interpretations of the argument that constitutes the puzzle. First:

(P4.27′)   *S* is morally responsible for *e* only if *S* was in control of *e*.

(P4.28′)   No event is such that anyone is ever in control of it.

Therefore

(P4.29)   No event is such that *S* is morally responsible for it.

Second:

(P4.27″)   *S* is morally responsible for *e* only if *S* was in complete control of *e*.

(P4.28″)   No event is such that anyone is ever in complete control of it.

Therefore

(P4.29)   No event is such that *S* is morally responsible for it.

But now, it seems to me, the puzzle disappears. I shall argue that neither version of the argument is persuasive.

Rejection of the first argument. The first version of the argument is easily dismissed. Both premises are problematic. In the last section we saw reason to reject (P4.27′), if by "control" is meant standard control. On the other hand, (P4.27′) seems true if by "control" is meant merely curtailed control. (As before, I here confine my attention to *strict* control.) But even so, (P4.28′) seems plainly false.[166] For it seems that I can now stop writing now; in addition, I can now continue writing now. Or again, I can now drink a glass of water thirty seconds from now; in addition, I can now do other than drink a glass of water thirty seconds from now.

Rejection of the second argument. The second version of the argument, while (I believe) unsound, is more interesting; though easily dismissed, it yet has undeniable force. Moreover, I suspect that it is this version that Feinberg, Williams, Nagel, and others have had in mind. Certainly, (P4.28″) seems true, even where "control" is understood to mean curtailed control. In this sense, it must be admitted, luck (whether situational or resultant) *is* an ineliminable part of existence. For example, I can now continue writing now, but this appears to depend (causally) on all sorts of things that are beyond anyone's control, such as: the world having come into existence (a situational matter), the world not ceasing to exist before the paper reacts appropriately to the ink's application (a resultant matter), and so on.

But even if (P4.28″) is true, (P4.27″) is surely false, although both Feinberg and Nagel appear at times to accept it. For instance, Feinberg writes:

If he [the champion of moral responsibility] is a rational man, he will admit that moral responsibility for external harm makes no sense and argue that moral responsibility is therefore restricted to the inner world of the mind, where the agent rules supreme and luck has no place. . . . Morals constitute a kind of internal law, governing those inner thoughts and volitions which are completely subject to the agent's control, and administered before the tribunal of conscience—the *forum internum.*[167]

(Of course, Feinberg goes on to say, quite rightly, that even the inner domain of one's thoughts and volitions is not immune to luck, in that even it is not under one's complete control.) And Nagel writes:

If the condition of control is consistently applied, it threatens to erode most of the moral assessments we find it natural to make. The things for which people are morally judged are determined in more ways than we at first realize by what is beyond their control. And when the seemingly natural requirement of fault or responsibility is applied in light of these facts, it leaves few pre-reflective moral judgments intact. Ultimately, nothing or almost nothing about what a person does seems to be under his control.[168]

And again:

How is it possible to be more or less culpable depending on whether a child gets into the path of one's car, or a bird into the path of one's bullet? Perhaps it is true that what is done depends on more than the agent's state of mind or intention. The problem then is, why is it not irrational to base moral assessment on what people do, in this broad sense? It amounts to holding them responsible for the contributions of fate as well as for their own—provided they have made some contribution to begin with. . . . If the object of moral judgment is the *person,* then to hold him accountable for what he has done in the broader sense is akin to strict liability, which may have its legal uses but seems irrational as a moral position.[169]

Although there is, I think, an important element of truth in all of this, it also seems to me, at bottom, importantly mistaken. After all, (P4.27″) is clearly false, if only because no one is in control of his being born—an event on which all of his decisions, actions, omissions, and the consequences thereof are contingent. And we all recognize this. Why should anyone think that our received conception of moral responsibility implies otherwise?

What Feinberg *et al.* have latched on to is an important fact, and that is that we tend, for example, to praise or blame someone for a good or bad decision more than one who did not make the decision, even though the one who did not failed to do so only because he was distracted.[170] Similarly, we tend to blame someone who collaborated with the Nazis more than someone who did not, even though the one who did not failed to do so only because he did not have the opportunity to do so.[171] Or again, we tend to praise someone who rescued a child from a burning building more than someone who did not, even though the one who did not failed to do so only because he did not have the opportunity to do so. These differential judgments, based on situational luck, have counterparts based on resultant luck. As Nagel notes, we tend to blame the reckless driver who hits a pedestrian more than the one who, through no merit of his own, avoids doing so; or again, we tend to praise the scientist who finds a cure for the common cold more than his colleague who, though equally dedicated to relieving the suffering of humanity, fails, through no moral fault of his own, to do so.[172] Such differential judgment seems hard to justify.

Indeed, such differential judgment would appear impossible to justify if the following principle were true:

(P4.30)   If (a) S brought about e,
              (b) S^* would have brought about e if e^* had occurred, and
              (c) e^* was not in S^*'s control,
              then whatever credit or discredit accrues to S for bringing about e accrues also to S^*.[173]

If (P4.30) were true, then, it seems, the Nazi collaborator would be no more culpable than the non-, but would-be, collaborator; the rescuer of the child would be no more laudable than the non-, but would-be, rescuer; the successful scientist would be no more laudable than the unsuccessful scientist; the "successful" reckless driver would be no more culpable than the "unsuccessful" reckless driver; and so on. And the principle need not be restricted to moral credit and discredit. The case of the two scientists, for example, can be easily recast so that its primary concern is intellectual credit. Similarly, if Arnold deserves athletic credit for hitting a round of 67, then so, it seems, does Arnold*, who would have done the same but for a splitting headache. (Of course, Arnold will win the prize and Arnold* will not, but there seems to be no good reason to attribute a degree of intrinsic athletic excellence, or skill, to Arnold and not to Arnold*.[174]) Or again, if the Sex Pistols deserve musical discredit for the cacophony they produced, then so, it seems, do the Sex* Pistols, who would have done the same but for chancing on the occasional euphonious chord.

Perhaps it is something like (P4.30) that Feinberg and others have in mind, and, indeed, its application to the foregoing cases seems to yield plausible judgments. But, of course, (P4.30) is false; it is too broad, too strong. Let S be Mother Teresa and bringing about e be the action of succoring cripples in Calcutta; let S^* be myself and e^* be the event of my acquiring the character of Mother Teresa. It seems plausible to think that, given these conditions, (P4.30) yields the result that I deserve the same credit that accrues to Mother Teresa. Or again, let S be Hitler and bringing about e be the action of exterminating millions of innocents; let S^* be myself and e^* be the event of my acquiring the character of Hitler. It seems plausible to think that, given these conditions, (P4.30) yields the result that I deserve the same discredit that accrues to Hitler. These are preposterous results.

Still, we must be careful to point up just what it is that is preposterous about these results. It is preposterous to hold Mother Teresa, Hitler, and me as equals with respect to moral (dis)credit *qua* admirability/reprehensibility. It is not *obviously* preposterous (although I am sure that it would be inaccurate) to hold us as equals with respect to moral (dis)credit *qua* laudability/culpability. For it seems to me not obviously preposterous to praise or blame me as much as them if I would have done what they did if only I had had their *given* character. On the other hand, insofar as I understand what it means to say this, it seems to me false that I would have done what they did if I had had their given character. (Of course, it *would* be preposterous to praise or blame me as much as them if I would have done what they did if, but only if, I had had their character *as so far formed*. For much of the "sum" that is left over when one "subtracts" their given character from their character as so far formed will be something for which they are in their own right responsible and for the lack of which I am in my own right responsible.[175])

Thus, even if (P4.30) is false, there is, I submit, something intuitively appealing about it, and perhaps some modification of it, where its antecedent is restricted by further conditions, is acceptable. But it is very difficult to figure out just what modification this is. One must beware of the trivial. For instance, the necessity of not engaging in differential judgment regarding Arnold and Arnold* would clearly be yielded by a version of (P4.30) whose antecedent included the condition that S and S^* possess the same athletic skills; such a version would be uninformative, however. I suspect that any interesting modifications of (P4.30) must be drawn up piecemeal: what is pertinent to athletic (dis)credit may not be pertinent to intellectual, musical, or moral (dis)credit, and so on. Henceforth, I shall concern myself solely with moral (dis)credit and solely with that sort which pertains to appraisability (rather than the virtues and vices).

Resultant luck. Rather than try to draw up a single version of (P4.30), which pertains to all types of situation concerning the implications of moral luck on the ascription of appraisability, I shall divide the task into two segments: the drawing up of such a principle first where it is resultant luck that is at issue and then where it is situational luck that is at issue.

The principle concerning resultant luck is this (where the control at issue is strict curtailed control and where the moral (dis)credit at issue is solely a matter of appraisability):

(P4.31)   If (a) S willed e, with purpose p and on the basis of belief b,
           (b) S thereby brought about f,
           (c) f's being a consequence of S's willing e was not in S's control (except insofar as S's willing e was in S's control),
           (d) S^* willed e, with purpose p and on the basis of belief b,
           (e) S did not thereby bring about f, and
           (f) f's being a consequence of S^*'s willing e was not in S^*'s control (except insofar as S^*'s willing e was in S^*'s control),
           then whatever moral credit or discredit accrues to S for bringing about e accrues also to S^*.[176]

This principle, undoubtedly deflationary with respect to common ascriptions of responsibility, is in keeping with all that has been said before concerning the parasitic nature of indirect freedom and the essential emptiness of indirect appraisability. Since direct freedom extends only to one's volitions and not beyond, one is in control of the consequences of one's volitions only insofar as one is in control of one's volitions. Thus resultant luck is ineliminable; even if (as is not the case) one were always in complete control of one's volitions, one would never be in complete control of the consequences of one's volitions.

All of this may be readily granted. A success confers no more appraisability than does a failed attempt. (See Section 4.3.) But of course this does not imply that the ultra-deflationary (P4.29) is true, that is, that no one is ever morally responsible for anything. All that emerges from the satisfaction of the antecedent of (P4.31) is that S is no more laudable or culpable than S^*; it does not follow that S is neither laudable nor culpable. This would follow only if S^* were neither laudable nor culpable, but this is not something that must be granted. Naturally, the question arises:

what is S^* appraisable *for?* The answer, of course, is: his willing e. Now S may be appraisable not just for willing e but also for bringing about f; but, as we saw in Section 4.3, the fact that S is thus appraisable for a greater *number* of events than S^* does not imply that he is appraisable to a greater *degree* than S^*.[177]

Of course, given that the successful driver is no more culpable than the unsuccessful driver, then it must be admitted that, from the point of view of ascribing moral responsibility, it does not matter whether or not the terrible event—the death—comes about as a result of the decision to drink and drive, as long as the decision itself occurs.[178] But, again, this does not imply that the successful driver is not culpable for the death. The death indicates the blemish on his record only indirectly, as it were, while the decision indicates it directly; but an indirect indication is still an indication. While the death that results is not itself the occasion of a fresh entry's being inscribed in the driver's ledger, it nevertheless reflects the fact that some entry is to be inscribed therein. Moreover, we may still say that the successful driver did something *wrong* that the unsuccessful driver did not do, namely, run over a pedestrian. For this reason we may accept that Nagel is *correct* in saying that there is something "morally significant" about the difference between reckless driving and manslaughter, while consistently cleaving to (P4.31), that is, while consistently denying that this makes a difference with respect to moral *appraisability.*[179]

In this connection, Williams's interesting remarks concerning what he calls agent-regret need to be addressed.[180] Williams seems to suggest that it is morally appropriate for the successful driver to regret what he has done more than the unsuccessful driver regrets what he has done. This is *true,* insofar as the former has done something *wrong,* which the latter has not. On the other hand, *anyone* should regret what the former has done more than what the latter has done; the appropriateness of such regret is not unique to the agent. Now, Williams seems to suggest otherwise; for he appears to believe that the successful driver is more *culpable* than the unsuccessful driver. Of course, I deny this, and so, in *this* respect, I believe that it is *not* morally appropriate for the successful driver to regret what he has done more than the unsuccessful driver regrets what he has done. In our world, such unsuccessful drivers are all too ready not to feel the appropriate degree of regret—or, better (in this context), of *remorse* (which is a matter not just of regretting but of acknowledging culpability).[181] At least, this is so for *intrinsic* appropriateness. We can, of course, admit that it can be *extrinsically* morally appropriate for a successful driver to feel a greater degree of remorse than an unsuccessful one. Suppose that the successful driver had not been at fault in causing the pedestrian's death. If (in an intrinsically appropriate manner) he had shown no more remorse than an unsuccessful driver would have done in similar circumstances, we might be warranted in being suspicious. For it is unlikely that anyone in such a position can turn remorse off in a manner that is intrinsically appropriate to the circumstances; and thus the successful driver's showing no remorse here would be an indication that he would have shown no remorse in circumstances where it was intrinsically called for.[182] But, to repeat, remorse would *not* be intrinsically appropriate here, no matter how hard it might be to convince the driver of this fact, and there is no call for him to regret what has occurred more than there is for anyone else (who is aware of what has occurred) to regret it.

Situational luck. But it might be thought that the foregoing betrays unwarranted complacency, that one cannot remain content with viewing the will as the stopping-place for the erosive power of luck with respect to appraisability; for luck may affect the will also.

It cannot be denied that luck affects the will. Feinberg stresses this point, and he is quite right to do so. One is never in complete control of the situations that one faces, either with respect to "external" matters such as being born, being of a certain physical constitution, being distracted by a loud noise, being in a certain geographical location, and so on, or with respect to "internal" matters such as being irascible, suffering from an Oedipus complex, having a kindly disposition, and so on. And all of these matters affect what one does. It is against them as a background that one makes the decisions that one does; indeed, without such a background, no decisions could be made.

But what are we to infer from this? Again, we are not committed to the claim that no one is responsible for anything. Consider again the collaborator and the noncollaborator. One could of course argue as follows (Argument I):

(P4.32)   The noncollaborator is as culpable as the collaborator.
(P4.33)   The noncollaborator is not culpable to any degree.
              Therefore
(P4.34)   The collaborator is not culpable to any degree.

But there are two other ways to go here. Either (Argument II):

(P4.32)   The noncollaborator is as culpable as the collaborator.
(not-P4.34) The collaborator is culpable to some degree.
                  Therefore
(not-P4.33) The noncollaborator is culpable to some degree.

Or (Argument III):

(P4.33)   The noncollaborator is not culpable to any degree.
(not-P4.34) The collaborator is culpable to some degree.

Therefore

(not-P4.32)   The noncollaborator is not as culpable as the collaborator.

Since I reject (P4.34), I reject Argument I. But which of Arguments II and III is to be accepted and which rejected? This is a tricky issue.

I am inclined to accept Argument III. Indeed, (P3.19) commits me to a rejection of (not-P4.33), and thus to a rejection of Argument II. After all, the noncollaborator made no decision, and hence there is nothing for which he is directly culpable (with respect to the episode in question). And, in response to the objection that acceptance of Argument III commits one to the acceptance of (not-P4.32) and that this conclusion is false, one must ask: why is (not-P4.32) false? The answer, presumably, would be that it is *unfair* to blame the collaborator more than the noncollaborator, since what distinguishes them is something over which they had no control. But the response to *this* might simply be: *"C'est la vie!"* After all, life just *is* "unfair." No one would think of praising or blaming a stone or some other inanimate object,[183] and yet such an object has ("unfairly"!) never had the opportunity to distinguish itself and thereby earn praise or ("fortunately"!) never had the opportunity to disgrace itself and thereby earn blame.[184] So, if the noncollaborator never had the opportunity to disgrace himself, he can thank his lucky stars. The collaborator might have cause for complaint (but complaint to whom? the gods? the stars?) for not being as lucky as the non-collaborator; but this does not imply that he is not culpable for his decision to collaborate, which, after all, was made strictly freely.

Although I am inclined, therefore, to accept Argument III, I also have some inclination to reject it and to accept (not Argument I but) Argument II. Acceptance of Argument III strikes me as perhaps too complacent. True, it would be absurd to praise or blame a stone, but is it absurd to hold the collaborator and the noncollaborator morally on a par with one another? Perhaps not.[185] But if not, then we must blame the noncollaborator, since the collaborator certainly is to blame. How might we account for this?

A first stab is to propose the following:

(P4.35)   If (a) S freely willed e, with purpose p and on the basis of belief b,

(b) S^* would have willed e, with purpose p and on the basis of belief b, if he had had belief b, and

(c) S^*'s not having b was not in his control,

then whatever moral credit or discredit accrues to S for willing e accrues also to S^*.

There are two major problems with this proposal, at most one of which I know how to overcome. The first problem, which I do not know how to overcome, concerns the fact that (P4.35) contains a subjunctive conditional, and it is notoriously difficult to settle on an acceptable account of the truth-conditions of such a conditional. Indeed, it sometimes appears as if some such conditionals lack a truth-value altogether. But here, for the sake of convenience and argument, I shall accept that all such conditionals have a truth-value, and that whatever difficulty one might on occasion have in assigning a truth-value to such a conditional is a purely epistemological difficulty. The second problem is this. (P4.35) is clearly too liberal. It would apparently permit us on occasion to praise and blame stones, something that has already been deemed inappropriate.

One way to try to overcome this second problem, a way that restores a link between freedom of the will and appraisability, is simply to modify the antecedent of (P4.35) as follows:

(P4.35′)   If (a) [as in (P4.35)],
            (b) [as in (P4.35)],
            (c) [as in (P4.35)], and
            (d) S^* was a free agent,
            then [as in (P4.35)].

By "a free agent" I mean someone who is strictly free to will something. This modification to (P4.35) would again rule out ever praising or blaming stones but rule in the possibility of blaming the noncollaborator. What would the noncollaborator be culpable *for?* Not collaboration, clearly; and in this case there is not even the *decision* to collaborate. In this regard the noncollaborator is significantly different from the unsuccessful driver.[186] But we could say that the noncollaborator is culpable for being such that he satisfies the relevant instantiation of clause (b) of (P4.35′). If so, we must admit that here we have an exception to the claim that, if S is culpable for e, then S was strictly free with respect to e; but, given clause (d) of (P4.35′), we may still accept that, if S is culpable for e, then, for some event f, S was strictly free with respect to f.

Should we accept (P4.35′)? I am not at all persuaded that we should. It would mean that culpability is far more widespread than we commonly think. This is ironic, insofar as much of this chapter has been devoted, in effect, to arguing that culpability is incurred less often, and to a lesser extent, than is commonly supposed, that is, that the proper account of responsibility is, in many respects, deflationary with respect to common ascriptions of responsibility. But, if (P4.35′) is accepted and incorporated into the present account of responsibility, this account turns out to be highly inflationary with respect to common ascriptions of responsibility. Still, perhaps this is right; perhaps we should rid ourselves of our complacency. Or perhaps it is wrong; perhaps the noncollaborator is merely reprehensible, but not strictly culpable, for being such that he would have collaborated under the conditions stipulated. But I am not sure of this; for the question of fairness raised earlier cannot be lightly dismissed.

Of course, if (P4.35') is correct, then (P3.19) requires modification. Let us say:

(P4.36) S is situationally culpable to degree x for e if and only if, for some event f,
(a) S would have willed f, with purpose p and on the basis of belief b, if he had had belief b,
(b) he would have been directly culpable to degree x for willing f, if he had had belief b,
(c) his not having belief b was not in his strict control,
(d) he was a free agent, and
(e) e is his being such that he would have willed f, with purpose p and on the basis of belief b, if he had had belief b.

We could then modify (P3.19) as follows:

(P3.19') S is culpable to degree x for e if and only if either
(a) S is directly culpable to degree x for e, or
(b) S is indirectly culpable to degree x for e, or
(c) S is conjointly culpable to degree x for e, or
(d) S is situationally culpable to degree x for e.

(P3.18) would call for analogous modification, and a similar principle for i-worthiness would need to be supplied. In addition, we should have to modify (P3.25) as follows:

(P3.25') S is substantially appraisable to degree x for e if and only if either
(a) S is directly appraisable to degree x for e, or
(b) S is situationally appraisable to degree x for e.

Note that clause (a) of (P3.25') is strictly redundant; for if S is directly appraisable for willing e (with purpose p and on the basis of belief b), then he is situationally appraisable for being such that he would have willed e (with purpose p and on the basis of belief b, if he had had b). The intriguing implication is that, with respect to situational appraisability, direct appraisability is superfluous—just as, with respect to direct appraisability, indirect appraisability is superfluous. However, I must repeat that I am not at all persuaded that this modification to (P3.25) is called for; indeed, I am inclined to say that it is not. But, more importantly, even if it is called for, given clause (d) of (P4.36) we may—and should—still insist that there is an essential connection between moral appraisability and strict freedom. Moreover, we may—and should—still resist the conclusion that no one is ever appraisable for anything. In fact, if (P3.25') is true, it would be closer to the truth to say that everyone is always appraisable for everything.[187] But, of course, this would still be a *gross exaggeration*, and the acceptance of situational appraisability by no means commits one to taking it literally.

NOTES

1. There is a fourth way to criticize my sort of account: to accept the equivalence of (some of) the statements tied by the biconditional (the "if and only if") but to reject the claim that the equivalence is tantamount to an *analysis*. Since I do not wish to get embroiled in the issue of just what an analysis requires beyond such equivalence, I shall not entertain objections of this sort.

2. For a representative analysis, see Chisholm (1977), p. 110. Perhaps only certain sorts of justification suffice for knowledge; I shall not discuss this here.

3. But see notes 7 and 15 to Chapter 2 for possible complications.

4. Here and henceforth I use "disbelief with respect to its being the case that *p*" to mean the lack of a belief that *p*, and *not* the presence of a belief that not-*p*.

5. See Broad (1946), p. 110.

6. See note 28 to Chapter 3. Such general unwillingness to do wrong seems to be part of what is at issue in Fingarette's important discussion of what he calls "accepting responsibility" in Fingarette (1967), Chapter 2, and I am in sympathy with much of what he says there. But I shall record here one point of disagreement. On p. 27 of that work, Fingarette seems to infer the claim that one who has not accepted responsibility *is* not responsible from the claim that it is *pointless to hold* someone responsible who has not accepted responsibility. The inference is unwarranted, even if both claims are true. This is clearly so if the responsibility at issue is appraisability; and, as I shall argue in Chapter 5, it is also so if the responsibility at issue is liability.

7. Aristotle, *Nicomachean Ethics,* 1111a.

8. Aristotle, *Nicomachean Ethics,* 1110b.

9. See Donagan (1977), p. 130.

10. *Cf.* Houlgate (1968), pp. 112–13. Saying this is compatible with saying that the agent is to blame for being such that he would have willingly done wrong, had he not been ignorant of his action. See Section 4.11 below on 'situational culpability.'

11. *Cf.* Chisholm (1977), pp. 20–23, on 'self-presenting states.'

12. For a strong contrast, see Aristotle, *Nicomachean Ethics,* 1110b, where it is apparently claimed that we are culpable for *all* our ignorance concerning what we ought to do. On the other hand, the law's position on the matter of legal liability for harm ignorantly brought about appears to be quite compatible with, indeed possibly to presuppose, the present position on moral culpability for ignorance. See Hughes (1958), p. 227.

13. *Cf.* Kleinig (1973), p. 95.

14. Donagan (1977), p. 136.

15. It might facilitate administration of the law, for example. *Cf.* Prosser (1971), pp. 152–53; Fingarette (1972), p. 154.

16. *Cf.* Keeton and O'Connell (1966), p. 85: "Some applications of modern negligence law quite regularly, rather than only occasionally, produce findings of negligence against defendants whom we would be unwilling to censure as morally blameworthy. A striking example of this is the liability of a mentally incompetent adult for harm caused by conduct falling below the standard of ordinary prudence."

17. This depends on whether volitions must be conscious. See Section 2.1.

18. *Cf.* Kenny (1978), p. 6: "Where there is negligence, there is voluntary unawareness of the nature of one's action."

19. In the law, "negligence" is sometimes applied to behavior that involves no

inadvertence. (See Hart (1968), pp. 137, 259–60.) But I think that our common usage of "negligence" is such that all negligence may be said essentially to involve inadvertence.

20. This is a stipulative use of the term "neglect," although such use is supposed to be suggestive. *Cf.* White (1964), pp. 83–84.

21. See Zimmerman (1986a), Section 1, for a fuller, but somewhat different, account.

22. On willing, see Section 2.1, including note 11.

23. See, *e.g.,* Austin (1873), p. 242.

24. Unless some volitions can be unconscious. See note 17, this chapter.

25. See note 17 to Chapter 3.

26. It is *not* conjoint. As characterized in (P4.7), neglectful action occurs as a consequence of, and does not include, the volition mentioned in (P4.6).

27. Hart reports Turner thus in Hart (1968), pp. 138 and 146ff.

28. In the preceding sentence I say "consistently with this" advisedly, since there can be some tension here. If the event in its original setting is highly unlikely then not seeking to prevent it is not very neglectful, but also there is little chance to reduce the degree of neglect further by taking precautions to prevent it. Just what the formula should be to resolve this tension, I am not sure.

29. This is in fact too rough a way of putting the point. See p. 45.

30. *Cf.* Brandt (1959), p. 462.

31. For a good general discussion of this matter, see Hughes (1967).

32. In Section 2.1, I explained that omissions may be either causal or simple consequences of other events. The manner in which they may be causal consequences differs somewhat from the manner in which "normal" events may be, but they may be causal consequences nonetheless.

33. *Cf.* Weinryb (1980). On p. 16, however, Weinryb appears to acknowledge an exception to premise (i).

34. *Cf.* Husak (1980), p. 320. Note that, while the argument as stated concerns responsibility for the consequences of omissions, it could have been extended so as to concern responsibility for omissions themselves. For example: (v) if one is not morally responsible for something that one has merely omitted to avert, then one is not morally responsible for merely omitting to avert it; hence, (vi) one is not morally responsible for merely omitting to avert harm.

35. See Harris (1980), Chapter 3.

36. See Green (1979), pp. 108–9.

37. *Cf.* Husak (1980), p. 320ff.; Steinbock (1980), p. 104. Contrast Donagan (1977), p. 46; Kleinig (1986), pp. 11–13.

38. The sort of control I have is *standard* and *contributory;* your opening the safe is a *simple* consequence of my holding a gun to your head, and my not holding the gun to your head would have had the simple consequence of your not opening the safe. See (P2.3), the discussion following (P2.15), and (P2.16) of Chapter 2.

39. See note 3 to Chapter 2.

40. See Steinbock (1980), p. 104.

41. See Weinryb (1980), p. 9ff.

42. This is one way to understand Green's contention in Green (1979), p. 109.

43. That there is sometimes such diminution certainly seems to be suggested, for example, in Cohen (1981), p. 75. Of a situation where a hundred people let some person die, none of the hundred could have prevented the death by himself, and not all of the hundred are required to act for the death to be prevented, Cohen talks explicitly of the *sharing* of responsibility and goes on to say: "[I]f there are a hundred independent defaulters . . . and one death, each carries a hundredth of the responsibility, not the whole of it. . . . [E]ach carries only one hundredth of a murderer's guilt."

44. I say "perhaps" for reasons given in note 6 to Chapter 2.

45. See note 29 to Chapter 2.

46. *Cf.* Feinberg (1970), pp. 181, 246.

47. The illustration is borrowed from Hart and Honoré (1959), p. 69.

48. See Hart and Honoré (1959), pp. 69, 129–30; Donagan (1977), pp. 45–47. Note that Hart and Honoré appear to reject the conclusion (on p. 78 of their work); and Donagan in fact explicitly rejects it, as we shall see. *Cf.* also Morris (1961), p. 282.

49. This would be denied by some. For example, Donagan—in Donagan (1977), p. 38—says that those events which go to make up a sufficient causal condition must all occur *at the same time*. This is surely false. See Hilbert (1983), pp. 8–9; Zimmerman (1984), pp. 61–62.

50. See note 3 to Chapter 2. At any rate, there is this distinction between the cases. In the case of the forest-fire, Smith's action contributes causally to the fire, but not by way of contributing causally to Jones's action. In the case of the torturing, if Smith's action contributes causally to the child's suffering at all, it does so only by way of contributing causally to Jones's action.

51. *Cf.* Feinberg (1970), pp. 138–39.

52. *Cf.* Husak (1980), pp. 324–26.

53. *Cf.* Hart and Honoré (1959), p. 71.

54. But here, I would say, "punish" is being used broadly. See Section 5.1.

55. See Hart and Honoré (1959), p. 69. *Cf.* Fitzgerald (1968), p. 140. This and related principles are examined in Feinberg (1970), Chapter 7.

56. I do not think that Hart and Honoré would accept (P4.12′), even if they accept (P4.10′); there is reason to believe that they would reject (P4.11). See Hart and Honoré (1959), p. 78. *Cf.* Fletcher (1978), p. 367.

57. On such an understanding of strict freedom, see Taylor (1966), pp. 109–12; Chisholm (1976), pp. 69–70; Donagan (1977), pp. 46–47; Zimmerman (1984), p. 228.

58. But see Zimmerman (1984), Chapters 11 and 12. See also note 3 to Chapter 2.

59. See notes 49 and 50, this chapter.

60. Donagan (1977), p. 47.

61. *Cf.* Fitzgerald (1968), p. 123, on servants and responsibility.

62. It should be stressed that, while (P4.10″) appears to have been accepted by Donagan at the time of his writing *The Theory of Morality,* he has since indicated (during a conference on his philosophy held at Illinois State University in November 1983) that he would reject it. He also indicated that he would accept some further modification of (P4.10); however, just what this modification is, I am not sure.

63. Donagan (1977), pp. 47–48.

64. *Cf.* Feinberg (1970), pp. 226–27, on the distinction between "bound" and "free" agents.

65. *Cf.* Fitzgerald (1968), p. 123 and Hart and Honoré, pp. 70, 94, and 251, on negligence and intervening agency. *Cf.* also Prosser (1971), pp. 172–73.

66. See note 44 to Chapter 3.

67. Or better, so as not to seem to be ascribing agency to a group as such: *A–C as a group* did wrong in both cases.

68. Contrast Frankfurt (1973), p. 82.

69. One could, of course, avoid whatever oddness there is in the claim that someone can be compelled to do something and yet not do it, by stipulating that *S* is compelled to degree *x* to bring about *e* just in case *S* is broadly unfree to degree *x* not to bring about *e and brings about e* (or, perhaps, brings about *e for this reason*). But this is a complication in which I shall not indulge here.

70. *Cf.* the *Royal Commission Report* (1953), p. 417.

71. According to some, this is not so. *Cf.* Feinberg (1970), p. 282; Thorp (1980), p. 134.

72. *Cf.* Fischer (1982), pp. 27–28.

73. Contrast Kenny (1978), p. 42.

74. See note 25 to Chapter 2. The one account of which I know where there is a

sustained effort to analyze irresistibility of impulse is that given in Neely (1974), p. 47. For reasons given in Mele (1986), pp. 674–76, this attempt is unsuccessful.

75. Contrast Frankfurt (1973), pp. 77–79.

76. *Cf*. Brandt (1959), p. 473, and, in the legal arena, LaFave and Scott (1972), pp. 374–75, 380–82. There it is said that duress and "necessity" can *justify* (note: not excuse) an otherwise unjustifiable action.

77. *Cf*. Flew (1973), p. 87.

78. I would put matters this way rather than—as in Audi (1974), p. 10ff.—as follows: whether or not there is compulsion is relative to the moral seriousness of the action in question. For difficulty in doing something is not a moral matter, and it seems to me that even nonmoral difficulty (of a particular sort, perhaps) serves to diminish or even eliminate broad freedom.

79. *Cf*. Aristotle, *Nicomachean Ethics*, 1110a.

80. *Cf*. Antony (1979), p. 67. Contrast Audi (1974), pp. 11–12. Note that there could be a diminution in *"situational"* culpability (see Section 4.11) if the agent would not have done the act which he believed wrong had he not had such a hard time resisting the compulsion to do it.

81. Szasz (1970), p. 15.

82. Szasz (1970), pp. 21–24.

83. *Cf*. Morris (1976), pp. 66–68.

84. *Cf*. Flew (1973), p. 61ff.

85. I concentrate here on the matter of *what* the agent believes, if anything, rather than on *how* he comes to believe it. The former has to do with the truth-values of his beliefs, the latter with their justification. While mental disorder surely can affect the justification of one's beliefs, for reasons given in Section 4.1 the issue of justification is irrelevant to the matter of appraisability.

86. Or consider a more dramatic case suggested to me by Douglas Husak: Green deliberately kills his mother in order to prevent her transmogrification into a succuba. Here, again, it is likely that Green believes that he is doing what is right, or even obligatory, and thus is not culpable for his misdeed.

87. *Cf*. Flew (1973), p. 75ff; Flew (1974), pp. 47–48.

88. *Cf*. Haksar (1965), p. 135ff.

89. *Cf*. Haksar (1964), p. 136ff.; Fingarette (1967), p. 23ff.; Murphy (1972), pp. 286–87; Pritchard (1974), p. 632; Duff (1977), pp. 191–92, 196; Milo (1984), pp. 61–62.

90. *Cf*. Fingarette (1967), pp. 25–26.

91. See Fingarette (1967), p. 23ff.; Pritchard (1974), p. 632ff.

92. Still, if it is logically possible for someone to understand the concept of wrongness, and to have beliefs concerning wrongdoing, without having a caring attitude, then there is no logical barrier that I can see to ascribing culpability to that person—contrary to the assertions of some. (See Murphy (1972), p. 291ff.)

93. This is a matter of degrees of strict freedom in the *extrinsic* mode.

94. Gross (1979), p. 306.

95. This points finds a partial echo in the *Royal Commission Report* (1953), p. 418, where it is pointed out that an insane person may lack, not so much the capacity to prevent himself from doing something, but rather the capacity to appreciate why he should prevent himself from doing it. Of course, if someone lacks this latter capacity, this is, or may well be, a matter of lacking strict freedom *with respect to appreciating the wrongness of one's action;* but it is not, or need not be, a matter of lacking strict freedom *with respect to the action itself.*

96. Culver and Gert (1982), pp. 116–17, distinguish between *compelled* and *compulsive* action. They appear to claim, for example, that the actions of a compulsive handwasher are not merely broadly but strictly unfree. If this is so, then of course an excuse is forthcoming. It seems that Culver and Gert would say that, in such a case, the agent's strict freedom has been confined.

97. See Feinberg (1970), p. 282ff. *Cf*. also Radden (1982), p. 359.

98. Perhaps there is no need to say here that I am not using "abnormal" pejoratively—but I shall say it. It should be noted that the compelling nature of a desire is not solely a function of its strength, but is rather a function of its strength *relative* to the strength of the agent's opposing desires. If it is the case that abnormal sexual desires are typically strongly opposed by other desires, then the case for saying that abnormal sexual desires are typically more compelling than normal ones is weakened.

99. See Fletcher (1978), p. 802; Radden (1982), p. 359; Radden (1985), p. 38.

100. *Cf.* Feinberg (1970), p. 273; Radden (1985), p. 9. Contrast Hall (1960b), p. 425. *Cf.* also Gross (1979), pp. 297–98.

101. See Feinberg (1970), p. 272; Cummins (1980), pp. 212–13; Radden (1982), p. 350. In Radden (1985), Chapter 9, there is some effort to reject this position by claiming that lack of reason itself provides an excuse. But all the plausible examples cited there seem to me to be cases where lack of reason excuses in the ordinary way, by virtue of affecting the agent's beliefs or freedom. (Contrast Fingarette (1972), pp. 155–56, where it is claimed that a psychotically schizophrenic mother who kills her child is to be excused, *even* if she believed her so doing was morally wrong.)

102. Feinberg (1970), pp. 283–88. *Cf.* Glover (1970), p. 119ff.

103. One example: Brandt (1958), p. 13ff.

104. In putting the matter thus, I do not wish to rule out the possibility that a character is some sort of organic unity, "greater than the sum of its parts," and hence not *merely* a set of properties. *Cf.* Mayo (1958), p. 175.

105. *Cf.* Brandt (1959), p. 466.

106. Perhaps it is one's character as so far formed that Gert has in mind when he says in Gert (1970), p. 153, that it is a "tautology" that one is responsible to some degree for one's character. This may be accepted, where it is *causal* responsibility that is at issue, but not where it is appraisability that is at issue.

107. *Cf.* Nagel (1979), p. 36.

108. A possible exception to this statement will be discussed in Section 4.11.

109. Contrast Aristotle, *Nicomachean Ethics,* Book III, Chapter 5. *Cf.* Glover (1970), pp. 11–12.

110. *Cf.* Edwards (1969), p. 80.

111. A common answer to this question—one advocated, *e.g.,* in Ross (1930), p. 155—is simply that the excellence and defectiveness concern *character*. This seems too sweeping to me. Quickness of wit is a character trait, but not a moral one.

112. The best recent treatment of many of these questions seems to me to be in Wallace (1978). *Cf.* also Gert (1970), Chapter 8. Of course, the most important classical treatment of them is in Aristotle, *Nicomachean Ethics,* Books II–V.

113. On the issue of responsibility for anger (and other emotions), see Sankowski (1977) and Adams (1985).

114. When I say "the virtues and vices," I am of course implicitly *excluding* laudability and culpability. Perhaps there is some common sense in which a laudable person is (to the extent that he is laudable) virtuous or a culpable person vicious. (One often encounters talk of "conscientiousness" in such a context. *Cf.* Brandt (1959), pp. 470–71.) But to allow such talk here would serve simply to obscure the distinction that I am trying to make between the two types of moral worth. See again the introduction to Chapter 3, where I note that a person may have a *number* of "moral records." *Cf.* also Prichard (1912), pp. 31–32, where a sharp distinction is drawn between the goodness of a conscientious act and the virtuousness of sympathetic, courageous, public-spirited, and other such acts.

115. See, among others: Rashdall (1907b), pp. 323–24; Brandt (1958), p. 15; Brandt (1959), p. 460ff.; Hunter (1973), p. 244; Nagel (1979), pp. 181–82; Wolf (1980), p. 156. The confusion is dramatically evident in two recent works: in Milo (1984), where very useful distinctions between various types of immorality are made, but where these distinctions cut insensitively right across the distinction that I wish to draw here (see especially Chapter 8 of that work); and in Adams (1985).

Perhaps it is this confusion that Kant sought to avoid in his enigmatic claim in Kant (1785), pp. 61–62, that only a good will is "good without qualification." (Cf. Aune (1979), p. 6.) Beardsley seems to be trying to avoid the confusion in Beardsley (1957), p. 319ff., and Beardsley (1979), pp. 580–81, although she appears to draw the distinction between the two types of moral worth in a way that I do not.

For a good, and early, example of a philosopher who does not succumb to the confusion, see Abelard, "Desire and Sin." More recent examples: Prichard (1912), pp. 31–32; Ewing (1929), pp. 37–38; Prichard (1949), pp. 11–12; Sankowski (1977), pp. 837–38; Blum (1980), pp. 178, 183, 186–90; van Inwagen (1984), p. 12.

116. See Foot (1978), p. 8.

117. Cf. Blum (1980), p. 172.

118. Quoted from van Inwagen (1984), p. 11. Contrast Wolf (1980), p. 156; Dennett (1984), pp. 133 and 157, n.3.

119. Cf. Oldenquist (1978), pp. 3–4.

120. The distinction between two types of moral worth helps resolve a puzzle posed in Foot (1978), p. 10. Foot says: "we both are and are not inclined to think that the harder a man finds it to act virtuously the more virtue he shows if he does act well." Might we not say that the one who finds it easy to act virtuously has a great deal of virtue and, thus, moral worth of one sort; while the one who finds it hard to act virtuously but does so nonetheless, if he chooses to do so for the sake of doing what he regards as right, shows a good deal of laudability and, thus, of moral worth of another sort? (Roberts (1984), pp. 233–34, comes close to saying just this, but in somewhat different terminology. Cf. Gert (1970), p. 163.)

121. See Adams (1985), pp. 3–4. Cf. Schlossberger (1986), p. 37ff.

122. Even Adams comes close to recognizing this. In Adams (1985), pp. 21–22, he recognizes that different overt responses are appropriate with respect to what he calls involuntary, as opposed to voluntary, sins. One wonders why this should be so, unless different inward, judgmental responses are also appropriate, serving as the ground for the difference in appropriateness of the overt responses.

123. Adams (1985), p. 19. Contrast Donagan (1977), p. 135.

124. Brandt, (1959), p. 473. Cf. Holborrow (1971–72), pp. 90–91.

125. Contrast Adams (1985), p. 12, and Schlossberger (1986), p. 47.

126. See, e.g., Broad (1950), p. 351; Frankena (1963), pp. 150–51; Chisholm (1964), pp. 149–50; Jackson (1985).

127. Cf. Sankowski (1977), pp. 834–36.

128. Cf. van Inwagen (1984), p. 11: "It might be that, while Washington was unable to lie in middle age, this is only because he had carefully schooled himself in veracity in his youth and early manhood. If this were so, then it would make good sense to say that he had once had a free choice about what sort of man he would be; and our praise of him would be directed at the sort of man he was."

129. Aristotle, Nicomachean Ethics, Book II, Chapter 5, and Book III, Chapters 5ff. See note 109.

130. In this respect, I am in agreement with Adams (1985), pp. 4–6.

131. Cf. the remarks on sympathy made in Bennett (1974), p. 22.

132. Frankfurt (1969), p. 829.

133. On the locution "something other than e," see note 28 to Chapter 2.

134. See Frankfurt (1969), p. 834ff.

135. Daniel Dennett has recently also argued that (P4.15) is false, but he appears to be primarily concerned with broad freedom. See Dennett (1984), Chapter 6.

136. Locke (1690), pp. 149–50; cf. Neely (1974), p. 38.

137. Note that an analogous example involving laudability rather than culpability could have been concocted.

138. Actually, for this to be so, it must also be true that, unbeknownst to him, Peter is unable to prevent Paul's waking up—by killing him, for example. So let us assume that this too is the case. (Paul is sleeping in the top bunk, say, and, if Peter were to try

to climb up, the ladder—the only means available to reach Paul—would break, and the noise of Peter's falling would wake Paul.)

139. Here, and elsewhere, I am of course using "remaining" and "annoyance" to refer to the issues of Peter's actions, and not the actions themselves.

140. *Cf.* Frankfurt (1969), pp. 835–36.

141. Moreover, it is, I think, possible to come up with a case where the agent is seen to have no alternative but to *act* in a certain way. See Blumenfeld (1971), p. 341, n.3; and see the discussion of (P4.17) further on.

142. It should be pointed out that those cases which Frankfurt—in Frankfurt (1969)—considers to be counterexamples to (P4.15) apparently fail to be counterexamples to (P4.16') just as the case of Peter, Paul, and the locked door does. For, although it seems plausible to say that, in Frankfurt's examples, an agent *S* "could not have done otherwise," it turns out on closer inspection that the sense in which this is true is apparently this: *S* has no *immediate* freedom with respect to doing otherwise, and not this: *S* had no *remote* freedom with respect to doing otherwise.

143. Again, we must also assume that Peter could not have rendered Paul unconscious prior to his (Paul's) annoyance. See note 138, this chapter.

144. But perhaps this is the tack taken in Audi (1974), pp. 4–5.

145. Again, on the locution "other than," see note 28 to Chapter 2.

146. *Cf.* Blumenfeld (1971), pp. 343–44; Naylor (1984), p. 249ff.

147. See Naylor (1984), p. 250ff.

Here it is worth noting that some philosophers have accepted that the principle of alternate possibilities is false but have advocated acceptance of certain closely related principles. Among these principles are the following:

(a) A person is not morally responsible for what he has done if he did it because he could not have done otherwise.

(b) A person is not morally responsible for what he has done if he did it only because he could not have done otherwise.

(c) A person is morally responsible for failing to perform an action only if he could have performed it.

(d) A person is morally responsible for an event only if he could have prevented it.

(a) is accepted in Blumenfeld (1971) and Cummins (1979). It is rejected in Frankfurt (1969), where (b) is advocated. (c) and (d) are advocated in van Inwagen (1983), Chapter 5, and (c) is advocated in Fischer (1985–86).

148. In Naylor (1984), p. 254ff., an argument is given which could be adapted for this purpose. But the argument seems to me to founder on a confusion between knowing what reasons an agent will in fact act on and rendering an agent strictly unfree to act on other reasons.

149. I am here overlooking the possibility that desires affect strict freedom. If they can, then they could in this way be relevant to questions of appraisability.

150. Frankfurt (1969), p. 830. *Cf.* Feinberg (1970), pp. 185–86, where it is claimed that "voluntariness does not entail avoidability." *Cf.* also Frankfurt (1978), where Frankfurt reiterates the claim that "the" principle of alternate possibilities is false, but where the principle apparently at issue is *not* (P4.15) or (P4.16) but something very much like (P4.23'). It is important to note that to deny that freely bringing about *e* entails being free to do other than bring about *e* is *not* also to deny that *un*freely bringing about *e* entails being *un*free to do other than bring about *e*. This latter claim is indeed true.

151. For a similar and instructive approach to this issue, see Fischer (1982).

152. I borrow the terminology from Fischer (1982).

153. On this issue, contrast Fischer (1985–86); *cf.* Fischer (1982), pp. 38–39.

154. Presentation of the details of which I shall, for obvious reasons, forgo.

155. Frankfurt (1969), pp. 838–39.

156. At least, this is so for the incompatibilist who takes determinism to be the claim that every event has an antecedent cause.

157. Again, for an incompatibilist account of strict freedom of action, see Zimmerman (1984), Chapter 11. However, if (P4.26) is true, then the account that I gave there of what it is to be strictly free to will something requires modification. Roughly, what I said was this (see D.11.2 of Chapter 11): S is strictly free to will e if and only if (a) there is no cause of his willing e and (b) there is no cause of his not willing e. In light of the foregoing, another clause must be added: (c) it is not the case that S would be caused not to will e if he were to show telltale signs of willing e. I do not pretend that a full spelling-out of what (c) amounts to, or of what it adds to (b), would be unproblematic.

158. At least, this seems to be the case in Feinberg (1970), pp. 34–37.

159. Nagel (1979), pp. 37–38. This is undoubtedly a simplistic and insensitive way of putting Nagel's point, but I am at a loss to understand the final two pages of an otherwise admirably lucid article. Cf. the note on p. 30 of Brandt (1958).

160. Williams (1981), p. 21ff, including n.11 on p. 36. Williams is concerned, not just with moral responsibility, but with morality in general; but I think that his view is not distorted by the present restriction of it. The restriction is important; I wish to allow for the possibility that what is to be said about the relation between luck and the moral responsibility of persons is not to be said about the relation between luck and other aspects of morality (such as the rightness and wrongness of actions).

161. Andre (1983), passim, especially pp. 206–7. Like Williams, Andre's concern is morality in general but, as with Williams, part of her concern is moral responsibility in particular.

162. The matters are not kept separate in Nagel (1979), p. 29. Of course, they are related.

163. Nagel (1979), p. 25.

164. What I call situational luck comprises what Nagel—in Nagel (1979), p. 28—calls constitutive luck, luck in one's circumstances, and luck in how one is determined by antecedent circumstances. What I call resultant luck corresponds with what Nagel calls luck in the way one's actions and projects turn out.

165. More restrictively, we might of course say that something which occurs as a matter of luck with respect to someone S is something which occurs beyond S's (complete) control.

166. Unless hard determinism is true—and I am assuming that it is not.

167. Feinberg (1970), p. 33.

168. Nagel (1979), p. 26.

169. Nagel (1979), p. 31.

170. Cf. Feinberg (1970), p. 35.

171. See Nagel (1979), p. 34. Nagel says: "We judge people for what they actually do or fail to do, not just for what they would have done if circumstances had been different." If "judge" is understood as "tend to judge," I would agree. But there is some indication that Nagel means not just "judge" but "ought to judge," and here I am not so sure. See (P4.35′) below and the commentary on it. Again, cf. the note on p. 30 of Brandt (1958).

172. Cf. Nagel (1979), p. 36, n.11.

173. Recall, with respect to clause (c), that whatever is not in one's control is ipso facto also not in one's complete control. Also, in (P4.30) "brought about e" is open to substitution by "helped to bring about e," and various such locutions having to do with omission.

174. Cf. Feinberg (1970), pp. 64 and 84.

175. To this extent, my not having their character as so far formed is in my control and is thus not a suitable substituend for "$e*$" in (P4.30).

176. Again, a similar principle in terms of helping to bring about f, etc., may be given. See note 173, this chapter.

177. This view of the relation between moral responsibility and resultant luck seems to be in keeping with what is said in: Morris (1976), p. 118; Jensen (1984), p. 327; and Parker (1984), pp. 270–74. *Cf.* also Feinberg (1970), p. 242.

178. *Cf.* Hart (1968), p. 135; Parker (1984), pp. 273–74.

179. I suspect that it is a confusion of these two moral spheres—right and wrong, on the one hand, and appraisability, on the other—that moves Nagel to assert a paradox where there is none.

180. See Williams (1981), pp. 27–30.

181. For a useful discussion of remorse and related concepts, see Thalberg (1963).

182. *Cf.* Nagel (1979), pp. 28–29. In this regard, we may compare what Smart says—in Smart (1973), p. 71—about an act-utilitarian (and Smart is one) who finds himself, according to his own beliefs, constrained to do what is unjust (Smart has in mind a case where punishing an innocent person is obligatory): "we should probably dislike and fear a man who could bring himself to do the right utilitarian act in a case of [this] sort. . . . Though the man in this case might have done the right utilitarian act, his act would betoken a toughness and lack of squeamishness which would make him a dangerous person. . . . [S]hould such a person be tempted to act wrongly he could act very wrongly indeed."

183. At least, nor normally. I am discounting pagan rituals.

184. On such "cosmic injustice," see Feinberg (1980), pp. 276–77, n.7. *Cf.* also Nagel (1979), pp. 33–34, including n.9.

185. *Cf.* once again the note on p. 30 of Brandt (1958). *Cf.* also Feinberg (1970), pp. 175–76, 191–92, and 243, and especially this passage on p. 176:

It might be said that mere predisposition does not constitute sufficient *culpability* for just punishment. But, from the moral point of view, there appears to be no significant difference between the person highly predisposed to act and the person highly predisposed who never finds his inducer. The locus of moral culpability in each *is* the predisposition, and what distinguishes the two is mere luck; for it is not to the credit of the one that he performed no criminal act if it was only an accident that he was never brought across the criminal threshold.

In addition, *cf.* Morris (1976), p. 122ff., and Richards (1986), pp. 204–5.

186. *Cf.* Feinberg (1970), p. 35, where Feinberg says (of feelings rather than decisions): "[A person] can no more be responsible for a feeling he did not have than for a death that did not happen."

187. See Morris (1976), Chapter 4.

5

LIABILITY

5.1 The Nature of Liability

I TURN NOW to that second variety of moral, retrospective, personal responsibility that I call liability. I borrow the term "liability" from the law. As it is used there, "liability" means liability to certain impositions being placed on one by certain legal officials. I shall use the term in a similar way, to mean the moral susceptibility to being acted on in certain ways—where the action in question has close ties with overt praising and blaming, that is, with the public expression of private appraisal. Let us look into this more closely.

Commendation and censure. Overt praising and blaming are acts of commendation and censure. They give expression to judgments concerning appraisability, that is, concerning laudability and culpability. (I suppose, too, that there can be actions that give expression to judgments concerning i-worthiness, but I shall not pursue this matter here.) I say "judgments *concerning* appraisability" rather than simply "judgments *of* appraisability," because there are two types of judgment to be distinguished here. First, there is the first-order judgment that consists simply in appraisal, that is, in inwardly praising (call this *lauding)* or inwardly blaming (call this *inculpating)* someone. One inwardly praises (or blames) someone for an event *e* just in case one judges *e* to indicate a credit (or debit) in that person's ledger.[1] Secondly, there is the second-order judgment which consists in finding someone to be appraisable, that is, worthy of appraisal. One judges someone to be laudable (or culpable) just in case one judges that it is correct, or true to the facts, to laud (inculpate) that person. (See the opening paragraph to Chapter 3.) Of course, the two judgments may very often accompany one another; one is unlikely to laud (or inculpate) someone whom one does not judge to be laudable (or culpable), and one cannot find someone laudable (or culpa-

148

ble) without lauding (or inculpating) him. Nevertheless, while both types of judgment *concern* appraisability, only the second-order judgment is strictly a judgment *of* appraisability. (See the commentary on (P3.25) in Section 3.5.)

There seem to me to be two main varieties of commendation and censure. (Other varieties could easily be distinguished, but I shall stick with these two. In this connection, it should be noted that, while I take my present uses of "commendation" and "censure" to be suitable for the concepts that I have in mind, I do not wish to insist either that no other terms would be suitable or that this is the only suitable use of the terms. Others have used such terms somewhat differently.[2]) I shall call them the *weak* and *strong* varieties. The first variety may be understood along the following lines:

(P5.1) S weakly commends S' for e if and only if S lauds S' for e and utters this judgment.

(P5.2) S weakly censures S' for e if and only if S inculpates S' for e and utters this judgment.

I take the utterance of a judgment to be an action (often, but not necessarily, verbal) which (under "standard" conditions, at least) is intended to convey to someone the content of the judgment. This is very rough, but perhaps familiar enough, and I shall not try to make it more precise.

Now, while S acts in weakly commending or censuring S', there is no necessity that he thereby *act on S'* (that is, that he commend or censure S' "in person") or that S' be aware of S's action. In this respect, and also in others, weak commendation and censure differ from strong commendation and censure, which may be understood roughly as follows:

(P5.3) S strongly commends S' for e if and only if
            (a) S judges S' to have some property F,
            (b) S lauds S' for e because he judges S' to have F,
            (c) S believes that S' deserves to experience pleasure because of his having F, and
            (d) for some event f, S brings about f in order thereby to cause S' to experience pleasure as he deserves.

(P5.4) S strongly censures S' for e if and only if
            (a) S judges S' to have some property F,
            (b) S inculpates S' for e because he judges S' to have F,
            (c) S believes that S' deserves to suffer because of his having F, and
            (d) for some event f, S brings about f in order thereby to cause S' to suffer as he deserves.

These statements require clarification.

First, what is the property F at issue in (P5.3) and (P5.4)? Well, in (P5.3) it is just that property in virtue of which S judges that e indicates a credit in S'''s ledger, *i.e.*, in virtue of which (clause (b)) S lauds S' for e.[3] And in (P5.4) F is that property in virtue of which S judges that e indicates a debit in S'''s ledger, *i.e.*, in virtue of which S inculpates S' for e.

Second, "pleasure" in (P5.3) and "suffer" in (P5.4) are to be understood to include the most diverse and the mildest of "positive" and "negative" experiences. What S believes that S' deserves may sometimes be merely some mild form of satisfaction or of imposition, and it might seem inappropriate to call this pleasure or suffering. On the other hand, what S believes that S' deserves may sometimes be some intense form of pleasure or suffering, and it might seem inappropriate merely to call this a form of satisfaction or imposition. For simplicity's sake, I shall use just one pair of terms here—"pleasure" and "suffer"—but with the explicit proviso that they are to be understood very broadly.

Third, strong commendation and strong censure are to be taken to include weak commendation and weak censure, respectively. Clause (b) of (P5.3) and (P5.4) ensures that there is actual lauding and inculpating; and clause (d) of (P5.3) and (P5.4) is to be understood in such a way that the bringing about of f constitutes a form of utterance of the judgment involved in clause (b).

But fourth, while strong commendation and strong censure are therefore to be understood to be expressions of judgments concerning appraisability, they are not merely this. For they give vent to the moral delight or disgust that standardly accompany such judgments; moreover, they are predicated not just on judgments concerning appraisability (clauses (a) and (b)) but on judgments concerning desert arising out of these judgments concerning appraisability (clause (c)); and they themselves involve the intention, and acting on the intention, to cause the person so judged to feel as he is judged to deserve (clause (d)). If I lavish praises (and perhaps gifts, or awards, or whatever) on you for some unselfish act, I do so not only to express my belief that you are laudable, but also because I believe that you deserve to feel pleasure and because I believe that I can thereby cause you to feel pleasure. If I sternly rebuke you (and perhaps humiliate you in the sight of others, or whatever) for some selfish act, I do so not only to express my belief that you are culpable, but also because I believe that you deserve to suffer and because I believe that I can thereby cause you to suffer. Thus strong commendation and censure are *very* complex phenomena.

Fifth, clause (d) of (P5.3) and (P5.4) indicates that strong commendation and censure can fail to be fully successful, insofar as S may fail to bring about f (in which case he fails to commend or censure at all) or to bring about the pleasure or suffering that he intends thereby to cause (in which case he succeeds in commending or censuring but nonetheless fails to do so "productively"); they are fully successful only if they have the "bite" intended.[4]

Sixth, I do not pretend that (P5.3) and (P5.4) capture the strongest senses of "commendation" and "censure." For example, one could say that S "very strongly" commends or censures S' only if S intends that S' be aware that he (S) is strongly (in the sense of (P5.3) and (P5.4)) commending or censuring him (S'). And, presumably, one could add even further restrictions.

Seventh, there can of course be degrees of strong commendation and censure (a fact not reflected in the rough formulations of (P5.3) and (P5.4)). Such degrees will correlate directly with the degree of pleasure or suffering which S intends to cause in S' and which is itself designed to correlate with the degree of S''s appraisability.

Finally, the matter of what exactly is involved in S's judging S' to *deserve* to have a certain experience is something that I shall take up in some detail in the next two sections.

Reward and punishment. Reward and punishment are simply restrictive forms of strong commendation and censure. I say this for two reasons: (i) if S rewards (or punishes) S' for $e,$ then S strongly commends (or censures) S' for $e;$ (ii) the reverse does not hold true.

Why do I accept (i)? I do so because I distinguish punishment, on the one hand, from mere penalty, discipline, or related forms of treatment, on the other. First, no opprobrium necessarily attaches to the latter, but it does to the former; punishment essentially involves the expression of disapproval and reprobation, resentment and indignation.[5] Of course, one can be penalized or treated "for" some event $e,$ in the sense that e prompts the penalty or treatment, as when animals or small children are disciplined; but in such a case there is no necessity that the person doing the penalizing or treating believe that the person on the "receiving end" is culpable for e and deserves to be so handled.[6] Analogous remarks pertain to reward. Secondly, when one punishes, there is the intention to cause suffering, not necessarily in order to achieve some further purpose thereby (although this might on occasion be an incidental aim[7]), but in order to give the person punished his due. This is not the case with related forms of treatment, such as those of penalty or discipline.[8] Again, analogous remarks pertain to reward. Of course, *none* of this is to deny that "reward" and "punishment" can be, and have been, used to refer to such related forms of treatment; it is to say only that there are these particular forms of treatment for reference to which "reward" and "punishment" are uniquely well qualified. Nor is it my purpose here to deny that we sometimes inculpate and, indeed, punish (in the full-blown sense of "punish," *i.e.*, that which implies inculpating) animals and small children. I am ashamed to confess that I have myself on occasion indulged in this. It is my purpose, however, to claim that such inculpation and punishment are a moral aberration, inasmuch as neither animals nor small children can be culpable.

It is perhaps worth pointing out explicitly that, in saying that punishment is a form of strong censure, I am *not* saying that a person can punish another only if he believes that other to satisfy the analysans of (P3.19). I *am* saying that a person can punish another only if he believes that other to be culpable. The point is, of course, that one person may punish another even when he (the former) does not subscribe to (P3.19); indeed, this is surely very common. In particular, it seems often to be thought that wrongdoing (either moral or legal, and under "normal" conditions, perhaps) suffices for culpability—something which of course I deny, and which is denied by (P3.19)—and it seems often to happen that one person punishes another simply for the reason that he believes the other to have done (either moral or legal) wrong. But this common occurrence does not undermine the claim that punishment is a form of strong censure; it simply highlights the fact that the punisher believes that culpability is incurred by wrongdoing.

As for (ii), sometimes punishment is taken to be a purely legal matter,[9] but this is clearly too restrictive; parents punish, headmasters punish, and so on. But there is undeniably something essentially official about punishment, as there is not about strong censure in general.[10] So, too, for reward. I shall not attempt here to spell out more precisely just when it is that commendation is tantamount to reward, or censure to punishment.

Liability. It would be a mistake to think of liability as simply worthiness of overt praise or blame, that is, worthiness of commendation or censure. Three factors spoil this neat analogy between appraisability and liability.

First, it is clear that the terms "desert" and "worthiness" serve a purpose in the context of *inward* praise and blame different from that which they serve in the context of *overt* praise and blame. In the former context, someone is deserving or worthy of such praise or blame just in case it is correct, or true to the facts, so to praise or blame him. And it is correct so to judge him just in case he has a credit or debit in his ledger. (See the opening paragraph of Chapter 3.) Here desert or worthiness is *not* a moral matter; rather, it is epistemological (a matter of true belief). But when it comes to being deserving or worthy of being acted on in some way, this clearly *is* a moral matter—just what sort of matter, we shall see in the next two sections.

Second, insofar as S's *weak* commendation or censure of S' does not require that S' be acted on by S in any way, or even that S intend to act on S' in any way, I am not sure that it makes sense to say that S' *deserves* to be weakly commended or censured by S (unless this is simply a misleading way of saying that S' nonmorally deserves the inward praise or blame which is implicit in S's weak commendation or censure of him). Of course, it remains true that, being an action, S's weak commendation or censure of S' is open to general judgments concerning its moral status as right or wrong, and so on; but it is unclear that it is open to any particular judgment of moral desert. Perhaps it is; perhaps one can morally deserve, *e.g.*, not to be stigmatized by weak censure, even when one is personally unaffected by it. At any rate, such doubts do not apply to S's *strong* commendation or censure of S', of course, since here S' is the recipient, or at least the intended recipient, of an action by S.

But this brings me to the third and perhaps most important point. Even if we do not think of moral liability as moral worthiness of weak commendation or censure, we cannot automatically think of it as moral worthiness of strong commendation or censure.[11] For notice part of what is involved in such worthiness; it is the worthiness of: being acted on in a certain way because one is believed to be worthy of having a certain experience. Strong commendation and censure already include acting on a judgment as to somebody's moral worthiness of something; thus to be worthy of such commendation or censure is to enjoy a sort of second-order worthiness. And I think that it would be a mistake to think of moral liability as essentially involving such second-order worthiness. In fact, it seems to me useful to distinguish two types of liability—which I shall call *basic* and *full*—the former of which requires only first-order worthiness, the second of which requires second-order worthiness. Somewhat more precisely:

(P5.5) S is basically liable for e if and only if S deserves, in virtue of having some relation to e, to experience pleasure or to suffer.

(Here "pleasure" and "suffer" are, as before, being used very broadly.)

(P5.6) S is fully liable for e if and only if S deserves, in virtue of having some relation to e, to be strongly commended or censured for e.

Full liability, then, constitutes a type of praise- or blameworthiness, but basic liability does not. Nevertheless, basic liability is closely tied to matters of praise and blame; for note that, given (P5.5) and clause (c) of each of (P5.3) and (P5.4), S strongly commends or censures S' for e only if S believes that S' is basically liable for e.[12]

Again, perhaps it is worth pointing out explicitly that, as before with "commend" and "censure," so here too I do not wish to pretend that (P5.5) and (P5.6) provide the only proper account of how to use the term "liable." On the contrary, this term may be, and has been, variously used, and I wish only to claim that the present use of it is a legitimate one.

Finally, a point that I have already made bears repeating. Each of (P5.1)–(P5.6) is only roughly stated. Each could be refined by attending to matters of time and degree; (P5.1)–(P5.4) could be refined by distinguishing direct, indirect, and other modes of commendation and censure; the uses of "because" in (P5.3) and (P5.4) could be clarified; (P5.3)–(P5.6) could be refined by distinguishing types of pleasure and suffering; and so on. But I shall not try here to undertake such refinement, for there is a more important task to which we must attend. This is a task upon which I shall now embark but which, for reasons that will emerge shortly, I do not know how to complete—the task of explaining just what is at issue when, as in (P5.3)–(P5.6), someone is said to *deserve* something.

5.2 Desert

Modes of desert. And so let us now look more closely into the matter of moral desert as it relates to appraisability, pleasure and suffering, commendation and censure. We should distinguish the following statements:

(P5.7)   The unlaudable do not deserve to experience pleasure.

("Unlaudable" is a barbarism; but it is useful.)

(P5.8)   The inculpable do not deserve to suffer.

(Instead of "inculpable," one might say "innocent." But "innocent" can also have other meanings, such as those of "having done no wrong," "not deserving to suffer (or be censured)," "deserving not to suffer (or be censured)," and so on. Analogously for "culpable" and "guilty.")

(P5.9)   The unlaudable deserve not to experience pleasure.

(P5.10)   The inculpable deserve not to suffer.

(P5.11)   The laudable do not deserve not to experience pleasure.

(P5.12)   The culpable do not deserve not to suffer.

(P5.13)   The laudable deserve to experience pleasure.

(P5.14)   The culpable deserve to suffer.

These are of course only roughly stated; but, so stated, their distinctness stands out. I shall now attend to their elucidation and refinement, but I must state here at the outset: I shall not provide a full analysis of (P5.7)–(P5.14), for I do not know how to do this.

To say that someone deserves to be acted on or to be treated in a certain way is to give an indication as to the type of grounds for this treatment. (Here I use "treatment" broadly, for any manner of acting on or toward someone; such use may be contrasted with that narrow use where "treatment" involves acting toward someone in a quasimedical way, handling him as a patient or, perhaps, as a subject of experimentation.) For, if someone is deserving of some treatment, this is, I think, always so in virtue of some *feature about himself*.[13] And, if someone is said to be not deserving of some treatment, this is always so in virtue of his lacking some feature. In the present context, of course, the features at issue just are those of laudability and culpability.[14] Thus, it seems that, in our effort to understand (P5.7)–(P5.14), we may take them, first, to be more precisely rendered as follows:

(P5.7′)   If S is not laudable for e, then S does not deserve (in virtue of being laudable for e) to experience pleasure.

(P5.8′)   If S is not culpable for e, then S does not deserve (in virtue of being culpable for e) to suffer.

(P5.9′)   If S is not laudable for e, then S deserves (in virtue of not being laudable for e) not to experience pleasure.

(P5.10′)   If S is not culpable for e, then S deserves (in virtue of not being culpable for e) not to suffer.

(P5.11′)   If S is laudable for e, then S does not deserve (in virtue of not being laudable for e) not to experience pleasure.

(P5.12′)   If S is culpable for e, then S does not deserve (in virtue of not being culpable for e) not to suffer.

(P5.13′)   If S is laudable for e, then S deserves (in virtue of being laudable for e) to experience pleasure.

(P5.14′)   If S is culpable for e, then S deserves (in virtue of being culpable for e) to suffer.

Given these more precise renditions of the original statements, we may now halve our labor by dismissing four of them—not as false, but as obviously true. These are (P5.7′), (P5.8′), (P5.11′), and (P5.12′)—the statements which concern themselves with "does not deserve" rather than "deserves." If someone has some feature F, then obviously he does not lack that feature; but then, of course, he cannot deserve anything in virtue of, or on the grounds of, his lacking that feature. Hence the statements just mentioned are true, and in a sense trivially so.

This is not to say that these statements are wholly insignificant, however. On the contrary, in relation to the remaining statements, (*i.e.*, (P5.9′), (P5.10′), (P5.13′), and (P5.14′), whose nontrivial truth-value will be a matter to which I shall return later), they have a dual significance. First, they serve to highlight the distinction between "not deserves" and "deserves not." It is surprising how often this crucial distinction has been overlooked.[15] But just compare: (P5.7′) with (P5.9′); (P5.8′) with (P5.10′); (P5.11′) with (P5.13′); and (P5.12′) with (P5.14′).[16] To be sure, everyday English is sloppy here. Just as "I don't want (to have) that" and "I don't believe that" are often substituted, respectively, for the more accurate "I want not to have that" and "I believe the negation of that," so "He doesn't deserve (to have) that" is often substituted for "He deserves not to have that." But such substitution is misleading. There is clearly a great difference between "not deserves" and "deserves not," between the absence of the desert of something and the presence of the desert of its "opposite." Of course, by no means all philosophers have failed to note this distinction. Consider, for example, the following remarks by Richard Wasserstrom:

> One argument goes something like this . . . [I]f we can understand so readily and clearly that it is unjust to punish the innocent, that can only be because it is also the case that it is just to punish the guilty. To understand that the innocent do not deserve punishment is also necessarily to understand that the guilty do deserve it. That justice requires the punishment of the guilty is but a different aspect of the widely accepted idea that justice forbids the punishment of the innocent.
>
> I find this a difficult claim to assess. I think there is something to it, but I am not certain how much. I do think that it is a fairly straightforward move from "It is unjust to punish the innocent," to "It is not unjust to punish the guilty," although I am uncertain of the strictness of the logical connection between the two expressions. But even if it is one of entailment, there seems to me to be an important difference in meaning between "It is not unjust to punish the guilty" and "It is just to punish the guilty."[17]

Secondly, once the distinction between "not deserves" and "deserves not" is made, it becomes apparent that there is a close relation between the "not deserves" statements and their *opposing* "deserves" statements, a relation that does *not* obtain between the "deserves not" statements and these same opposing "deserves" statements. I have in mind the relation between: (P5.7′) and (P5.13′); (P5.8′) and (P5.14′); (P5.11′) and (P5.9′); and (P5.12′) and (P5.10′). For simplicity, let us consider just the last of these pairs. Suppose that (P5.10′) is true; then (P5.12′), while trivially true, gains a certain significance in light of the truth of (P5.10′). For (P5.12′) serves to emphasize the absence of a condition (that of not being culpable for *e*), a condition which is recognized (in (P5.10′)) as being a genuine desert-basis. (This is what is at issue in the following statement by Wasserstrom: "I am clear that there is a special injustice in punishing the innocent such that *that* injustice is not present when the guilty are punished. In this sense, at least, it is true that it is not unjust to punish the guilty."[18]) Notice that this relation between (P5.12′) and (P5.10′) does *not* obtain between (P5.14′) and (P5.10′)—a fact that once again serves to point up the difference between (P5.12′) and (P5.14′).

(P5.7)–(P5.14) concern themselves with desert as it relates to pleasure and suffering. This is the stuff of basic, but not of full, liability. In connection with full liability there are again eight statements initially to be distinguished:

(P5.15)   The unlaudable do not deserve to be strongly commended.

(P5.16)   The inculpable do not deserve to be strongly censured.

(P5.17)   The unlaudable deserve not to be strongly commended.

(P5.18)   The inculpable deserve not to be strongly censured.

(P5.19)   The laudable do not deserve not to be strongly commended.

(P5.20)   The culpable do not deserve not to be strongly censured.

(P5.21)   The laudable deserve to be strongly commended.

(P5.22)   The culpable deserve to be strongly censured.

Once again, these may be more precisely rendered thus:

(P5.15′)   If S is not laudable for e, then S does not deserve (in virtue of being laudable for e) to be strongly commended for e.

(P5.16′)   If S is not culpable for e, then S does not deserve (in virtue of being culpable for e) to be strongly censured for e.

(P5.17′)   If S is not laudable for e, then S deserves (in virtue of not being laudable for e) not to be strongly commended for e.

(P5.18′)   If S is not culpable for e, then S deserves (in virtue of not being culpable for e) not to be strongly censured for e.

(P5.19′)   If S is laudable for e, then S does not deserve (in virtue of not being laudable for e) not to be strongly commended for e.

(P5.20′)   If S is culpable for e, then S does not deserve (in virtue of not being culpable for e) not to be strongly censured for e.

(P5.21′)   If S is laudable for e, then S deserves (in virtue of being laudable for e) to be strongly commended for e.

(P5.22′)   If S is culpable for e, then S deserves (in virtue of being culpable for e) to be strongly censured for e.

And, once again, four of these statements may be dismissed as trivially true, namely, (P5.15′), (P5.16′), (P5.19′), and (P5.20′), although these statements, like their trivially true predecessors, are not wholly insignificant.

There remain eight statements to try to render still more precise. All seem to me to have some plausibility; but only one strikes me as very plausible, and so let me start with it. The statement that I have in mind is (P5.18′). It concerns itself with censure, but makes no mention of the following dimensions of censure: time, degree, and source. Nor does it concern itself with time of desert. All four items, as we shall see, are important. In the case of (P5.18′) it seems that they are easily supplied. That is, (P5.18′) seems open to the following more precise rendition:

(P5.18″)   If S is not culpable for e, then, for any times T and T', any degree of censure d, and any source of censure s:
S deserves (in virtue of not being culpable for e) at T not to be strongly censured for e at T' to degree d by s.[19]

I think that (P5.18″) is true—as, I am sure, do many others—although I am not sure how best to argue for it, beyond pointing out that strong censure of the inculpable, by virtue of the stigmatization it involves, would appear to violate the respect that is their due.[20]

If (P5.18′) may be transformed into (P5.18″), are the other statements open to analogous transformations? In the case of (P5.17′), (P5.10′), and (P5.9′), I think that the answer is a qualified "Yes"; but in the case of (P5.13′), (P5.14′), (P5.21′), and (P5.22′), I think that the answer is "No." Let us look at the former group first.

Consider (P5.17′) and its transformation into (P5.17″) (a transformation that I shall not give explicitly, since it mirrors (P5.18″)). Perhaps an advocate of (P5.17′) means to advocate (P5.17″); I am not sure. Perhaps, indeed, (P5.17″) is true; again, I am not sure. Certainly, it is *not* open to the same sort of defense as that just given to (P5.18″). To strongly commend someone who is not laudable is to misrepresent him, but it is not to stigmatize him, and for this reason it is not clear to me that he *deserves* not to be so misrepresented. Perhaps he does; but, if so, it is not, I think, because of considerations of *respect*. It seems to me that I do not fail to respect S if I commend him when he is not laudable. This disparity between (P5.17″) and (P5.18″) will be mentioned again in the next subsection, where the relation between desert and rights is discussed.

Consider next (P5.10′) and its transformation (in which I explicitly include a variable ranging over *ways* of suffering):

(P5.10″)   If S is not culpable for e, then, for any times T and T', any way of suffering w, any degree of suffering d, and any source of suffering s:
S deserves (in virtue of not being culpable for e) at T not to be caused to suffer at T' in way w, to degree d, by s.

I am not sure whether an advocate of (P5.10′) means to advocate (P5.10″). Note that, while a source of censure is necessarily a person, a source of suffering is not. Nature cannot censure you, but it can make you suffer.[21] For this reason, (P5.10″) strikes me as false. It may be that I *do not deserve* to suffer at the "hands" of nature; but I do not think that I *deserve not* so to suffer. After all (to invoke the rationale given for (P5.18″)), nature cannot be disrespectful; only a person can be. Moreover, so as not to be committed to saying, for example, that a person innocent of spitting on the sidewalk when a youngster deserves not to be caused to suffer twenty years later by being denied employment, it seems that the advocate of (P5.10′) would do well to stipulate that the person who is not culpable for *e* deserves not to be caused to suffer *for e*. Of course, it is a delicate question just what is involved in making someone suffer *for* an event. Presumably, this has to do with somehow using that event as a pretext for causing the suffering, but it is unclear to me just what this amounts to. On one restrictive understanding, this would amount to strongly censuring, in a fully successful way, the person for the event; in such a case, of course, (P5.10″) would be modified in such a way as simply to become a strengthened version of (P5.18″). On a less restrictive understanding, making *S* suffer for *e* might be said to consist in using the occurrence of *e* as a reason for making *S* suffer, without grounding this in the claim that *S deserves* to suffer in virtue of the occurrence of *e*. So that a version of (P5.10′) may be drawn up which is less restrictive than (P5.18″), let us therefore modify (P5.10″) as follows, where this less restrictive understanding of "being caused to suffer for *e*" is presupposed:

(P5.10″a)   If *S* is not culpable for *e*, then, for any times *T* and *T*′, any way of suffering *w*, any degree of suffering *d*, and any agent *S*′:
S deserves (in virtue of not being culpable for *e*) at *T* not to be caused to suffer at *T*′ in way *w*, to degree *d*, by *S*′ for *e*.

This statement strikes me as true, so far as I understand it (and, again, it is the small addition of "for *e*" which creates the problems in understanding it), and perhaps it is what the advocate of (P5.10″) has in mind. I am not sure how best to defend it but, as before, an appeal to respect seems to me appropriate.

It might be thought that (P5.10″a) is too restrictive. If *S*′ makes *S* suffer but *not* for *e*, surely *S*′ has treated *S* in a way that *S* deserves not to be treated. I agree with this (I think, although perhaps we should add something about *S*′'s making *S* suffer "without due cause"—whatever that is supposed to amount to), but the point is strictly irrelevant. For *S*'s deserving not to be so treated by *S*′ is *not* grounded in his *inculpability* with respect to any event *e*, and so is not the sort of desert at issue in (P5.10′). That is, even someone who *is* culpable with respect to some event would appear to deserve not to be made to suffer by someone (without due cause, perhaps) in such a manner that the imposition of suffering is *not* for that event.

Finally, consider (P5.9′). This may be transformed into (P5.9″) in a manner which mirrors (P5.10″). I think that (P5.9″) is false, as (P5.10″) is. However, just as (P5.10″) was restricted in the form of (P5.10″a), so (P5.9″) may be restricted in the analogous form of (P5.9″a). But whether or not (P5.9″a) is true, I am not sure; my doubts here are the same as those which I had concerning both (P5.17″) and (P5.10″a).

Let us now turn to those transformations which I have said *cannot* be given along the same lines, or even close to the same lines, as (P5.18″). Consider (P5.14′). Presumably, someone who advocates acceptance of this statement is *not* advocating that we accept the following:

(P5.14″)   If S is culpable for e, then, for any times T and T', any way of suffering w, any degree of suffering d, and any source of suffering s:

S deserves (in virtue of being culpable for e) at T to be caused to suffer at T' in way w, to degree d, by s.

(P5.14″) is wildly implausible. More to the point, it is surely much stronger than anything that an advocate of (P5.14′) wishes to claim. Some restrictions are in order. But what restrictions? This is an extremely important question, I think, and one to which I shall return in the next section. Here we should simply note that, while the restriction of (P5.10″) in terms of (P5.10″a) is fairly straightforward, no such easy remedy presents itself with respect to (P5.14′). The same holds true of (P5.13′), (P5.21′), and (P5.22′). And so the question remains: just what is it that an advocate of these statements is advocating?

Desert and rights. I have not attempted a full analysis of any of (P5.7′)–(P5.22′), nor shall I attempt one. But one way to try to elucidate these statements is to compare and contrast them with analogous statements concerning rights. Here I shall concern myself with (P5.7′)–(P5.14′)—in fact, just with those among them which are not trivially true; what I say about them can be applied, *mutatis mutandis,* to (P5.15′)–(P5.22′).

Like desert, rights too are best understood in terms of moral considerations grounded in personal features. Feinberg warns us against thinking of moral desert in terms of moral rights; he insists that there is a distinction to be drawn between that of which a person is worthy or deserving and that to which a person is entitled or has a right.[22] The example is given of a president-elect who is entitled to, but does not deserve, the presidency; the runner-up deserves it, for he is better qualified.[23] The force of this example is unclear to me. Of course, it must be accepted that the president-elect has a right to the presidency; and this right is moral (for there is an institutional promise to the effect that the president-elect will gain the presidency). And it would be wrong to think that such entitlement confers desert. But all that follows from this is that a person may have a moral right to something without morally deserving that thing; it does not follow that a person may morally deserve something without having a moral right to it. It might, of course, be that the runner-up deserves the presidency but has no moral right to it; but does he *morally* deserve it? I think not. Just as some rights are nonmoral, so is some desert, and this seems to me to be a case of nonmoral desert only. To give someone what he deserves is to give him his due. When a person deserves something, he has somehow earned it; he has it coming.[24] Now, from what we might call a presidential point of view, the runner-up may have earned the presidency (by virtue of his superior qualifications). But I doubt whether we should say that *morally* he has it coming. If he does not, then, although this case shows us that moral entitlement does not confer moral desert, it does not show us that moral desert does not confer moral entitlement.

Nevertheless, it must be admitted that there is sometimes something infelicitous in inferring statements about moral rights from statements about moral desert. Consider the following:

(P5.9*)   If *S* is not laudable for *e*, then *S* has a right (in virtue of not being laudable for *e*) not to experience pleasure.

(P5.10*)   If *S* is not culpable for *e*, then *S* has a right (in virtue of not being culpable for *e*) not to suffer.

(P5.13*)   If *S* is laudable for *e*, then *S* has a right (in virtue of being laudable for *e*) to experience pleasure.

(P5.14*)   If *S* is culpable for *e*, then *S* has a right (in virtue of being culpable for *e*) to suffer.

Two types of formal oddity attach to these statements. One type is fairly easily remedied, at least in one instance; the other, is not.

The first type of oddity is this. Rights (of the sort at issue here, namely, claim-rights) are rights held by someone *against someone else*. But there is no specification in any of the four foregoing statements of any person against whom *S* holds his right. Such specification is needed, since the thing to which *S* is said to have a right can be gained or lost by means other than the actions of other agents. This is, however, just the same point, in somewhat different guise, that was raised earlier when discussing (P5.10″). The remedy applied then may be applied now. That is, (P5.10*) may be better rendered thus:

(P5.10*a)   If *S* is not culpable for *e*, then *S* has a right (in virtue of not being culpable for *e*) against everyone not to be made by them to suffer for *e*.

It seems to me that (P5.10′) implies (P5.10*a) and that noting this fact helps us to understand (P5.10′).

But can (P5.13*) be similarly treated? Not quite, and perhaps not at all.

Earlier, doubts were registered about what the exact content of (P5.13′) is supposed to be, and these doubts may be reapplied to (P5.13*). To use terminology that is rough but widespread and perhaps useful in the present context: considerations of desert are, in part, considerations of what ought to *be,* while considerations of rights are considerations of what someone ought to *do.*[25] Now, in the case of the relation between (P5.10′) and (P5.10*), we have what is, so to speak, an implication by default of an ought-to-do by an ought-to-be; that is, the ought-to-be imposes an ought-(not-)to-do on *everyone.* But (P5.13′) does not have any such global implication (surely *S* does not have, in virtue of being laudable for *e,* a right against *everyone* that he be made to experience pleasure), and it is unclear to me whether it has any more restricted implication concerning rights. (Could we say this: *S* has, in virtue of being laudable for *e,* a right against *everyone in a position to make him experience pleasure* that he be made to experience pleasure? This, too, would strike many as far too strong a claim.)

It might at first appear that (P5.9*) is no more problematic than (P5.10*), while (P5.14*) is just as problematic as (P5.13*). But in fact a second type of formal oddity attaches to both (P5.9*) and (P5.14*). Normally, to say that someone has a right to something is in part to say that that thing is or would be in fact, or is or would be regarded by the person in question to be, beneficial in some way to that person.[26] But, *pace* Hegel and some others, being made to suffer, or not being made to experience pleasure, seem to me not essentially to be something of this sort—a strange right, one so readily waived![27] (This is not to say that Hegel may not have had a proper point to make in saying that we sometimes have a right to be punished; only that this is not the proper way to express this point. I shall return to this issue later.) I do not mean by this that one cannot truthfully claim that *S* deserves something that is not beneficial to him, or deserves not to have something that is beneficial to him. All that I mean is that, if there is such desert, it is not normally a matter of right.

Overall justification. Desert is a *prima facie* matter. To say that someone morally deserves a certain treatment is in part to say that there is a moral consideration in favor of his being so treated. (This is so, even if desert in some cases imposes no ought-to-do; for, even where it fails to impose an *ought*-to-do, it nonetheless provides a *good-reason*-to-do.) But it is not to say that there is a *conclusive* moral consideration in favor of his being so treated. Desert constitutes just *one* moral consideration, and the force of its presence or absence can in principle be overridden by other considerations.[28]

This obvious truth is all too often overlooked. What follows from it, though, is very important. For what follows is this: the *desert* of a certain form of treatment is not only not a *sufficient* condition for the *overall justification* of the treatment, it is also not a *necessary* condition for such justification. For example, some thug may deserve punishment, and yet his punishment may be overall unjustified since to administer it would trigger a riot. Or again, some inculpable person (an insane person, perhaps) may not deserve (indeed, deserve not) to be punished (or made to suffer as if punished), and yet his punishment may be overall justified since not to administer it would pose grave danger to the community.[29] (Perhaps the consideration concerning danger must be very weighty in order to override the consideration of desert; but that is another matter, and one on which I would not care to speculate at this point.[30]) Indeed, once it is recognized that desert constitutes just one moral consideration, it becomes clear that it may also clash with another consideration *of desert*. In principle, at least, there seems to be nothing to preclude the possibility of an agent's deserving some treatment in virtue of his having some feature F and also deserving *not* to have this same treatment in virtue of his having some other feature G. For example, perhaps (P5.14), suitably qualified, is true; but perhaps (P5.10) is also true (in the form of (P5.10″a), as I have suggested); and, as we noted in Chapter 3, one can be both culpable and inculpable (even with respect to the same event). Or it could be, I suppose (although I believe this to be false), that a vicious criminal deserves, in virtue of his reprehensibility, to be made to suffer, even though he is inculpable and (given (P5.10)) thereby also deserves not to be made to suffer.[31] Or it might be true (but again I believe otherwise) that someone who has done wrong—who is *causally* responsible, say, for some harm—deserves to be made to suffer, even though he is inculpable. Or, again, if (P5.22) is true, a person will deserve to be censured because he is culpable; but, if there is no provision for ensuring that censure is properly administered, so that any censure that the person would receive would be in some way (unduly) disrespectful to him, then he will also deserve, for this reason, not to be censured. Or, somewhat differently, one person S may deserve something x while also another person S' deserves x, and yet x is indivisible. Here, clearly, either S or S' will fail to get what he deserves, and yet it seems plausible to say that a person in the position to grant x to either S or S' can do what is overall right, perhaps even overall obligatory, in failing to grant x to one or the other.[32] And so on and so forth.

It might, of course, happen on occasion that S's deserving to be treated in such-and-such a way by S' is the most important moral consideration that is pertinent, and thus that S' ought, all things considered, so to treat S. This might be true due to other considerations having some, but less, force than this consideration of desert; or it might be true (as some absolutist moral theories would have it) due to this consideration of desert preempting all conflicting considerations, such that the latter, while normally having some force, in the present instance have no force at all. But this seems to me quite unlikely, especially in the area of punishment. Usually, I would think, if it is justifiable to punish someone, then that person deserves the punishment, or at least does not deserve not to receive it; but even if he deserves it, this consideration will be secondary to considerations concerning vindication of the law and the preservation of civil society, and will constitute more the absence of a stumbling-block to justification (the stumbling-block being that of deserving not to be so punished) rather than the presence of a major factor in such justification.[33] At any rate, we may safely say that desert *in general* affords only a partial, and not an overall, justification for acting in a certain way. In light of this we can see that, even if one accepts (P5.14) or (P5.22), one is *not* committed to accepting Kant's celebrated, and celebratedly extreme, claim that, should a civil society resolve to dissolve itself, the last murderer lying in prison ought nevertheless to be executed before the dissolution takes place, so that everyone "may realize the desert of his deeds."[34]

Thus, if utility has anything to do with what makes an act overall right or wrong (as I believe it does), it is clearly morally appropriate on occasion to raise the question as to whether it would be useful to *hold* someone responsible for a certain deed (that is, to commend, censure, reward, or punish him for it). But, this granted, it cannot be too strongly emphasized that this question is quite distinct from the question as to whether the person concerned *is* responsible for the deed. Very often these questions have been conflated—most often, by claiming that someone is responsible just in case his behavior is modifiable by his being held responsible—and this seems to me a terrible confusion.[35]

5.3 Retributivism

Two types of retributivism. The term "retributivism" has been very widely and variously used. I shall not undertake a survey of its uses here,[36] but it should be noted that the term has been used to characterize many radically different theories—theories of annulment (punishment somehow negates a wrongdoing), of placation (punishment placates some deity), of blood-lust (punishment satisfies the thirst for vengeance), and other theories too. Since I do not wish to advocate—indeed, even to discuss— any such theory, I would be quite happy to drop the term "retributivism" entirely. Unfortunately, this term has also traditionally been used to characterize theories concerning the *desert* of punishment, and so, saddled with this tradition, I reluctantly acknowledge that the foregoing, and the ensuing, discussion have to do with retributivism, in one common sense of the term.

Even where we confine our attention to matters of desert, however, we may distinguish between two types of retributivism, which I shall call *logical* and *moral*. I admit to being a logical retributivist. A logical retributivist is one who believes that strong commendation and censure are, *by definition,* predicated on ascriptions of desert—more precisely, on ascriptions of basic liability.[37] My advocacy of (P5.3) and (P5.4) confirms me as a logical retributivist. In my opinion, there can be no quarrel with this; commendation and censure, reward and punishment, just are intended as ways of giving someone "his due," of giving him "what he has coming to him."[38] (As noted in Section 5.1, it seems often to be believed—falsely, in my opinion—that wrongdoing suffices for culpability and thus that punishment is "due" someone simply in virtue of that person's doing wrong.) This is *not* to say that it is impossible to punish the innocent, as some contend,[39] but it is to say that it is impossible to punish someone that one regards as innocent, *i.e.,* inculpable.[40] Of course, to say this is *not* to say that it is impossible to inflict suffering on someone that one regards as innocent.

Moral retributivism is different. It consists in the claim that, if *S* is appraisable for *e,* then *S* is liable for *e.* It cannot be too strongly emphasized that this thesis of moral retributivism is far from trivial. It concerns two quite distinct species of moral responsibility and asserts that there is a significant connection between them. The truth of the claim, if it is true, is far from obvious and is, or would be, most important.[41] For it is simply not analytic that, for example, the culpable deserve to suffer or be censured, and so we *must* accept at least the conceptual possibility that a person be inwardly blameworthy to a high degree but overtly blameworthy to no degree at all. Moreover, it should be noted that the thesis of moral retributivism has, conceptually at least, *nothing* to do with vengeance. While I am sure that it is true that some people are prone to rationalize their lust for vengeance by disguising it in terms of the thesis (witness the frequent cries of victims, or their next of kin, for "justice"), the fact remains that the thesis itself concerns vengeance not at all.[42]

Two species of moral retributivists may in fact be distinguished: those who concern themselves with basic liability (and thus claim (P5.13) and (P5.14) to be true), and those who concern themselves with full liability (and thus claim (P5.21) and (P5.22) to be true). A logical retributivist, such as myself, need *not* be a moral retributivist. For all I have said so far, (P5.13), (P5.14), (P5.21), and (P5.22) may be false; nothing that I have said—including my acceptance of (P5.3) and (P5.4)—commits me to accepting any of these four statements.

Of course, the interesting question here is: are any of these four statements true? I know that, in my everyday judgments, I often rely on them, or something like them; and I am sure that many others do also.

But I do not know how best to defend such reliance. Indeed, it seems to me that, on inspection, such reliance may well be mistaken, and what I want to do here is to discuss some of the reasons why I think that it may be so. For most of this section I shall concern myself with basic liability, and thus with (P5.13) and (P5.14); in fact, I shall concern myself explicitly only with (P5.14), the truth-value of which is a practically more pressing matter than that of (P5.13). What I shall say about (P5.14) can, I think, be applied, *mutatis mutandis,* to (P5.13)—despite the disparity noted earlier between (P5.13*) and (P5.14*). At times, however, I shall have occasion also to mention full liability, and thus to discuss (P5.22).

The barrier to accepting (P5.14) which concerns me is the conceptual one noted earlier: what exactly is it that would be thus accepted? (P5.14) may be transformed into (P5.14′), we noted, but (P5.14′) is *not* to be transformed into (P5.14″). Restrictions are called for, in terms of time of desert, time of suffering, way of suffering, source of suffering, and degree of suffering. But *what* restrictions? If no clear answer to this question is forthcoming, then (P5.14′) is surely suspect. I propose now to look into this matter piecemeal.

Time of desert and time of suffering. It might seem reasonable to say that, if S deserves to suffer for e because he is culpable for e, then the times at which S deserves this are those times at which he is so culpable. But in fact this is not reasonable. In Section 3.1, it was noted that appraisability is in fact not essentially retrospective, even if ascriptions of appraisability are in fact typically so, and that, if S is culpable for e, then he is culpable for it at all times after its occurrence, and quite possibly at all other times also. But, insofar as liability is grounded in appraisability, are we therefore constrained to say that, if S is culpable for e, then he is liable for it at all times after its occurrence, and quite possibly at all other times also? Surely this would be an outrageous thing to say; for surely there is a *limit to the degree of suffering* which S deserves in virtue of being culpable for e—a matter that I shall take up shortly. If S has passed this limit, he no longer deserves to suffer.

This consideration suggests the following modification to the foregoing suggestion: if S deserves to suffer for e because he is culpable for e, then S deserves at all times, at which he is so culpable, so to suffer, up until he has reached the appropriate limit concerning degree of suffering. I find this modification quite plausible, although two issues cause me to hesitate to accept it.

The first issue is this. Is it possible, in general, for S at T to morally deserve something without being alive at T?[43] If not, then the formula just given must be modified still further, since there is, as far as I can see, no need for S to be alive in order for it to be true that there is a debit in his ledger.

The second issue concerns personal identity. If S is distinct from S', and S is culpable for e but S' is not, then, even if S deserves to suffer for e because of *his* culpability, S' does not deserve to suffer for e because of any culpability for e on his part. This seems clearly true, where S is *wholly* distinct from S'. But can S be distinct, but not wholly distinct, from S'? That is, can there be *degrees* of personal identity? If so, how does this affect the alleged moral desert to suffer? For example, am I now wholly identical with "myself" when a youth? If not, do I now deserve to suffer for those culpable misdeeds performed by me then for which I have yet to suffer? If so, to what extent? Or again, does a Nazi war criminal still, forty years after his crimes, deserve to suffer for them?[44] Or, finally, does an insane person deserve to suffer for misdeeds culpably performed when sane?[45]

I do not know how to answer these questions. If personal identity comes in degrees, and if these (and other such) cases are cases where someone is not wholly, and is perhaps not even partially, identical with his former self, then there does seem to be some plausibility to the claim that, in such cases, the agent is not wholly, and is perhaps not even partially, liable for the misdeed in question.[46] But I do not know whether personal identity comes in degrees, and I certainly do not propose to investigate this issue here.

Of course, it is open to someone to claim this: I am wholly identical with myself as a youth, but I *still* do not now deserve to suffer for my culpable misdeeds then (at least, not to the extent that I deserved to do so then), even though I have not yet suffered for them; so too for the Nazi war criminal; so too for the insane person. But I am not at all sure *why* someone would want to say this. One reason that might be proffered is this: the war criminal and I have since turned over entirely new leaves, and the insane person no longer "has a leaf" at all, and it would be pure vindictiveness, or blood-lust, or whatever, now to dredge up the past; making us suffer now would be morally inappropriate to our present moral state, no matter how appropriate it would earlier have been to our then moral state. There seems to me something attractive about this reply, to which there are, I think, three basic responses.

The first response is to take the reply seriously. Desert of suffering for past deeds is a function not just of culpability for those past deeds but of present culpability or nonculpability for those past deeds. What might this mean? Perhaps we can invoke the concept of *situational culpability* here (see (P4.36)) and say: if the war criminal, the insane person, and I no longer have our old leaves, we remain culpable for our previous misdeeds, but we are not in addition situationally culpable for them.[47] Of course, for this response to have any pertinence, it must in addition be contended that desert of suffering is a function of situational as well as of nonsituational culpability. This is a bold contention, insofar as it seems that hardly anyone has entertained, let alone accepted, it. Nonetheless, if there is such a thing as situational culpability, then substantial culpability is surely a function of it—indeed, *solely* a function of it (see the final paragraph of Chapter 4)—and so the contention (insofar as the notion of situational culpability has plausibility) would seem to have at least as much plausibility as the contention that desert of suffering is a function of nonsituational culpability.

The second response is to agree that there is reason to make the war criminal, the insane person, and me suffer less now, but this is not a reason based on considerations of desert. We still *deserve* to suffer as much as we always did, but there are now certain "independent mitigating factors."[48]

The third response is to reject the reply.

It is not clear to me which response is the best. The first response, of course, is acceptable only if there is such a thing as situational culpability (about which I expressed my doubts in Section 4.11). The third response strikes me as unduly harsh. Perhaps the second response is best, from the point of view of the advocate of (P5.14′). But the fact that there is a question as to which response is best shows that there is a question as to just how (P5.14′) is to be understood.

Suppose, however, that this issue concerning time of desert has been resolved. There remains a question as to when it is that a person, who (at some time) deserves to suffer, is to suffer. It might seem that there is no problem with asserting the following in this regard: if S deserves at T to suffer, then he deserves at T to suffer at T. But in fact this seems too strong; for it implies that, if S deserves at T_1 to suffer, does not suffer then but does suffer at some later time T_2, then some moral consideration has been flouted. More plausible, it seems to me, is the claim that, if S deserves at T to suffer, then he deserves at T to suffer at some time T'. But this claim is put too roughly, being open to two interpretations. I do not mean by this claim that, if S deserves at T to suffer, then (i) there is some time T' such that S deserves at T to suffer at T'; rather, I mean (to put it somewhat awkwardly) that, if S deserves at T to suffer, then (ii) he deserves at T that there be a time T' such that he suffers at T'. Statement (ii) is clearly fairly weak. I think that it can be plausibly strengthened, without going as far as statement (i), by modifying it thus: (ii′) S deserves (in virtue of being culpable for e) at T that there be a time T' such that he suffers at T', and there is no time T' (at which it is true that S is culpable for e) such that S deserves (in virtue of being culpable for e) at T not to suffer at T'.

In this connection, it should be noted that, while liability (like appraisability) is not in fact essentially retrospective, there is nevertheless in all, or almost all, cases a very good reason (one, however, not based on considerations of desert grounded in culpability) not to censure anyone, or to make anyone suffer, for some event e, unless e has already occurred. The reason for this is that, while it may be true at or before e's occurrence that S is appraisable for e, I take it that no one is ever in a position to judge, and so to act on the judgment, that S is appraisable for e, until after e has occurred. In saying this, I leave aside questions of God and omniscience; but also, in saying this, I am not denying the possibility of knowledge of any proposition about the future, but simply denying the possibility of our knowing in advance that propositions about appraisability are true. This seems reasonable to me, although I accept that it is debatable; but I shall not debate it here.

Way of suffering and source of suffering. Suppose that it has been determined that S deserves (in virtue of being culpable for e) at T to suffer at T' (where this rough formula is understood along the lines just mentioned). In what *way* does he deserve to suffer?

The dictum, "An eye for an eye, a tooth for a tooth" suggests this: if S deserves (in virtue of being culpable for e) to suffer, then he deserves to suffer in just that way in which he made another suffer. This position is obviously absurd. First, it might be impossible to make S suffer in just that way in which he made another suffer. (What is one to do with an offender, caught for the third time, who has a penchant for cutting off other people's hands?[49]) Secondly, even if this is not impossible, the offender may not suffer to the same degree as the person caused to suffer. (What if a sadist is also a masochist?[50]) But, thirdly, the greatest problem with this view is simply that a culpable person need not have caused suffering, nor even have intended or foreseen doing so.

This third problem also shows that the common claim that culpability grounds the obligation to make reparation (a matter of *prospective* responsibility) is problematic. For a culpable person may have done nothing which requires reparation. What, however, if a culpable person *has* done something which requires reparation? Does he *then* have an obligation to make reparation? Perhaps he does, but I am inclined to think that this is still not an exceptionless truth. What does seem plausible is (roughly) this: if someone who is innocent (*i.e.* (here), deserves not to be harmed) is harmed, then that person deserves reparation; a culpable person deserves to suffer; if a culpable person harms such an innocent person, then often (but not necessarily) the best way to try to ensure that each receives what he deserves is to require that the former compensate the latter. (Perhaps, in such a case as this, it is even true to say that the former has an *obligation* to make reparation to the latter; but, even if so, this is still only an obligation which often, but not necessarily, arises.)

Presumably (recalling what was said concerning time of suffering) we may reject this: if S deserves to suffer, then (i) there is some way of suffering w such that he deserves to suffer in way w; while we may accept this: if S deserves to suffer, then (ii) he deserves that there be a way of suffering w such that he suffers in way w. But can we strengthen (ii) thus: (ii') S deserves (in virtue of being culpable for e) that there be a way of suffering w such that he suffers in way w, *and* there is no way of suffering w such that S deserves (in virtue of being culpable for e) not to suffer in way w (consistent, of course, with not exceeding the appropriate *degree* of suffering)? I am not sure; I shall return to this in a moment.

Notice, first, that similar positions may be distinguished concerning the source of suffering, as follows. If S deserves to suffer, then: (i) there is some source of suffering s such that he deserves to be made to suffer by $s;$ (ii) he deserves that there be some source of suffering s such that he is made to suffer by $s;$ and (ii') he deserves (in virtue of being culpable for e) that there be some source of suffering s such that he is made to suffer by s, *and* there is no source of suffering s such that he deserves (in virtue of being culpable for e) not to be made to suffer by s.

There is reason to think that some advocates of (P5.14') would reject (ii') in the cases of way of suffering and source of suffering, whereas they would not in the case of time of suffering. Why? They claim that there must be limits to the ways in which, and the sources by which, suffering may be caused; that the suffering that is imposed be imposed *for* the event for which the agent is culpable. In brief, some would claim that the sort of modification made to (P5.10″) to produce (P5.10″a) be applied also to (P5.14').

But why accept such a modification to (P5.14')? One answer that might be given is this. "Not all suffering that a person undergoes can be viewed as going some way toward meeting what demands there are (if any) that justice has with respect to his suffering. For, if this were so, then all sorts of natural (and, perhaps, not-so-natural but still non-penal) disasters would serve justice; worse, there could be 'pre-emptive suffering' which would permit a person, who has suffered in the past, to do culpable wrong without incurring any further liability. Clearly, then, not just any form or way of suffering will satisfy the demands of justice."[51] But *is* this so clear? Not to me. First, we often do say that a person "has suffered [or even: has been punished] enough already" when, as a result of some culpable misdeed of his, some misfortune has befallen him prior to any official censure.[52] It is hard to see what "enough" can mean here, if not that the demands of justice have been satisfied. Secondly, while there clearly is good reason to try to ensure that suffering prior to an offense not be viewed as "pre-emptive," that is, to ensure that it not be viewed as some sort of license to do wrong, this fact is consistent with saying that any additional suffering meted out *after* the wrongdoing is not *deserved*.[53] Thirdly, what I have just said is consistent with what I said in the last section when rejecting (P5.10″) in favor of (P5.10″a), namely, that a person can at best be said *not to deserve* to suffer at the "hands" of nature, rather than *to deserve not* so to suffer. For the view that nonpenal suffering can meet the demands of justice requires only that such suffering not be otherwise deserved, and not that the person otherwise deserve that it not occur. Now, none of this is to say that this view is correct; it is only to say that it is plausible. Frankly, I do not pretend to know whether the view is true or false or how best to argue for or against it. My aim here is simply to point out that how one interprets (P5.14') depends in part on what its advocate's position is on this matter.

Some advocates of (P5.14') appear nonetheless to urge an even more restrictive rendition of that formula. They appear to claim that the suffering which is deserved by the culpable must be not only in the form of suffering *for* the event for which they are culpable, but also be meted in such a manner that there is an implicit recognition that it is *deserved* because of the agent's culpability. In short, they appear to claim that deserved suffering must be censure-induced, that (P5.14') is true only insofar as (P5.22') is true.[54] One reason that might be given for this claim is this: "To say that (P5.14') is true, but that (P5.22') is not, is to sanction vigilantism." But this is unpersuasive. If (P5.14') were true but (P5.22') not, all that would follow is that someone who deserves to suffer because culpable does not *deserve* to be censured. It does not follow from this that just anyone may, *all things considered,* cause the suffering that is deserved, in any way that he chooses, *even if* this ranks as making the culpable person suffer *for* the event for which he is culpable. On the contrary, there are obviously very good reasons for ensuring that suffering that is brought about is done so by persons in a position of authority and in certain ways that have been authorized.[55] Indeed, it might be that any suffering that is thus brought about ought, all things considered, to be brought about in the form of censure. But none of this implies that the culpable person *deserves,* simply in virtue of being culpable, to be made to suffer by way of being censured.

Another reason to claim that (P5.14') is true only insofar as (P5.22') is true can be derived from one interpretation of Hegel's view of punishment. According to this interpretation, only if the culpable are censured does the suffering that is inflicted on them not violate the respect that is due them as free and rational agents (a status which, being culpable, they necessarily enjoy). Thus the culpable, on this view, have a "right to censure," in the sense that they have a *conditional* right to be censured, namely, a right to be censured *if* they are made to suffer at all.[56] Perhaps, too, on this view the right extends to being censured by those in a position to make a judicious assessment of culpability—I am not sure.

The question that now arises is of course this: why does making a culpable person suffer other than by means of censure fail to show him the respect that is his due, while making him suffer by means of censure does not? Perhaps there is a good answer to this question; I would not care to speculate. (Of course, there may well be—indeed, surely are—disrespectful ways to treat a person, even a person who deserves to suffer.[57] But this does not take us very far; for it does not allow us to infer that the *only* respectful way to cause such a person to suffer is to censure him.)

Let me, finally, give a reason for thinking that it is *not* the case that, insofar as a culpable person deserves to be made to suffer, this is so because he *deserves* to be *strongly censured* for the event for which he is culpable. The reason is this. If the claim were true, then, if (P5.4) is to be accepted as a (rough) analysis of what it is for S to strongly censure S', the belief (mentioned in clause (c) of (P5.4)) which S has with respect to S'''s deserts must (on pain of circularity) be false or, at best, incomplete. Thus the claim at issue here would imply that, if S' is culpable for e and deserves to be made to suffer, then he *deserves* to be treated by someone, S, who has (by definition) a false or incomplete belief with respect to his deserts. It seems to me that an advocate of (P5.14') should reject this implication and thus reject (P5.22').[58]

Degree of suffering. So far we have met only with what I would call relatively minor stumbling-blocks in the interpretation, and so to the eventual acceptance, of (P5.14'). But now we meet with a major one, one which is quite possibly insurmountable.

A common, and certainly intuitively appealing, claim is that "the punishment should fit the crime," or, more generally, that the suffering of a culpable person should "fit" his culpability. No doubt, it is this intuition which underlies the misguided dictum, "An eye for an eye." Of course, just what is supposed to "fit" what is unclear, but I take it that at least the following is often implied: there should be a match, a proportion, between degree of suffering and degree of culpability. Moreover, I take it that this is something which the advocate of (P5.14') wishes to advocate, since, as noted earlier, he would (quite correctly) declare (P5.14'') false, rejecting it as a proper interpretation of his claim.

Now, it is a commonplace that there are fundamental conceptual, and not just practical, problems in determining such a match or proportion. It is not that there are difficulties in assessing degree of suffering; of course there are, but this is beside the present point.[59] Nor is it that there are difficulties in assessing degree of culpability; of course there are, but again this is beside the present point (except for one instance to be mentioned shortly). The problem is simply this: how, even in principle, are we to *match* culpability to some degree x with suffering to some degree y? I do not know how to begin to answer this question.[60] Some have claimed that degree of suffering should be determined by sounding out popular opinion, so that a great degree of culpability is matched with what is *generally felt* to be a great degree of suffering, and so on.[61]

Perhaps there is no better guideline than this, but surely it can, in principle, mislead. After all, popular opinion is not infallible. In addition, one should ask: on what basis is popular opinion formed, if not on some proposed solution to the very puzzle with which we began? If such a solution is forthcoming, why not appeal directly to it, rather than to some opinion formed on the basis of it? And if such a solution is not forthcoming, then the popular opinion in question would appear baseless; so why heed it?

Of course, a proponent of (P5.14′) can at least say this: the greater the degree of culpability, the greater the degree of suffering deserved, and the less the degree of the former, the less the degree of the latter. But without a solution to the problem of how to match at least one specific degree of culpability to some specific degree of suffering, this does not take us very far; and even if we had one such specific match, our ranking of degrees of culpability and degrees of suffering would then be correlated only ordinally, so that further specific cardinal cross-matches would not automatically drop out of the original specific cross-match.[62]

This problem becomes more acute when it is recognized (as it was in Section 3.3) that one can be multiply appraisable for one and the same event. Indeed, it becomes even more acute still when it is recognized (as it was in Section 3.1) that the degree to which someone is culpable may not be determinate; that there can be, and often is, a genuine objective indeterminacy concerning a person's moral worth. How is one to match suffering to *that?* I have simply nothing illuminating to contribute here.[63]

The status of retributivism. The remarks made in the last subsection might suggest that (P5.14) (and (P5.13)) and (P5.22) (and (P5.21)) are hopelessly vague and, for this reason, to be rejected, while the other statements among (P5.7)–(P5.22), despite the initial appearance of similarity of form, are not hopelessly vague and not to be rejected for that reason. (Notice that (P5.13) and (P5.21) *are* affected by the foregoing considerations. If the notion of desert of suffering, censure, or punishment is problematic, so too is the notion of desert of pleasure, commendation, or reward. Are those who are prepared to reject the former notion just as prepared to reject the latter? They should be.[64]) Or, at least, my remarks might suggest that, even if (P5.14) and (P5.22) are not hopelessly vague, I have found no reason to believe otherwise and *I,* for one, should reject them for that reason. But I am not yet prepared to do this. The reason is that the problem just noted with (P5.14) and (P5.22) is not confined to them but, as it were, spills over to (P5.10) and (P5.12) (in the area of basic liability) and to (P5.18) and (P5.20) (in the area of full liability)—all of which I have said seem acceptable (when properly interpreted); indeed, two of which I have said are trivially true. Let me try to explain why.

Consider (P5.10) and (P5.12). I have said that (P5.10) (when understood in terms of (P5.10″a)) seems true to me; and I am sure that many accept it. But if someone who is not culpable to any degree for *e* deserves, *in virtue of this inculpability*, not to be made to suffer to any degree for *e*, then someone who *is* culpable to some degree for *e* cannot deserve, *for this same reason*, not to be made to suffer to any degree for *e*. This is just the trivial truth involved in (P5.12). And yet I am sure that those who accept (P5.10) would also want to claim that the culpable deserve, in virtue of their being culpable to some degree *x* (and so, of their not being culpable to a degree greater than *x),* not to be made to suffer to an "excessive" degree. Of course, the advocate of (P5.10) (and its trivial concomitant, (P5.12)) is not logically committed to accepting this, but I think that in spirit he is. So *he* does not avoid the problem of matching degree of suffering to degree of culpability, either; for he too must give an account of what amounts to an "excessive" degree of suffering.[65] Now, the advocate of (P5.10) might of course respond to this challenge by claiming that *any* degree of suffering is *always* excessive, and thereby seek to provide an easy solution to our puzzle; but such a claim seems implausible, insofar as it implies that the wholly inculpable and the culpable-to-degree-*x* (where *x* is greater than zero) are equally deserving with respect to being made to suffer. No other solution seems easy, however; for every other solution requires a genuine attempt to match degree of suffering to degree of culpability (and we are of course assuming that there can be a nonzero degree of culpability). Similar remarks pertain to (P5.18) (and its trivial concomitant, (P5.20)).

Thus, while moral retributivism is in a sorry plight, so too is the view—which we might call *moral protectionism*—according to which (P5.10) and/or (P5.18) is true. But moral protectionism seems to me to be a view which has strong appeal; in particular, it appeals to many who would wish to reject moral retributivism. Now, there may be good, independent reason to reject moral retributivism while accepting moral protectionism, but the problem with vagueness—in particular, the problem with matching degree of suffering to degree of culpability—is not, I think, such a reason.[66]

It is also worth noting that the foregoing problem with evaluating moral retributivism also affects our evaluation of logical retributivism. If it is unclear what it really means to say that someone deserves suffering or censure, then this affects both species of retributivism equally. For, if logical retributivism is true, then, given this unclarity, it is also not clear what is really involved in the strong commendation or censure, and thus in the reward or punishment, of someone. (It is clause (c) of each of (P5.3) and (P5.4) that is the crux of the problem here.) Thus, not only must we wonder whether or not punishment is *deserved,* we must wonder what punishment *is.*

At this point I shall cease my evaluation of (P5.7)–(P5.22). I have deliberately kept to the level of a structural analysis of these statements; while venturing opinions as to the truth of the nontrivial among them, I have not sought to support these opinions with any systematic argumentation. For this would have demanded a full and separate inquiry.[67] Even so, the results of the evaluation have been inconclusive (a full analysis has by no means been achieved), a fact which I would like, but do not know how, to alter.

In the remainder of this section I shall concern myself with two special issues which arise in the context of (P5.7)–(P5.22).

Mercy. Is mercy ruled out by any of (P5.7)–(P5.22)? It is not; but just why it is not depends on precisely what we mean by "mercy."

In one, strong sense of "mercy," mercy is the failure to make someone suffer, or to censure someone, to the extent that he deserves.[68] If retributivism is true, then clearly there is necessarily a moral consideration in favor of *not* showing mercy (in the present sense of "mercy").[69] But, given the *prima facie* status of desert, this fact is consistent with there also being a moral consideration (even, possibly, a consideration of *desert*[70]) in favor of showing mercy; and if on some occasion this latter consideration overrides the former, then it is right, and perhaps obligatory, all things considered, to show mercy on that occasion.[71]

In another, weaker sense, mercy is the failure to make someone suffer, or to censure someone, to an extent to which he does *not* deserve *not* to suffer. (Consider, for example, a judge's exercising discretion, where (if this is possible) an offender deserves some form of punishment *within a certain range* of severity, and the judge opts for the least severe punishment in that range. Or consider a judge's showing mercy to the family of the offender by passing a lenient sentence.[72] Or consider the plea to Shylock for mercy with respect to his right to exact a pound of flesh from Antonio.[73]) Clearly, in this sense, mercy does *not* necessarily flout any moral consideration. Still it *may,* of course—as when, for example, one person is shown mercy, while another person, relevantly similarly situated, is not.[74]

In both the strong and weak senses, showing mercy is equivalent to granting a pardon. But now suppose that a person deserves suffering or censure to some degree y, but the only means open to someone are to make him suffer or to censure him to a lesser degree x or to a greater degree z. If the officially prescribed standard is suffering or censure to degree z, then perhaps it may be said that someone, in choosing censure to degree x, shows mercy in not adhering to the standard.[75] It would be misleading to think of this as a case of granting a pardon, however. Clearly, far from lack of mercy being called for by considerations of desert, mercy is called for by these considerations—at least, insofar as suffering or censure to degree z is proscribed (by protectionism), even if suffering or censure (merely) to degree x is not prescribed (by retributivism).

Finally, it must be recognized that, strictly, mercy is quite distinct from forgiveness, with which it is nonetheless often confused. Forgiveness is a personal attitude which one person bears to another whom he believes (perhaps falsely) to have (perhaps culpably) wronged him; it is an attitude of nonresentment. Forgiveness is an essentially private affair, and it does not essentially concern the reduction of suffering or censure; on both these counts, it is to be distinguished from mercy.[76]

Strict liability. "Strict liability" is, strictly, a legal term, whose definition is roughly this:

(P5.23) S's legal liability for an *actus reus* is strict if and only if its imposition is not conditional upon S's being found to have possessed *mens rea* with respect to that act.[77]

Some writers claim such strict liability to be morally repugnant[78]—at least often, if not always[79]—although some seem not to regard it this way,[80] and many accept its utility. But whether or not it is repugnant can hardly be determined in the absence of a clarification of the key terms *"actus reus"* and *"mens rea."*

An *actus reus* is a legal offense, an act that is proscribed by law. But just what *mens rea* is supposed to be is far from clear.[81] Literally, *"mens rea"* means "a guilty mind"; some have taken it to mean "guilty intent." But neither account helps. Are we here concerned with moral or legal guilt? Ostensibly the latter; but what then is the source of the *moral* repugnance of strict legal liability? What sort of intent is at issue? Intent to do (moral, legal) wrong; or merely intent to do something, something that is in fact (morally, legally) wrong? And why restrict the matter to *intent?* What of negligence, recklessness, and so on?

Since we are not here concerned with the law, we are at liberty to drop legal terminology; and in this case I think it would be wise to do so. We may still quite easily conjure up at least one source of repugnance that I take to be commonly associated with strict legal liability. We may, that is, talk of *strict victimization* in the following ways:

(P5.24) S's victimization for e is genuinely strict if and only if it is imposed in the absence of S's being culpable for e.

(P5.25) S's victimization for e is quasistrict if and only if it is imposed in the absence of S's being found to be culpable for e.

"Victimization," here, is a technical term used to cover either making someone suffer (call this *weak* victimization) or strongly censuring someone (call this *strong* victimization).[82] If protectionism is true, then genuinely strict victimization is, barring one condition to be mentioned shortly, clearly morally repugnant; for it violates the right of S not to be so treated (see (P5.10*a)).[83] Similarly, quasistrict victimization is, in such a case, in a way derivatively repugnant, since, even if S is culpable, his being victimized is not predicated on this fact. Another, secondary source of repugnance involved in quasistrict victimization is this: where the victimization is strong, there is an element of hypocrisy, insofar as the censure is not properly grounded in a finding of culpability.[84]

It will not have escaped the reader's attention that if, as I claim, liability is grounded in culpability and if the conditions of culpability are as I have set them out in Chapter 3, then it seems likely that *very many* people who commit legal offenses fail to be culpable for so doing and thus that *very many* of those who are punished for committing legal offenses are, in effect, *strictly victimized* by the law. Of course, I have no hard empirical data to back up this claim, but I would simply call here on the reader's own judgment. I am thinking in particular of the distinction between culpability and wrongdoing. How often does it happen that someone who (wrongly, let us agree) breaks the law *believes* that he is or may be doing something morally wrong? I would venture to say: not very often. Indeed—ironically—it seems to me that, the more serious the legal offense, the less likely it is that the offender believes that he is or may be doing something morally wrong. Of course, there will be exceptions to this, even if it is in general true. But the fact—if it is a fact—that this is a general truth surely points up an extremely important fact about our system of legal justice, to wit, that to a large extent it is morally repugnant.

There are four responses to this charge which can be made here.

First, it might be claimed that protectionism is not true, and hence that there is not the moral repugnance alleged. Without argument, but with what I believe many will accept as a high degree of plausibility, I shall here simply claim protectionism to be true. Thus I reject this first response.

Second, it might be claimed that, while protectionism is true, something *other* than culpability can serve as a desert-basis for censure (or for the imposition of suffering that is typical of censure), so that, even if a person deserves, in virtue of being inculpable, *not* to be censured, he *also* deserves, in virtue of having some other feature, *to* be censured. In particular, it might be claimed that moral wrongdoing and/or moral reprehensibility (of the sort discussed in Section 4.9) can serve as such a basis, and that many legal offenders satisfy one or the other of *these* conditions. Again, I would deny this, and so I reject this second response. But, again, I shall not try to provide an argument for my denial, although I would urge anyone inclined to make this second response to ensure that any case that he concocts in order to try to back up the response be one

where there is wrongdoing *without any trace of culpability* and/or reprehensibility *without any trace of culpability*. Only then will this second
response be properly established. But, if this is done, I think that the
plausibility of this second response will in fact tend to disappear. Surely,
if an agent has a *wholly* undiluted excuse (enjoys *total* exculpation, is
thoroughly blameless) for a certain event, then the fact that this event
nonetheless involves wrongdoing or reprehensibility does not serve as a
desert-basis for censuring him.

Third, it might be claimed that a person can waive his right not to be
strictly victimized and that it is in fact quite plausible to view many so-
called strict liability offenses in this light; that is, to view them as
involving the imposition of some penalty in the absence of culpability, or
at least in the absence of being found culpable, but where the person
penalized has in advance given up his right not to be so treated.[85] I think
that there is something to this. For example, as Feinberg notes, all milk
producers are "put on notice by one statute that, if any of their marketed
product is found to be adulterated, they will be subject to penalty."[86]
Insofar as these producers are *put* on notice, then they would seem to
assume voluntarily the risk of such penalty when they engage in the
production and marketing of milk products. There is perhaps good reason
to regard this as tantamount to a waiving of their right not to be strictly
victimized for marketing adulterated milk products. This seems to me to
constitute an exception to the general moral repugnance of strict victimization. But here we meet with another ironic fact, and that is that those
offenses which are currently recognized to be strict liability offenses are
less likely (insofar as they involve giving explicit prior notice to potential
offenders) to involve a morally repugnant form of strict victimization than
those offenses *not* already so recognized. Of course, there are exceptions
to this too—in both directions. First, some offenses currently not taken
to be strict liability offenses may perhaps be seen in the same light,
insofar as they may perhaps be taken to involve the waiving of one's right
not to be strictly victimized in virtue of prior notice to the effect that
what one plans to do will put one at risk of being so victimized. A
plausible example of this is the commission of a legal offense as a matter
of conscientious objection.[87] At least, this seems plausible to me when
the offense is committed in a democratic society, where it is reasonable
to believe that the offender has recourse to an alternative, law-abiding
mode of protest and the government's representatives have the moral
authority to impose the penalty in question. (Of course, this is a very
complex question; I present it here solely for purposes of illustration.)
Second, some offenses currently taken to be strict liability offenses
perhaps may not be seen in this light. At least, we must recognize the fact
that giving prior notice to a potential offender that what he plans to do
will put him at risk of being strictly victimized does not, in and of itself,

guarantee that, if he does what he plans to do despite this warning, then he has either waived or otherwise forfeited his right not to be so victimized. Consider, for example, a kidnapper's telling his victim that, if he (the victim) tries to escape, he (the kidnapper) will shoot him. If the victim does try to escape, it would be perverse to say that he has thereby "brought the penalty (*i.e.,* his being shot) on himself"; for he has not thereby waived or otherwise forfeited his right not to be shot by the kidnapper.

Finally, even where there has been no waiving of the right not to be victimized in a strict manner, it of course remains an open question just how morally repugnant the victimization is. I ventured the opinion earlier that the right of the inculpable not to be made to suffer or to be censured is a weighty one; but I did not back this statement up, and it is certainly not very precise. Moreover, it certainly seems plausible to say that, on some occasions perhaps, strict victimization is justified, all things considered, even if repugnant due to the infringement of a right. (See the discussion of overall justification above.)

5.4 The Justification of Punishment

In this final section I shall briefly address the issue of when it is that punishment is, not merely deserved, but overall justified. This is a huge topic, the adequate treatment of which would require both a detailed theory of what makes an act justified or unjustified and also access to a wealth of empirical data concerning such issues as the efficacy of certain forms of treatment (including both punishment and alternatives to punishment), the accuracy of inferences from overt behavior to inner thoughts, the accuracy of ascriptions of strict (un)freedom, and much more. Clearly, I am not in a position to supply such a theory or such data. I must rest content, therefore, with a few general observations which, while sweeping and hardly rigorous, are nevertheless, I hope, sensible. If what follows is, as I fear, replete with platitudes, perhaps there is some consolation to be found in the fact that platitudes have the virtue of being true. (If you have survived *this* platitude, you should survive the rest.)

Why even broach such a complex topic? Simply for this reason. Many of the conclusions that I have reached in the foregoing pages are, I have contended, fairly radical; they undermine much of our common practice of ascribing responsibility. The question naturally arises: what would life be like if we modified our practice accordingly? My answer is: I do not know. The reason that I do not know is that the conclusions that I have reached concern only questions of desert. But one of the things that makes the topic of the justification of punishment so difficult is the fact that considerations of desert are, as noted in Section 5.2, merely *prima facie* and thus in principle subject both to supplementation and to being overridden. This fact opens up the possibility that many of the factors shunned in Chapter 4 as irrelevant to appraisability (and hence also to liability, which is grounded solely in appraisability) may nevertheless be relevant to the overall justification of punishment. Thus it is extremely difficult to determine the extent to which the radical conclusions that I have reached should modify our general practice of ascribing responsibility; for their subversive nature can be diluted by extraneous considerations. So that this point may be fully appreciated, let us now very briefly investigate certain key issues pertaining to the overall justification of punishment.

Wrongdoing. Wrongdoing has not been mentioned as a condition of liability, for the by-now-familiar reason that it is not a condition of culpability. Being neither a necessary nor a sufficient condition of the latter, wrongdoing is immaterial to the truth or falsity of any of (P5.7)–(P5.22). Of course, this does not imply that it is immaterial to an overall justification of punishment; all that it implies is that it is immaterial insofar as such a justification is grounded in the desert-basis of culpability.

But we saw in the last section that there can be very good reasons not to cause a culpable person to suffer except by way of authorized censure, even if (P5.22) false; for vigilantism is obviously undesirable in civil society. Moreover, if moral protectionism is acceptable (as I believe, but have not argued), then there would seem to be very good reason for assuming that, in general, it is wrong to punish someone who has not done wrong. For, while a person who has done no wrong may deserve punishment, evidence of such desert will in general prove very hard to come by[88]; and if we proceed to punish in the absence of such evidence, then, given the truth of protectionism, we may very well be punishing someone who deserves not to be so treated.

Of course, the (moral) retributivist can retort: "If you insist on wrongdoing as a necessary condition for punishment, many persons deserving of suffering and/or punishment will avoid receiving their due." This is true (if retributivism is true) but seems not to count against the general guideline just mentioned. For to say that:

(P5.26)   In general we overall ought not to punish someone who has not done wrong,

is *not* to say that:

(P5.27)   We overall ought never to punish someone who has not done wrong.

(P5.26) affords only a *general* rule, and clearly there can be and are exceptions to it. (Indeed, as we shall see, attempts of a certain sort seem to constitute a *general* exception to this general rule.) What the acceptance of (P5.26) amounts to is the acceptance of this conservative guideline: on the whole, one is less likely to do wrong by not punishing, rather than by punishing, someone who has not done wrong; so, unless it is clear that it is not wrong to punish someone who has not done wrong, do not punish him.[89]

But the retributivist might still complain: "Merely distinguishing (P5.26) from (P5.27) is not good enough. You still have not explained why (P5.26) is to be accepted. Why be so conservative, when you thereby run the risk of failing to give the culpable their due? Why favor the desert of the inculpable over the desert of the culpable?" There is a twofold response to this. First, I am more sure of the truth of protectionism than I am of the truth of retributivism; but I recognize that this hardly meets the retributivist's complaint head-on. Secondly, however, even if one grants the truth of retributivism, one must also acknowledge that giving the inculpable their due is to fail to bring suffering into the world, while giving the culpable their due is to bring suffering into the world (not only the suffering of the culpable, but also of those who care for them or depend on them); and, even if such suffering (or some of it) is deserved, there is surely something bad—intrinsically bad, I would say—about it. Hence the conservatism of (P5.26) seems to me justified.

(P5.26) is also to be distinguished from the following:

(P5.28)   In general we overall may punish someone who has done wrong.

The conservatism underlying (P5.26) requires that we *reject* (P5.28); for it is clear that wrongdoers can be inculpable, and such people (given the truth of protectionism) deserve not to be punished. Of course, this is *not* to say that the following is true:

(P5.29)   We overall ought never to punish someone who is inculpable.

But it is to say that, if it is ever justifiable to punish an inculpable person, this is so *despite* his deserving not to be so treated. (See the discussion of strict victimization in the last section.) Now, it might on occasion be overall morally justifiable to punish someone who deserves not to be punished; and, indeed, the fact that a person has done wrong might provide such an overriding reason. Why? Because one of the primary purposes of punishing someone is to prevent further wrongdoing by both him and others; this is a good purpose, and achieving (or approaching) it may be accomplished by means of rehabilitation, deterrence, and suchlike, all of which, for their effectiveness, would appear in general to require that punishers focus their attention (though perhaps not exclusively) on actual wrongdoers. But I should add that I think that this goal of preventing further wrongdoing very seldom, if ever, provides a consideration of sufficient weight to override the desert of an inculpable person not to be so treated; still one should not, I think, rule out this possibility. On the other hand, we should note that, even if it never provides an overriding reason, it does provide a supplementary reason to focus one's attention, even when one is dealing with culpable persons, on those who have done wrong; and this provides further support for (P5.26).[90]

In keeping with my established practice, I have so far been using "wrongdoing" to refer to *moral* wrongdoing. But there is of course good reason to restrict *legal* punishment (that is, punishment prescribed and administered by legal officials) to punishment for *legal* offenses. The relation between moral and legal offenses is a complicated one. First, not all moral offenses are legal offenses; I may gratuitously insult you but I thereby break no law. If I am (indirectly) culpable for the result, and if (moral) retributivism is true, I am liable for it. Perhaps it is also true that I ought, all things considered, to be censured for it. But I doubt whether it is true that I ought to be legally punished for it. If the law is to operate successfully in the long run, it seems that, if legal punishment for certain moral offenses is desirable, they should be made legal offenses, that is, proscribed by law. (Whence the dictum: *nulla poena sine lege*.[91]) For, whatever the reasons for there being law at all (and, let us assume, the existence and upholding of law are in general good), it is in general enforceable only where legal sanctions (including punishment) apply to and *only* to the commission of legal offenses. This is not, of course, to say that every moral offense should be proscribed by law; there ought to be limits to the law's intrusion into our lives. Secondly, not all legal offenses are moral offenses; a German soldier who refused to participate in the extermination of Jews did no moral wrong. Of course, many acts become morally offensive simply in virtue of becoming legally offensive; in the absence of a law prescribing driving on the right, there is likely to be nothing morally wrong with driving on the left, but the creation of such a law also gives birth to the moral offensiveness of breaking it.[92] It is a vexed question just when the commission of a legal offense constitutes the commission of a moral offense. The case of the soldier just given is not difficult in this regard, nor is the case of driving on the left when the law proscribes it. But in the middle lie such cases as that of morally conscientious civil disobedience. In such a case, it is clear that no moral wrongdoing is intended or foreseen in the breaking of the law, and (given the truth of protectionism) the agent deserves no punishment, including legal punishment; and, given the dubious moral status of the act, it is far from clear that there would normally be an overriding moral reason to inflict punishment anyway, although the fact that it is clearly proscribed by law *might* provide such a reason.[93]

In addition to (P5.26), then, we may also say this:

(P5.30)   In general we overall ought not to legally punish someone
           who has not done legal wrong.

Conjointly, (P5.26) and (P5.30) yield this:

(P5.31)   In general we overall ought not to legally punish someone
           who has not done both legal and moral wrong.

We should now ask: *insofar as* (P5.26) and (P5.30) (and (P5.31)) hold,
what follows?

Justification and excuse. One thing that follows is this: certain modified
versions of Table I of Chapter 3 concerning justification and certain types
of excuse are acceptable. Recall Table I (slightly amended for purposes
of clarification):

Table Ia

		LO	&	LLi	iff	LJ	&	LE
Case	1	yes		yes		no		no
	2	yes		no		no	←	yes
	3	no	→	no		yes	→	no

This is to be read as follows. Case 1: in bringing about *e*, *S* commits a
legal offense (LO) (*i.e.*, does legal wrong) and is *legally liable (LLi)* to
penalty or punishment for so doing (*i.e.*—in this case—the law does not
prescribe not penalizing or punishing *S*), if, and only if, being charged
with bringing about *e*, he has neither a *legal justification (LJ)* nor a *legal
excuse (LE)* for bringing about *e;* similarly for cases 2 and 3.[94] The arrows
indicate implication; in particular, case 3 tells us that, if no offense is
committed, no liability is incurred.

A modified version of Table Ia, incorporating (P5.26), may be con-
structed thus:

Table IV

		MW	&	MP	iff	MJ	&	ME
Case	1	yes		yes		no		no
	2	yes		no		no	←	yes
	3	no	→	no		yes	→	no

This is to be read as follows. Case 1: in bringing about *e*, *S* does *moral
wrong (MW)* and is *morally* open to *punishment (MP)* for so doing (*i.e.*,
it is not the case that we overall ought not to punish him for so doing), if,
and only if, being charged with bringing about *e*, he has neither a *moral
justification (MJ)* nor a *moral excuse (ME)* for bringing about *e* (where in
this case a moral excuse constitutes a sort of moral immunity from

punishment; *i.e.,* one has such an excuse just in case one has done moral wrong but overall ought not to be punished for it anyway); similarly for cases 2 and 3. (P5.26) is captured by the first arrow of case 3.

Similar tables incorporating (P5.30) and (P5.31) may be drawn up. The uses of "excuse" in such tables are perhaps a little stilted, but I think that Table Ia establishes a precedent for them. In particular, the stipulation that, wherever there is an excuse there is no justification, and *vice versa,* may seem somewhat artificial, but it seems harmless enough. More importantly, we should note that, even if Tables Ia and IV and similar tables are acceptable *(as general guidelines),* it is certainly *not* acceptable to say this: whenever someone has done a legal wrong, then that person is morally open to—has no moral excuse or immunity from—legal punishment. This claim is *not* an implication of any of the tables, which is just as well. For, given the truth of protectionism, it is clearly false, even if we restrict it to voluntary or intentional legal wrongdoing. Unfortunately, some philosophers seem to think some such claim true.[95]

Luck. But perhaps the most important implication of (P5.26) and (P5.30) is simply this: insofar as these rules hold, luck is a significant factor in the overall justification of punishment. It is not that those, who according to the rules may be punished, are unlucky; it is that those, who are culpable but according to the rules ought not to be punished, are lucky.[96] For many culpable persons will luckily avoid doing moral wrong, and thus luckily escape punishment; and many of those who do moral wrong will luckily avoid doing legal wrong, and thus luckily escape legal punishment. Here, then, we again find good reason for the remark made in Section 4.11 to the effect that there can indeed be a morally significant difference between, for example, the "successful" and "unsuccessful" reckless drivers, even though there is nothing to distinguish them with respect to appraisability (and so, too, with respect to liability).[97]

Compulsion and mental disorders. I noted in Section 4.6 that compulsion might be thought to diminish the wrongness of an act. If this is in fact the case, then, where such diminution is tantamount to elimination, (P5.26) implies that in general we overall ought not to punish the agent—despite the by-now-familiar fact that such an agent may nevertheless be culpable. And an arguable corollary to (P5.26) would imply that, where there is such diminution but it is not tantamount to elimination, perhaps we overall may punish the agent, but still we overall ought not to punish him to the extent to which we would be justified in punishing him if there were no compulsion at all.

But I am doubtful that compulsion diminishes wrongness. (See the penultimate paragraph to Section 4.6.) If it does not, (P5.26) is inapplicable. Nonetheless, if it is commonly *believed* that compulsion diminishes wrongness (as it may well be), *evidence* as to a person's culpability (and hence liability) in doing what he was compelled to do will still in general be lacking (since in general there will be no evidence that the person who acted under compulsion did not subscribe to this common belief). And even if what is commonly believed is simply that acting under compulsion tends to *minimize the risk* of doing wrong (as I suggested in Chapter 4), evidence as to a person's culpability (and hence liability) in doing what he was compelled to do will likewise in general be lacking (see clause (b) of (P3.1')).

But while all this may be so in general, there appear to me to be certain types of compulsion that do not, and are not commonly believed, substantially to diminish the wrongness of performing, or the risk of doing wrong in performing, certain actions prompted by the compulsions. Among such compulsions are those characteristic of certain mental disorders—pedophilia, I venture to say, being a salient example. But even if I am right in this, and so the general reason not to punish such compulsive wrongdoers is not applicable in this sort of case, the nature of the disorder *itself* may be such as to preclude punishment. For while the disorder at the time of the action may not render the agent inculpable and thus deserving of no punishment, its being a *current* disorder (if we assume that the agent continues to suffer from it) may well override his desert of punishment (if, as retributivism asserts, he does deserve it), such that it would seem best not to punish him but to treat him in some other way in an attempt to cure him.[98]

This issue of how to treat those who currently suffer from mental disorders is a very complicated one. I shall make just four observations here. First, there can be no general formula adequate to all cases; this is so simply because of the large variety of mental disorders. Secondly, if the person is not culpable for a particular event *e,* then to use *e* as a pretext for punishing or otherwise similarly treating him is to treat him as he deserves not to be treated (given the truth of protectionism). Thirdly, even if a person was once culpable for *e,* if his present mental disorder is such as to render him a "new person," then to punish him for *e* may well be to treat him as he deserves not to be treated. (See the discussion of degrees of personal identity in the last section.) Finally, if the mental disorder itself constitutes a form of suffering, then perhaps it itself suffices as "punishment" for whatever it is for which the person is culpable. (See the discussion of source of suffering in the last section.[99]) All in all, then, it seems that there can be very serious obstacles to the overall justifiability of punishing a person who is currently suffering from a mental disorder; in addition, the person may well deserve not to be otherwise forcibly treated, although this is not to say that, in such a case, it would necessarily be overall wrong so to treat him.

Omissions. We have seen, then, some reason to concentrate on actual wrongdoers when meting out punishment. There is also reason to concentrate on those who do wrong by *acting* (that is, those who strictly *do* wrong) rather than on those who do wrong by omitting. For evidence of wrongdoing is, in general, more easily come by in the case of action than in the case of omission. Clearly, one can do wrong simply by virtue of omitting to do something. (Again, whether or not in general one does *as much wrong* by omitting as by acting is an issue that I shall leave to one side. See Section 4.4.) But, while it can be very obvious that *S did not* bring about *e*, it may not be at all obvious that *S omitted* to bring about *e*, and hence not at all obvious that *S wrongly* omitted to bring about *e*.[100] For wrongful omissions often leave no telltale physical evidence, while wrongful actions often do. For this reason it seems in general wise to concentrate on punishment for actions rather than for omissions.

There can also be practical disadvantages to adopting a policy of punishing people for culpable, wrongful omissions. Often, but by no means always, the effects of such punishment may be to encourage several people to "lend a hand" at once, thereby prompting confusion and serving in effect to exacerbate, rather than to alleviate, the problem in question. Or again, the effects of such punishment may be to encourage people to try to lend a hand where they are not in a position to do so helpfully, again exacerbating the problem in question. These and other issues need to be taken into account when contemplating the drawing-up of "Good Samaritan" legislation. Some careful drafting is required to circumvent the problems—which is not to say that they cannot be circumvented.

Punishment without wrongdoing. As already mentioned, where evidence of culpability is available in the absence of wrongdoing, there may be no need to be bound by the general rule embodied in (P5.26). For instance, those who are successful but not completely so—those who make narrow, *i.e.*, observable culpable attempts that end in failure—seem to me as open to investigation of liability and, ultimately, as open to punishment as those who succeed in their endeavors. And this is so whether or not, in making their attempts, they have in fact done wrong. Certainly, no diminution of appraisability rides on lack of ultimate success (see Section 4.3), and so no diminution of liability rides on it either. And when one looks for an *overall* justification for diminution of punishment owing to lack of success in one's endeavor, it is remarkably hard to find.[101] I certainly have not found it.[102]

To say that punishment for narrow attempts can well be justified is not to say that punishment for mere thoughts can be justified. For narrow attempts are not broad attempts, which are a species of mere thoughts. The idea of punishment for thoughts strikes many as quite horrible, and, on the whole, I am of the same opinion. But we must be careful to point out just what it is that is horrible about the idea.

For the most part, thoughts are not in our strict control, even indirectly. Hence we cannot be culpable for them, even indirectly. Thus, if protectionism is true, punishment for them would, for the most part, go counter to our desert. This is a genuine source of horror.

But we can indirectly control some of our thoughts (as when we do mental arithmetic, force ourselves to concentrate, allow ourselves to daydream, and so on) and, if having such thoughts leads to wrongdoing, we should control them. In such a case, we may incur liability. This can be equally well expressed in terms of (i) conjoint culpability for not ensuring the nonoccurrence of the thoughts, (ii) indirect culpability for the thoughts themselves, or (iii) indirect culpability for the wrongdoing that results from the thoughts. Even if we put matters in terms of (ii), we should beware the misleading talk of culpability for *mere* thoughts, which suggests that it is the thoughts themselves that are the source of culpability, rather than the willful refusal to avoid or banish them. So, even if it is justifiable to punish someone for failing to control his thoughts, we should not talk of this as punishment for mere thoughts.

There is, however, one species of mere thoughts for which one may be directly culpable. These are, of course, volitions, *i.e.,* attempts in the broad sense. So what makes punishment *merely* for having such thoughts unwelcome is *not,* as before, that it must be punishment in the absence of culpability, but rather that, the world being as it is (and in particular, as it is with respect to the availability of evidence), it must be punishment in the absence of adequate evidence of culpability.[103] In short, such punishment would be quasistrict (see (P5.25)); hence the foregoing emphasis on *narrow* attempts as fit occasions for punishment.

I shall end with an illustration of another type of case where it seems that one ought not to invoke the general rules embodied in (P5.26) and (P5.30). The illustration is provided by the interesting case of *Summers v. Tice.*[104] Harold Tice and Ernest Simonson were hunting quail; both of them negligently fired, at the same time, at a quail and in the direction of Charles Summers. (For our purposes, let us assume that the sort of negligence at issue here is that analyzed in (P4.8); *i.e.,* it is culpable.) Summers was struck in the eye by a shot from one of the guns; but there was no evidence as to which of the guns it was. In this case, both Tice and Simonson were found to have broken the law and were ordered to compensate the victim. Whether or not this was a sound legal judgment I shall not say. There was some concern for the moral culpability of both defendants; but there was also concern for the plaintiff's being compensated, which is a separate matter. Had there been evidence that pointed to, say, Tice's gun, rather than Simonson's, as the one from which the shot in question issued, then perhaps there would have been good reason—even good moral reason—to saddle Tice with the entire compensation[105]; perhaps not. The point remains that Tice and Simonson (their frames of mind being assumed to have been essentially the same) would have remained equally culpable and thus (given the truth of retributivism) equally liable. This would be one occasion—a comparatively rare one, presumably—where there is no obvious indirect culpability (for the injury, at least) that rides on direct culpability and no apparent need to adhere to the general rules concerning wrongdoing (or at least, wrongdoing with respect to that event which afforded the initial evidence of culpability). Indeed, there is an apparent need *not* to invoke these rules. For, even if we believe that the defendant who in fact did not injure Summers did not actually do wrong, he is as open to punishment as the other defendant, who certainly did actually do wrong.

Thus, while there may in general be good moral reason to punish only those who have succeeded in doing wrong, we must not forget that this is so *despite* the facts that culpability does not require wrongdoing and that liability, to the extent that it is implied by appraisability at all, owes nothing to indirect appraisability, which is essentially empty. In addition, there may sometimes (though, I believe, not often) be good moral reason to punish (or "punish"[106]) someone who has done wrong but is not culpable for this; but, again, this is so only *despite* the truth of protectionism. And so it can on occasion be overall justifiable to commit injustices, to perform actions which run counter to an individual's desert. But it is imperative that we not let our common practice of ascribing responsibility (including our common practice of punishment), which tends to run roughshod over the crucial distinctions between appraisability and liability, direct and indirect appraisability, and culpability and wrongdoing, blind us to the fact that many actual instances of punishment (*and* of the failure to punish) would seem indeed to be unjust. For, if we recognize this, I believe that we will also recognize that many of these instances are, in addition, overall unjustifiable. While the extreme complexity of the question of the overall justifiability of punishment prevents my giving a detailed account of how our practice of punishment should be modified in light of the account of responsibility that I have presented, I think that it must be agreed that it should be very different from the way it is now.

NOTES

1. Just as direct appraisability is to be distinguished from indirect and other forms of appraisability, one could distinguish direct lauding (or inculpating) from other forms of appraisal. Thus, and for example, if one holds to the account of Chapter 3, one will directly laud someone just in case one judges that he satisfies the analysans of (P3.6').

2. See, *e.g.*, Beardsley (1969).

3. For example, if it were a matter of direct laudability, and if S were to accept the account given in Chapter 3, then F would be the property of satisfying the analysans of (P3.6′). See note 1, this chapter; and, again, see the commentary on (P3.25) in Section 3.5.

4. *Cf.* Kleinig (1973), p. 24.

5. *Cf.* Flew (1951), p. 85ff.; Baier (1955), p. 130ff.; Feinberg (1970), pp. 98ff., 263–64; Wasserstrom (1977), pp. 179, 189–90; Baier (1984), p. 249. Contrast Feinberg (1960), p. 156, and Honderich (1969), pp. 1, 5.

6. *Cf.* Glover (1970), p. 141; Wasserstrom (1977), p. 179; French (1984), pp. 166–67.

7. Contrast Hobbes (1651), p. 230, on pain being inflicted "without respect to the future good."

8. *Cf.* Baier (1955), p. 132. I shall not consider here the matter of distinguishing suffering by dint of some "positive evil" being visited upon one and suffering by dint of the "deprivation" of some "good." *Cf.* Mabbott (1955), p. 117.

9. See, *e.g.,* Mabbott (1939).

10. *Cf.* Hobbes (1651), pp. 229–30; Hart (1968), p. 4ff.; Wasserstrom (1977), p. 179.

11. Again, I do not wish to rule out the possibility of desert of weak commendation or censure; I wish simply to point out its dubious nature and, henceforth, not to concentrate on it. For one of my main concerns here will be the desert and justification of *punishment,* which I have already claimed to be a variety of *strong* censure.

12. Or rather, this is so for any rational S who accepts (P5.5).

13. *Cf.* Feinberg (1970), pp. 58–59; Kleinig (1973), p. 55; Pincoffs (1977), p. 76.

14. In fact, what is at issue is of course *substantial* laudability and culpability (see (P3.25) and (P3.26)). But I shall not complicate matters still further by explicitly introducing this.

15. This has usually taken the form of failing to distinguish between (P5.12′) and (P5.14′) (or similar statements). See, *e.g.,* Kant (1797), pp. 103–4; Lewis (1948–49), pp. 301–3; Raphael (1955), p. 142; Ezorsky (1974), pp. 112–13. Ezorsky also appears to fail to distinguish between (P5.8′) and (P5.10′).

16. Where "ought" and "may" are used broadly (to express what is sometimes called the "ought-to-*be*"), we could say that "deserves" in part expresses what "ought" expresses while "does not deserve not" in part expresses what "may" expresses. Thus (P5.7′) says, roughly, that it is not the case that the unlaudable ought to experience pleasure, while (P5.9′) says that the unlaudable ought not to experience pleasure; (P5.11′) says, roughly, that the laudable may experience pleasure, while (P5.13′) says that the laudable ought to experience pleasure; and so on.

17. Wasserstrom (1977), pp. 190–1. *Cf.* Ewing (1929), pp. xiv, 44–45; Kleinig (1973), p. 72.

18. Wasserstrom (1977), p. 191.

19. Perhaps this should read "for any times T (during S's lifetime) and T' . . . ," since it is admittedly odd to ascribe desert to someone that does not exist. But this is tricky. There are occasions where it seems plausible to ascribe desert to someone who does not exist but has existed. *E.g.:* "George Washington deserves the reputation that he has." And perhaps it is even plausible sometimes to ascribe desert to entities that do not exist, have never existed, and perhaps never will exist. *E.g.:* "Members of future generations deserve a clean environment."

20. Just what constitutes respecting or disrespecting a person is, of course, a *very* difficult question, and one that I shall not broach here, beyond pointing out the need to distinguish genuinely (dis)respectful behavior (which is in part a function of *attitude*) from merely outwardly (dis)respectful behavior.

21. *Cf.* Hobbes (1651), p. 230, on "natural evil consequences [being] no punishments."

22. Feinberg (1970), pp. 85–86. *Cf.* Kleinig (1973), pp. 59–60.

23. *Cf.* Hospers (1977), p. 24; Pincoffs (1977), pp. 79–80.

24. Desert is not *just* a matter of what ought to be, or of what is fitting or appropriate. Contrast Feinberg (1970), p. 86.

25. *Cf.* Kleinig (1973), pp. 51–52, on "raw" versus "institutionalized" desert claims; *cf.* also Wolfgast (1985). See also notes 16 and 24, this chapter.

26. *Cf.* Moberly (1968), p. 158; Lyons (1969).

27. *Cf.* Quinton (1954), p. 57; Gendin (1970), p. 5.

28. *Cf.* Ewing (1929), p. 15ff.; Coddington (1946); Flew (1951), p. 95; McCloskey (1965), p. 122; Feinberg (1970), pp. 60, 83–85, 127–29; and Hospers (1977), p. 24.

29. *Cf.* Ten (1967), p. 253; Glover (1970), p. 169; Prosser (1971), pp. 152–53; Kleinig (1973), p. 63. Contrast, to some extent: Sprigge (1974), pp. 73, 78–79; Hospers (1977), p. 22.

30. *Cf.* Kleinig (1973), p. 85ff.

31. *Cf.* Schlossberger (1986), pp. 52–55. On reprehensibility, see Section 4.9. *Cf.* also Adams (1985), pp. 21–22, and note 122 to Chapter 4.

32. *Cf.* Feinberg (1970), p. 79.

33. *Cf.* Coddington (1946), pp. 339–40.

34. See Kant (1797), pp. 105–6.

35. See, *e.g.*: Schlick (1939), p. 61; Smart (1973), p. 54; Dennett (1984), p. 162. Contrast Blumenfeld and Dworkin (1965); Kleinig (1973), pp. 100–1; Morris (1976), p. 119.

36. For a useful survey, see Cottingham (1979). See also Feinberg (1970), p. 216, n.20.

37. *Caveat:* see note 12, this chapter.

38. One might claim that, in (P5.3) and (P5.4), I have succumbed to an error of which I have just accused others, namely, that of failing to distinguish between "not deserves" and "deserves not." For one might claim that, in (P5.3) and (P5.4), I should be talking, not of S'''s *deserving* to experience pleasure (or to suffer), but of S'''s *not deserving not* to experience pleasure (or to suffer). But I deny this. When one strongly commends or censures someone for something, it is because one believes a certain treatment to be this person's due, and not merely because one believes that it is not his due not to receive such treatment.

39. See, *e.g.*, Mundle (1954), p. 63; Quinton (1954), p. 58.

40. *Cf.* Quinton (1954), p. 59ff.; Baier (1955), pp. 132, 135; Armstrong (1961), pp. 146–47; and Flew (1967), pp. 102–3. It is Flew's position which is closest to mine here. *Cf.* also Ewing (1963), p. 138ff.; Locke (1963), p. 569; Feinberg (1970), pp. 71, 112; Kleinig (1973), pp. 13, 34, 70; Wasserstrom (1977), p. 179; and Baier (1984), p. 249. In saying that it is impossible to punish someone that one regards as inculpable, I am talking of doing "one's own" punishment. There is, I concede, a secondary sense of "punish" where S' punishes S^* *on* S's *behalf* and where S' need *not* regard S^* as culpable. (*Cf.* Baier (1955), p. 135.) In such a case, however, I would insist that S himself *must* regard S^* as culpable.

41. *Cf.* Feinberg (1970), pp. 127–29, on the "second and third stages."

42. *Cf.* Coddington (1946), p. 341; Mundle (1954), pp. 67–68; Kleinig (1973), p. 3; Hospers (1977), p. 22; Nozick (1981), pp. 366–69.

43. See note 19, this chapter.

44. According to Kleinig (1973), p. 67, he does.

45. See McInerney (1984), pp. 6–8, on what he calls "Past Self" cases.

46. *Cf.* Smart (1968), p. 222ff., especially pp. 226–27, and Parfit (1984), p. 326.

47. Perhaps this is close to what Nozick has in mind when he talks of "connecting with values." See Nozick (1981), pp. 384–85.

48. See McInerney (1984), pp. 4–5. With respect to insanity, see Gross (1979), pp. 315–16 and also Section 5.4.

49. *Cf.* Armstrong (1961), p. 154.

50. *Cf.* Hart (1968), p. 161.

51. *Cf.* Gendin (1970), p. 3; Ezorsky (1972c), p. 366; Kleinig (1973), p. 17.

52. *Cf.* Card (1972), p. 201ff., on "poetic justice." *Cf.* also Baier (1984), p. 248. Given the truth of logical retributivism, the use of "punish" here is irregular. Such irregular uses are commonplace. One often hears, for instance, of the "punishing" heat, and so on. *Cf.* the metaphorical "blaming" of the weather mentioned in Section 1.1.

53. *Cf.* Ezorsky (1972b), pp. xxiv–v.

54. It is possible, of course, that censure cause no suffering; and so it is conceivable, I suppose, that someone should accept (P5.22) while rejecting (P5.14). But I can think of no good reason for believing that someone may be fully liable without being basically liable. Feinberg (1970), pp. 115–16, discusses the possibility of stigmatizing by censure without causing (unnecessary) suffering. While there might be some reason to engage in such stigmatizing, I find it hard to see why someone should be said to *deserve* it.

55. On this issue, see: Mundle (1954), p. 69ff.; Feinberg (1970), p. 71; Kleinig (1973), p. 39; Hospers (1977), p. 35ff.

56. See Morris (1968). *Cf.* Hegel (1821); McTaggart (1896), pp. 40–41. *Cf.* also Ewing (1929), p. 44; Moberly (1968), pp. 110–1; Feinberg (1970), pp. 72–74; Fried (1978), p. 32; Jensen (1984), p. 324.

57. I have in mind in particular the evils of "rehabilitation," which are in a way all the more sinister because usually well-motivated. There is no need to document these evils here, or to point out the often-misguided basis on which the "theory" of rehabilitation is founded. For discussion of these issues, see Lewis (1948–49); Hart (1968), Chapter 8; Goldstein (1968), pp. 190–91, 196; Murphy (1969); Szasz (1970), p. 103ff. and Chapter 9; Kleinig (1973), p. 99ff.; Gendin (1974); Morris (1976), p. 71. Of course, if rehabilitation is advocated in the *absence* of culpability—as it, in fact, usually is (*cf.* Wootton (1963), p. 141)—then its evil nature is all the more apparent: it violates the right at issue in (P5.10*a). Having said this, it is worth pointing out that rehabilitation is not *necessarily* disrespectful and does not *necessarily* violate a person's rights; it is only that it runs a very grave risk of being and doing so, especially when touted, as in the past, as a panacea.

In this connection, we may raise the interesting question of whether a person may waive his conditional right to punishment. What if, for example, he agrees to subject himself to some form of experimentation in lieu of the punishment that he would otherwise receive? This is a very complicated issue. I shall list here just some of the points that need to be borne in mind. (i) Supposing that the person has the conditional right in question, does he have the moral authority to waive it? (ii) Even if he has in general this authority, could he, in light of the coercive nature of the situation, truly waive the right? (iii) Even if he could, would it be right of him to do so? (iv) Would it be right of his punishers to act according to his request? (*Cf.* Kant (1797), p. 104.)

58. This is not to say that an advocate of (P5.14′) ought to deny that a culpable person deserves to be strongly censured, but that he ought to deny that a culpable person, *simply in virtue of his culpability,* deserves to be strongly censured.

59. It is worth noting that time, way, and source of suffering can all affect degree of suffering, both positively and negatively. (*Cf.* Feinberg (1970), p. 114.) But this is a complication that I shall leave aside here.

60. *Cf.* Honderich (1969), p. 17, where it is flatly stated: "the distress of a penalty and the culpability of an offender are not commensurable." *Cf.* also Rashdall (1907a), p. 289; Ewing (1929), p. 36ff.; Maclagan (1939), p. 290; Feinberg (1970), pp. 117–18; Ezorsky (1972b), p. xxiii.

61. *Cf.* Moberly (1968), p. 94; Gross (1979), pp. 439–40; Davis (1985), p. 132.

62. *Cf.* Pincoffs (1977) on what he calls the "anchoring" and "interval" problems. *Cf.* also Hart (1968), pp. 162, 233–34. Kleinig (1973), p. 115ff., notes the need for at least *two* specific cross-matches in order for the "interval" problem to be resolved.

63. In Kleinig (1973), p. 123ff., the following solution is proposed: determine the

upper and lower limits of human depravity; determine the upper and lower limits of humane punishment; cross-match these limits; and then simply scale other wrongs and punishments in between these limits. But this seems to me to face three problems. By what criterion is depth of human depravity to be measured? By what criterion is humaneness of punishment to be measured? And what is one to do about cases of culpability whose degree is indeterminate? The second question seems to me the especially important one in this context. In Davis (1985), a more detailed proposal, but one essentially similar to Kleinig's, is given. On the crucial matter of the (in)humaneness of punishment, all that is said by Davis is this (p. 132): "An inhumane . . . penalty is one . . . [to which] most members of the society [in question] object . . . on principle (and independent of its utility within the criminal law)." I do not find this illuminating. See note 61, this chapter, with its surrounding commentary.

64. *Cf.* Oldenquist (1978), pp. 61–62.

65. Indeed, it is surely common to arrive at (P5.10) *by way of* the general view that a person who is culpable-to-degree-*x* deserves not to be made to suffer excessively. For inculpability is simply culpability-to-degree-zero, in which case any and all suffering is excessive.

66. The conceptual distinction between moral retributivism and moral protectionism—between (P5.14) and (P5.10), and between (P5.22) and (P5.18)—has often been overlooked (but by no means always: *cf.* Brandt (1960), pp. 106–8). Many self-professed antiretributivists, such as Wootton (1963), have openly attacked (P5.14) and (P5.22), while seeming to think that any success they enjoy in so doing serves also to undermine (P5.10) and (P5.18). This, of course, is not so. Wootton's detractors (such as Hart (1968), Chapter 8) have often been guilty of a parallel fallacy. They have openly defended (P5.10) and (P5.18), while seeming to think that any success they enjoy in so doing serves also to support (P5.14) and (P5.22). Again, this is, of course, not so. This problem is exacerbated simply by virtue of the fact that many philosophers, on both sides of the fence, have used "retributivism" to refer not only to what I have called retributivism but also to what I have called protectionism. (*Cf.* Hart (1968), p. 9ff.)

67. For just a very small sampling of recent discussions of the desert of punishment in particular, see: Pincoffs (1966); Morris (1976), Chapter 2 (contrast Morris (1981)); Card (1973); Wasserstrom (1977), p. 191ff.; Nozick (1981), p. 363ff.; and Burgh (1982). I shall not discuss the matter further.

68. See Smart (1968), Sections 2 and 3; Kleinig (1973), pp. 88–89.

69. Armstrong (1961), pp. 155–56, is wrong to say that, on retributivism, a punisher merely has the right, and not the duty, to punish. He is here in effect confusing (P5.20) and (P5.22).

70. *Cf.* Card (1972), p. 184ff.

71. *Cf.* Ewing (1929), pp. 30–31. Contrast Rashdall (1907a), p. 306ff.

72. *Cf.* Kleinig (1973), p. 88.

73. *The Merchant of Venice*, Act IV, Scene I. I am grateful to Deborah Berlyne for this reference.

74. *Cf.* McCloskey (1967), pp. 108–9.

75. See Smart (1968), Section 1. *Cf.* Kleinig (1973), p. 88.

76. *Cf.* Downie (1965), pp. 131–32; O'Shaughnessy (1967), p. 337ff.; Kleinig (1973), pp. 91–92.

77. *Cf.* Wasserstrom (1959–60), p. 199; Kenny (1978), p. 6.

78. *Cf.* Hart (1968), p. 136 and elsewhere; Feinberg (1970), p. 111.

79. See Feinberg (1970), pp. 223–24.

80. See Wootton (1963), p. 139.

81. *Cf.* Hart (1968), pp. 139–40. *Cf.* also: Williams (1953a), p. 132; Williams (1953b), p. 218; Hughes (1958), p. 226; Hall (1960a); Jeffery (1967), p. 7ff.; Hart (1968), pp. 36, 91; Kenny (1978), p. 7.

82. *Cf.* Kleinig (1973), p. 34.

83. Some have claimed that strict strong victimization is more repugnant than strick weak victimization because of the representation of culpability involved in the former. See, *e.g.*: Feinberg (1970), pp. 111–13; Gross (1979), p. 364. Clearly, if strong victimization involves the same degree of suffering as weak victimization *plus* the stigma of being represented as culpable, this claim is plausible. But where the degree of suffering varies, the claim seems moot to me.

84. *Cf.* Feinberg (1970), p. 110ff. Indeed, given the truth of logical retributivism, we should strictly not speak of (strong) censure but of the pretense of (strong) censure.

85. *Cf.* Wasserstrom (1959–60), p. 210; Feinberg (1970), pp. 223–25; and also, to some extent, Gross (1979), pp. 343, 346, 372ff.

86. Feinberg (1970), p. 224.

87. *Cf.* Fingarette (1972), p. 155.

88. *Cf.* Dworkin and Blumenfeld (1966), p. 401.

89. Note that, if (P5.26) is true, we finally have a reason to concentrate on the sort of hybrid personal-*cum*-causal responsibility mentioned in Section 1.1; for much wrongdoing involves causal responsibility for some untoward event.

90. Even so, one should be very careful just *how* rehabilitation, deterrence, and so on are promoted. See note 57, this chapter.

91. For a discussion of this dictum, see Husak (1987), pp. 7–8 and 212–15.

92. See Fried (1987), p. 138; *cf.* pp. 99 and 139. *Cf.* also Hart (1968), p. 37.

93. Why? To try to ensure that the agent and the general populace obey the law, such obedience being (we have assumed) in general a good thing. But this can be counterproductive; for if the law is seen to be at odds with what morality requires, respect for it will be diminished, and thereby obedience to it will tend to diminish also. There is also the issue of whether the offender has waived, implicitly or explicitly, his right not to be strictly victimized. See the last section.

94. But see notes 61, 67, and 70 to Chapter 3.

95. See Mabbott (1939), *Cf.* Hart (1968), p. 37.

96. *Cf.* Feinberg (1970), pp. 219–20; Jensen (1984), p. 327ff.; Richards (1986), p. 199.

97. See the subsection on resultant luck, including note 182. See also note 162 to Chapter 4.

98. But again see notes 57 and 90, this chapter.

99. I put "punishment" in quotation marks to signal that its use here, given the truth of logical retributivism, is irregular.

100. I submit that *S* cannot wrongly *not bring about e* without wrongly *omitting to bring about e*. For, given the account of omissions in (P2.10), this would imply that *S* can wrongly not bring about *e* even though he (strictly) cannot bring about *e*. I think that this is impossible; for I believe that "ought" implies "can." See Zimmerman (1987b), Section 1.

101. *Cf.* Dworkin and Blumenfeld (1966), p. 396ff.; Hart (1968), pp. 129–31; Kleinig (1973), pp. 132–33; Carr (1981).

102. Of course, I am talking of genuine attempts here, and not of half-hearted efforts (whose failure is often attributable to this half-heartedness). For half-heartedness can signal a diminution of culpability—either with respect to the original volition itself, or with respect to sustaining, or re-endorsing, the original volition—and where there is a diminution of culpability, there is a diminution of liability. *Cf.* Kleinig (1973), p. 133; Morris (1976), p. 123ff.

103. Again, *cf.* Dworkin and Blumenfeld (1966), p. 401.

104. Supreme Court of California (1948). 33 Cal.2d 80, 199 P.2d 1.

105. *Cf.* Thomson (1984), p. 104ff.

106. See note 99, this chapter.

Bibliography

This bibliography is restricted to those items to which reference is made in the foregoing pages.

Abelard, Peter. "Desire and Sin." In Sommers: 246–54.

Acton, H. B., ed. 1969. *The Philosophy of Punishment*. London: Macmillan.

Adams, Robert Merrihew. 1985. "Involuntary Sins." *Philosophical Review* 94: 3–31.

Andre, Judith. 1983. "Nagel, Williams, and Moral Luck." *Analysis* 43: 202–7.

Antony, Louise. 1979. "Why We Excuse." *Tulane Studies in Philosophy* 28: 63–70.

Aristotle. *Nicomachean Ethics*. In *The Basic Works of Aristotle,* edited by Richard McKeon. New York: Random House, 1941.

Armstrong, K. G. 1961. "The Retributivist Hits Back." In Acton, 1969: 138–53.

Audi, Robert. 1973. "Intending." *Journal of Philosophy* 70: 387–403.

———. 1974. "Moral Responsibility, Freedom, and Compulsion." *American Philosophical Quarterly* 11: 1–14.

———. 1982. "Believing and Affirming." *Mind* 91: 115–20.

Augustine. 400. "The Depths of Vice." In Sommers, 1985: 241–45.

Aune, Bruce. 1979. *Kant's Theory of Morals*. Princeton: Princeton University Press.

Austin, J. L. 1956–57. "A Plea for Excuses." In Feinberg and Gross, 1975: 12–25.

Austin, John. 1873. "Negligence, Heedlessness, and Rashness." In Morris, 1961: 359–61.

Ayer, A. J. 1984. *Freedom and Morality and Other Essays*. Oxford: Clarendon Press.

Baier, Kurt. 1955. "Is Punishment Retributive?" In Acton, 1969: 130–37.

———. 1965. "Action and Agent." *Monist* 49: 183–95.

———. 1970. "Responsibility and Action." In *The Nature of Human Action,* edited by Myles Brand. Glenview: Scott, Foresman: 100–16.

———. 1984. "The Concepts of Punishment and Responsibility." In Sterba, 1984: 248–55.

———. 1985. "Moral and Legal Responsibility." Unpublished.

Bates, Stanley. 1970–71. "The Responsibility of 'Random Collections.' " *Ethics* 81: 343–49.

Bayles, Michael D. 1972. "A Concept of Coercion." In Pennock and Chapman (1972): 17–26.

———. 1974. "Coercive Offers and Public Benefits." *Personalist* 55: 139–44.

195

Beardsley, Elizabeth L. 1957. "Moral Worth and Moral Credit." *Philosophical Review* 66: 304–28.

———. 1969. "A Plea for Deserts." *American Philosophical Quarterly* 6: 33–42.

———. 1979. "Blaming." *Philosophia* 8: 573–83.

Beck, Lewis White. 1960. *A Commentary on Kant's Critique of Practical Reason.* Chicago: University of Chicago Press.

Benditt, Theodore. 1977. "Threats and Offers." *Personalist* 58: 382–84.

Bennett, Jonathan. 1974. "The Conscience of Huckleberry Finn." In Sommers, 1985: 20–34.

Berofsky, Bernard. 1980. "The Irrelevance of Morality to Freedom." In Bradie and Brand, 1980: 38–47.

Blatz, Charles V. 1973. "Mitigating and Meliorating Defenses." *American Philosophical Quarterly Monograph Series* 7: 1–16.

Blum, Lawrence A. 1980. *Friendship, Altruism, and Morality.* London: Routledge & Kegan Paul.

Blumenfeld, David. 1971. "The Principle of Alternate Possibilities." *Journal of Philosophy* 68: 339–45.

Blumenfeld, David, and Gerald Dworkin. 1965. "Necessity, Contingency, and Punishment." *Philosophical Studies* 16: 91–94.

Bradie, Michael, and Myles Brand, eds. 1980. *Action and Responsibility.* Bowling Green: Bowling Green State University.

Brand, Myles, and Douglas Walton, eds. 1976. *Action Theory.* Dordrecht: D. Reidel.

Brandt, Richard B. 1958. "Blameworthiness and Obligation." In *Essays in Moral Philosophy,* edited by A. I. Melden. Seattle: University of Washington Press: 3–39.

———. 1959. *Ethical Theory.* Englewood Cliffs: Prentice-Hall.

———. 1960. "The Conditions of Criminal Responsibility." In Friedrich, 1960: 106–15.

———. 1969. "A Utilitarian Theory of Excuses." *Philosophical Review* 78: 337–61.

Broad, C. D. 1946. "Some of the Main Problems of Ethics." *Philosophy* 21: 99–117.

———. 1950. "Obligations, Ultimate and Derived." In *Broad's Critical Essays in Moral Philosophy,* edited by David R. Cheney. London: George, Allen and Unwin, 1971: 351–68.

Burgh, Richard W. 1982. "Do the Guilty Deserve Punishment?" *Journal of Philosophy* 79: 193–210.

Card, Claudia. 1972. "On Mercy." *Philosophical Review* 81: 182–207.

———. 1973. "Retributive Penal Liability." *American Philosophical Quarterly Monograph Series* 7: 17–35.

Carr, Charles R. 1981. "Punishing Attempts." *Pacific Philosophical Quarterly* 62: 61–66.

Castañeda, Hector-Neri. 1975. *Thinking and Doing.* Dordrecht: D. Reidel.

Cederblom, J. B., and William L. Blizek, eds. 1977. *Justice and Punishment.* Cambridge: Ballinger.

Chisholm, Roderick M. 1964. "The Ethics of Requirement." *American Philosophical Quarterly* 1: 147–53.

———. 1976. *Person and Object.* La Salle: Open Court.

———. 1977. *Theory of Knowledge,* 2nd edition. Englewood Cliffs: Prentice-Hall.

Coddington, F. J. O. 1946. "Problems of Punishment." In Grupp, 1971: 333–53.

Cohen, Jonathan L. 1981. "Who Is Starving Whom?" *Theoria* 47: 65–81.

Cooper, D. E. 1968. "Collective Responsibility." *Philosophy* 43: 258–68.

———. 1969. "Collective Responsibility—Again." *Philosophy* 44: 153–55.

Cottingham, J. G. 1979. "Varieties of Retribution." *Philosophical Quarterly* 29: 138–46.

Culver, Charles M., and Bernard Gert. 1982. *Philosophy in Medicine.* London: Oxford University Press.

Cummins, Robert. 1979. "Could Have Done Otherwise." *Personalist* 60: 411–14.

———. 1980. "Culpability and Mental Disorder." *Canadian Journal of Philosophy* 10: 207–32.

Dahl, Norman O. 1967. " 'Ought' and Blameworthiness." *Journal of Philosophy* 64: 418–28.

D'Arcy, Eric. 1963. *Human Acts.* Oxford: Oxford University Press.

Davidson, Donald. 1963. "Actions, Reasons and Causes." In Davidson, 1980: 3–19.

———. 1971. "Agency." In Davidson 1980: 43–61.

———. 1980. *Essays on Actions and Events.* Oxford: Clarendon Press.

Davis, Lawrence H. 1979. *Theory of Action.* Englewood Cliffs: Prentice-Hall.

Davis, Michael. 1985. "How to Make the Punishment Fit the Crime." In *Criminal Justice,* edited by J. Roland Pennock and John W. Chapman. New York: New York University Press: 119–55.

Dennett, Daniel C. 1984. *Elbow Room.* Cambridge: The MIT Press.

Donagan, Alan. 1977. *The Theory of Morality.* Chicago: University of Chicago Press.

Downie, R. S. 1965. "Forgiveness." *Philosophical Quarterly,* 15: 128–34.

———. 1969. "Collective Responsibility." *Philosophy* 44: 66–69.

Duff, Antony. 1977. "Psychopathy and Moral Understanding." *American Philosophical Quarterly* 14: 189–200.

Dworkin, Gerald. 1970. "Acting Freely." *Noûs,* 4: 367–83.

Dworkin Gerald, and David Blumenfeld. 1966. "Punishment for Intentions." *Mind* 75: 396–404.

Edwards, Rem B. 1969. *Freedom, Responsibility and Obligation.* The Hague: Martinus Nijhoff.

Ewing, A. C. 1929. *The Morality of Punishment.* Montclair: Patterson Smith, 1970.

———. 1963. "On 'Retributivism.' " In Ezorsky, 1972a: 137–41.

Ezorsky, Gertrude, ed. 1972a. *Philosophical Perspectives on Punishment.* Albany: State University of New York Press.

———. 1972b. "The Ethics of Punishment." In Ezorsky, 1972a: xi–xxvii.

———. 1972c. "Retributive Justice." *Canadian Journal of Philosophy* 1: 365–68.

———. 1974. "Punishment and Excuses." In Goldinger, 1974: 99–115.

Feinberg, Joel. 1960. "On Justifying Legal Punishment." In Friedrich, 1960: 152–67.

———. 1970. *Doing and Deserving.* Princeton: Princeton University Press.

———. 1980. *Rights, Justice, and the Bounds of Liberty.* Princeton: Princeton University Press.

Feinberg, Joel, and Hyman Gross, eds. 1975. *Responsibility.* Encino: Dickenson.

Fingarette, Herbert. 1967. *On Responsibility.* New York: Basic Books.

———. 1972. *The Meaning of Criminal Insanity.* Berkeley: University of California Press.

Fischer, John Martin. 1982. "Responsibility and Control." *Journal of Philosophy* 79: 24–40.

———. 1985–86. "Responsibility and Failure." *Proceedings of the Aristotelian Society* 86: 251–70.

Fitzgerald, P. J. 1968. "Voluntary and Involuntary Acts." In *The Philosophy of Action,* edited by Alan R. White (Oxford: Oxford University Press): 120–43.

Fletcher, George P. 1978. *Rethinking Criminal Law.* Boston: Little, Brown.

Flew, Antony. 1951. "The Justification of Punishment." In Acton, 1969: 83–102.

———. 1967. Postscript to "The Justification of Punishment." In Acton, 1969: 102–4.

———. 1973. *Crime or Disease?* London: Macmillan.

———. 1974. "Delinquency and Mental Disease." In Goldinger, 1974: 39–55.

Foot, Philippa. 1978. *Virtues and Vices and Other Essays in Moral Philosophy.* Berkeley: University of California Press.

Frankena, William K. 1963. "Obligation and Ability." In *Philosophical Analysis,* edited by Max Black. Englewood Cliffs: Prentice-Hall: 148–65.

Frankfurt, Harry G. 1969. "Alternate Possibilities and Moral Responsibility." *Journal of Philosophy* 66: 829–39.

———. 1973. "Coercion and Moral Responsibility." In *Essays on Freedom of Action,* edited by Ted Honderich. London: Routledge & Kegan Paul: 65–86.

———. 1978. "The Problem of Action." *American Philosophical Quarterly* 15: 157–62.

French, Peter A., ed. 1972. *Individual and Collective Responsibility.* Cambridge: Schenkman.

———. 1984. *Collective and Corporate Responsibility.* New York: Columbia University Press.

Fried, Charles. 1978. *Right and Wrong.* Cambridge: Harvard University Press.

Friedrich, Carl J., ed. 1960. *Responsibility.* New York: The Liberal Arts Press.

Gardiner, P. L. 1955. "On Assenting to a Moral Principle." In Mortimore, 1971: 100–17.

Gendin, Sidney. 1970. "A Plausible Theory of Retribution." *Journal of Value Inquiry* 5: 1–16.

———. 1974. "A Critique of the Theory of Criminal Rehabilitation." In Goldinger, 1974: 17–37.

Gert, Bernard. 1970. *The Moral Rules.* New York: Harper and Row.

———. 1972. "Coercion and Freedom." In Pennock and Chapman, 1972: 30–48.

Ginet, Carl. 1966. "Might We Have No Choice?" In *Freedom and Determinism,* edited by Keith Lehrer. New York: Random House: 87–104.

Glover, Jonathan. 1970. *Responsibility.* London: Routledge & Kegan Paul.

Goldinger, Milton, ed. 1974. *Punishment and Human Rights.* Cambridge: Schenkman.

Goldman, Alvin I. 1970. *A Theory of Human Action.* Princeton: Princeton University Press.

———. 1976. "The Volitional Theory Revisited." In Brand and Walton, 1976: 67–84.

Goldstein, Abraham S. 1968. "The Mentally Disordered Offender and the Criminal Law." In *The Mentally Abnormal Offender,* edited by A. V. S. de Reuck and Ruth Porter. London: J. and A. Churchill: 188–200.

Gosselin, Phillip D. 1979. "Is There a Freedom Requirement for Moral Responsibility?" *Dialogue* 18: 289–306.

Green, O. H. 1979. "Refraining and Responsibility." *Tulane Studies in Philosophy* 28: 103–13.

Greene, Theodore M. 1934. "The Historical Context and Religious Significance of Kant's *Religion.*" In Kant, 1793: ix–lxxviii.

Greenspan, Patricia S., 1978. "Behavior Control and Freedom of Action." *Philosophical Review* 87: 225–40.

Gross, Hyman. 1979. *A Theory of Criminal Justice*. New York: Oxford University Press.

Grupp, Stanley E., ed. 1971. *Theories of Punishment*. Bloomington: Indiana University Press.

Haksar, Vinit. 1964. "Aristotle and the Punishment of Psychopaths." *Philosophy* 39: 323–40.

———. 1965. "The Responsibility of Psychopaths." *Philosophical Quarterly* 15: 135–45.

Hall, Jerome. 1960a. "*Mens Rea* and Personal Guilt." In Morris, 1961: 214–18.

———. 1960b. "Mental Disease." In Morris, 1961: 425–35.

Hare, R. M. 1952. *The Language of Morals*. Oxford: Oxford University Press.

Harris, John. 1980. *Violence and Responsibility*. London: Routledge & Kegan Paul.

Hart, H. L. A. 1968. *Punishment and Responsibility*. Oxford: Oxford University Press.

Hart, H. L. A., and A. M. Honoré. 1959. *Causation in the Law*. Oxford: Clarendon Press.

Haydon, Graham. 1978. "On Being Responsible." *Philosophical Quarterly* 28: 46–57.

Hegel, G. W. F. 1821. "Punishment as a Right." In Ezorsky, 1972a: 107–8.

Heintz, Lawrence L. 1981. "The Logic of Defenses." *American Philosophical Quarterly* 18: 243–48.

Held, Virginia. 1972a. "Coercion and Coercive Offers." In Pennock and Chapman, 1972: 49–62.

———. 1972b. "Moral Responsibility and Collective Action." In French, 1972: 103–18.

———. 1986. "Corporations, Persons, and Responsibility." Forthcoming.

Henson, Richard G. 1979. "What Kant Might Have Said." *Philosophical Review* 88: 39–54.

Hilbert, David. 1983. "Novus Actus Interveniens in *The Theory of Morality*." Unpublished.

Hobbes, Thomas. 1651. *Leviathan*. London: Collier-Macmillan, 1962.

Holborrow, L. C. 1971–72. "Blame, Praise and Credit." *Aristotelian Society Proceedings* 72: 85–100.

Honderich, Ted. 1969. *Punishment: The Supposed Justifications*. New York: Harcourt, Brace and World.

Hospers, John. 1977. "Punishment, Protection, and Retaliation." In Cederblom and Blizek, 1977: 21–50.

Houlgate, Laurence D. 1968. "Knowledge and Responsibility." *American Philosophical Quarterly* 5: 109–16.

Hughes, Graham. 1958. "Omissions and *Mens Rea*." In Morris, 1961: 226–30.

———. 1967. "Attempting the Impossible." In Feinberg and Gross, 1975: 60–68.

Hunter, J. F. M. 1973. "Acting Freely and Being Held Responsible." *Dialogue* 12: 233–45.

Husak, Douglas N. 1980. "Omissions, Causation and Liability." *Philosophical Quarterly* 30: 318–26.

———. 1987. *Philosophy of Criminal Law*. Totowa: Rowman and Littlefield.

Jackson, Frank. 1985. "On the Semantics and Logic of Obligation." *Mind* 94: 177–95.

Jeffery, C. R. 1967. *Criminal Responsibility and Mental Disease*. Springfield: Charles C. Thomas.

Jensen, Henning. 1984. "Morality and Luck." *Philosophy* 59: 323–30.

Kant, Immanuel. 1785. *Groundwork of the Metaphysic of Morals*, translated and analyzed by H. J. Paton. New York: Harper and Row, 1964.

———. 1793. *Religion within the Limits of Reason Alone*, translated by Theodore M. Greene and Hoyt H. Hudson. New York: Harper and Row, 1960.

———. 1797. "Justice and Punishment." In Ezorsky, 1972a: 103–6.

———. "Jealousy, Envy, and Spite." In Sommers, 1985: 272–9.

Keeton, Robert E. and Jeffrey O'Connell. 1966. "Why Shift Loss?" In Feinberg and Gross, 1975: 84–8.

Kenner, Lionel. 1967. "On Blaming." *Mind* 76: 238–49.

Kenny, Anthony. 1966. "Intention and Purpose." *Journal of Philosophy* 63: 642–51.

———. 1978. *Freewill and Responsibility*. London: Routledge & Kegan Paul.

Kim, Jaegwon. 1973. "Causes and Counterfactuals." *Journal of Philosophy* 70: 570–2.

Kleinig, John. 1973. *Punishment and Desert*. The Hague: Martinus Nijhoff.

———. 1986. "Criminal Liability for Failures to Act." *Law and Contemporary Problems* (forthcoming).

LaFave, Wayne R., and Austin W. Scott, Jr. 1972. *Criminal Law*. St. Paul: West.

Lemos, Ramon M. 1980. "Duty and Ignorance." *Southern Journal of Philosophy* 18: 301–12.

Lewis, C. S. 1948–49. "The Humanitarian Theory of Punishment." In Grupp, 1971: 301–8.

Lewis, H. D. 1972. "The Non-Moral Notion of Collective Responsibility." In French, 1972: 121–44.

Locke, Don. 1963. "The Many Faces of Punishment." *Mind* 72: 568–72.

Locke, John. 1690. *An Essay Concerning Human Understanding*, abridged and edited by Maurice Cranston. New York: Collier, 1965.

London, Perry. 1969. *Behavior Control*. New York: Harper and Row.

Lukes, Steven. 1965. "Moral Weakness." In Mortimore, 1971: 147–59.

Lyons, Daniel. 1975. "Welcome Threats and Coercive Offers." *Philosophy* 50: 425–36.

Lyons, David. 1969. "Rights, Claimants, and Beneficiaries." *American Philosophical Quarterly* 6: 173–85.

Mabbott, J. E. 1939. "Punishment." In Acton, 1969: 39–54.

———. 1955. "Professor Flew on Punishment." In Acton, 1969: 115–29.

Maclagan, W. G. 1939. "Punishment and Retribution." *Philosophy* 14: 281–98.

Matson, W. I. 1956. "On the Irrelevance of Free-Will to Moral Responsibility." *Mind* 65: 489–97.

Mayo, Bernard. 1958. "Virtue or Duty?" In Sommers, 1985: 171–76.

McCloskey, H. J. 1965. "A Non-Utilitarian Approach to Punishment." In Ezorsky, 1972a: 119–34.

———. 1967. "Utilitarian and Retributive Punishment." *Journal of Philosophy* 64 (1967): 91–110.

McInerney, Peter. 1984. "Diminishing Responsibility for Past Actions." Unpublished.

McTaggart, J. E. 1896. "Hegel's Theory of Punishment." In Ezorsky, 1972a: 40–55.

Mele, Alfred R. 1986. "Is Akratic Action Unfree?" *Philosophy and Phenomenological Research* 46: 673–79.

Mellema, Gregory. 1984. "On Being Fully Responsible." *American Philosophical Quarterly* 21: 189–93.

Milo, Ronald D. 1984. *Immorality*. Princeton: Princeton University Press.

Moberly, Sir Walter. 1968. *The Ethics of Punishment*. Hamden: Anchor Books.

Moore, G. E. 1912. *Ethics*. London: Oxford University Press, 1965.

Morris, Herbert, ed. 1961. *Freedom and Responsibility*. Stanford: Stanford University Press.

———. 1976. *On Guilt and Innocence*. Berkeley: University of California Press.

———. 1981. "A Paternalistic Theory of Punishment." *American Philosophical Quarterly* 18: 263–71.

Mortimore, G. W., ed. 1971. *Weakness of Will*. London: Macmillan.

Mundle, C. W. K. 1954. "Punishment and Desert." In Grupp, 1971: 58–75.

Murphy, Jeffrie. 1969. "Criminal Punishment and Psychiatric Fallacies." In *Punishment and Rehabilitation*, edited by Jeffrie Murphy. Belmont: Wadsworth: 197–210.

———. 1972. "Moral Death: A Kantian Essay on Psychopathy." *Ethics* 82: 284–98.

Nagel, Thomas. 1979. *Mortal Questions*. Cambridge: Cambridge University Press.

Naylor, Margery Bedford. 1984. "Frankfurt on the Principle of Alternate Possibilities." *Philosophical Studies* 46: 249–58.

Neely, Wright. 1974. "Freedom and Desire." *Philosophical Review* 83: 32–54.

Nell, Onora. 1975. *Acting on Principle*. New York: Columbia University Press.

Nesbitt, Winston, and Stewart Candlish. 1973. "On Not Being Able to Do Otherwise." *Mind* 82: 321–30.

Nozick, Robert. 1969. "Coercion." In *Philosophy, Science and Method*, edited by Sidney Morgenbesser *et al.* New York: St. Martin's, 1969: 440–72.

———. 1981. *Philosophical Explanations*. Cambridge: Harvard University Press.

Oldenquist, Andrew G. 1978. *Moral Philosophy*, 2nd edition. Prospect Heights: Waveland Press.

O'Shaughnessy, R. J. 1967. "Forgiveness." *Philosophy* 42: 336–52.

Parfit, Derek. 1984. *Reasons and Persons*. Oxford: Clarendon Press.

Parker, Richard. 1984. "Blame, Punishment, and the Role of Desert." *American Philosophical Quarterly* 21: 269–76.

Pennock, J. Roland, and John W. Chapman, ed. 1972. *Coercion*. Chicago: Aldine and Atherton.

Pincoffs, Edmund L. 1966. "Classical Retributivism." In Sterba, 1984: 267–74.

———. 1977. "Are Questions of Desert Decidable?" In Cederblom and Blizek, 1977: 75–88.

Plato. *Meno, Protagoras,* and *Gorgias.* In *Plato: The Collected Dialogues,* edited by Edith Hamilton and Huntington Cairns. Princeton: Princeton University Press, 1961.

Prichard, H. A. 1912. "Does Moral Philosophy Rest on a Mistake?" *Mind* 21: 21–37.

———. 1949. *Moral Obligation*. Oxford: Clarendon Press.

Pritchard, Michael S. 1974. "Responsibility, Understanding, and Psychopathology." *Monist* 58: 630–45.

Prosser, William L. 1971. *The Law of Torts*. St. Paul: West.

Quinton, Anthony. 1954. "On Punishment." In Acton, 1969: 55–64.

Radden, Jennifer. 1982. "Diseases as Excuses: Durham and the Insanity Plea." *Philosophical Studies* 42: 349–62.

———. 1985. *Madness and Reason*. London: George Allen and Unwin.

Raphael, D. Daiches. 1955. "Justice." In Ezorsky, 1972a: 142–44.
Rashdall, Hastings. 1907a. *The Theory of Good and Evil*, volume I. Oxford: Clarendon Press.
———. 1907b. *The Theory of Good and Evil*, volume II. Oxford: Clarendon Press.
Rescher, Nicholas. 1983. *Risk*. Lanham: University Press of America.
Richards, Norvin. 1986. "Luck and Desert." *Mind* 95: 198–209.
Roberts, Robert C. 1984. "Will Power and the Virtues." *Philosophical Review* 93: 227–47.
Ross, W. D. 1930. *The Right and the Good*. Oxford: Clarendon Press.
———. 1960. *Foundations of Ethics*. Oxford: Clarendon Press.
Royal Commission Report. 1953. "Legal Insanity." In Morris, 1961: 410–22.
Russell, Bertrand. 1910. *Philosophical Essays*. London: Longmans, Green.
Sankowski, Edward. 1977. "Responsibility of Persons for Their Emotions." *Canadian Journal of Philosophy* 7: 829–40.
Schlick, Moritz. 1939. "When Is a Man Responsible?" In *Free Will and Determinism*, edited by Bernard Berofsky. New York: Harper and Row, 1966: 54–63.
Schlossberger, Eugene. 1986. "Why We Are Responsible for Our Emotions." *Mind* 95: 37–56.
Sellars, Wilfrid. 1976. "Volitions Re-Affirmed." In Brand and Walton, 1976: 47–66.
Silber, John R. 1960. "The Ethical Significance of Kant's *Religion*." In Kant, 1793: lxxix–cxxxiv.
Smart, Alwynne. 1968. "Mercy." In Acton, 1969: 212–27.
Smart, J. J. C. 1973. "An Outline of a System of Utilitarian Ethics." In *Utilitarianism: For and Against*, by J. J. C. Smart and Bernard Williams. Cambridge: Cambridge University Press: 3–74.
Smith, Holly. 1983. "Culpable Ignorance." *Philosophical Review* 92: 543–71.
Sommers, Christina Hoff, ed. 1985. *Vice and Virtue in Everyday Life*. San Diego: Harcourt Brace Jovanovich.
Sprigge, T. L. S. 1974. "Punishment and Moral Responsibility." In Goldinger, 1974: 73–97.
Squires, J. E. R. 1968. "Blame." In Acton, 1969: 204–11.
Steinbock, Bonnie. 1980. "Causing Death and Allowing to Starve." In Bradie and Brand, 1980: 102–10.
Sterba, James, ed. 1984. *Morality in Practice*. Belmont: Wadsworth.
Szasz, Thomas S. 1970. *Ideology and Insanity*. Garden City: Anchor.
Taylor, Richard. 1966. *Action and Purpose*. Englewood Cliffs: Prentice-Hall.
———. 1976. "Action and Responsibility." In Brand and Walton, 1976: 293–309.
Ten, C. L. 1967. "Mr. Thompson on the Distribution of Punishment." *Philosophical Quarterly* 17: 253–54.
Terry, Henry T. 1915. "Negligence." In Morris, 1961: 243–46.
Thalberg, Irving. 1963. "Remorse." *Mind* 72: 545–55.
———. 1978. "Hierarchical Analyses of Unfree Action." *Canadian Journal of Philosophy* 8: 211–26.
Thomson, Judith Jarvis. 1984. "Remarks on Causation and Liability." *Philosophy and Public Affairs* 13: 101–33.
Thorp, John. 1980. *Free Will*. London: Routledge & Kegan Paul.
Tuomela, Raimo. 1984. *A Theory of Social Action*. Dordrecht: D. Reidel.
VanDeVeer, Don. 1977. "Coercion, Seduction, and Rights." *Personalist* 58: 374–81.

van Inwagen, Peter. 1983. *An Essay on Free Will*. Oxford: Clarendon Press.

———. 1984. "Comments on Dennett's 'I Could Not Have Done Otherwise—So What?' " Unpublished: presented at the Eastern Division meeting of the American Philosophical Association, December 30, 1984.

Wallace, James D. 1978. *Virtues and Vices*. Ithaca: Cornell University Press.

Waller, Bruce N. 1985. "Deliberating about the Inevitable." *Analysis* 45: 48–52.

Wasserstrom, Richard. 1959–60. "Strict Liability in the Criminal Law." In Ezorsky, 1972a: 196–212.

———. 1977. "Some Problems with Theories of Punishment." In Cederblom and Blizek, 1977: 173–96.

Weinryb, Elazar. 1980. "Omissions and Responsibility." *Philosophical Quarterly* 30: 1–18.

White, Alan R. 1964. *Attention*. Oxford: Basil Blackwell.

Williams, Bernard. 1981. *Moral Luck*. Cambridge: Cambridge University Press.

Williams, Glanville, 1953a. "The Criminal Act." In Morris, 1961: 125–34.

———. 1953b. "Intention in the Criminal Law." In Morris, 1961: 218–26.

Wolf, Susan. 1980. "Asymmetrical Freedom." *Journal of Philosophy* 77: 151–66.

Wolff, Robert Paul. 1973. *The Autonomy of Reason*. New York: Harper and Row.

Wolgast, Elizabeth H. 1985. "Intolerable Wrong and Punishment." *Philosophy* 60: 161–74.

Wootton, Barbara. 1963. "Eliminating Responsibility." In Feinberg and Gross, 1975: 135–50.

Zimmerman, Michael J. 1982. "Moral Responsibility, Freedom, and Alternate Possibilities." *Pacific Philosophical Quarterly* 63: 243–54.

———. 1984. *An Essay on Human Action*. New York: Peter Lang.

———. 1985a. "Intervening Agents and Moral Responsibility." *Philosophical Quarterly* 35: 347–58.

———. 1985b. "Sharing Responsibility." *American Philosophical Quarterly* 22: 115–22.

———. 1986a. "Negligence and Moral Responsibility." *Noûs* 20: 199–218.

———. 1986b. "Subsidiary Obligation." *Philosophical Studies* 50: 65–75.

———. 1987a. "Luck and Moral Responsibility." *Ethics* 97: 374–86.

———. 1987b. "Remote Obligation." *American Philosophical Quarterly* 24: 199–205.

Index of Names

204

Index of Subjects

Action, 86–87, 121, 129, 131, 149–51, 161; appraisability for, 60, 85, 95–96, 113, 118–19, 123, 125; desert of, 152–53, 155, 171, 185; group, 10, 19, 24, 34, 96–98, 103–4; and intention, 21–22, 27–28, 123; and issue, 17, 19, 28–29, 35, 43, 61, 69–70, 123, 125, 145; nature of, 6–7, 13, 17–21, 23, 65, 69–70, 72–73, 78–79, 85, 93, 121, 125, 127, 186; voluntary, 100–102, 144. *See also* Intention, Volition, Willingness
Actus reus, 176
Admirability, 11, 115–19, 124, 132
Advertence. *See* Inadvertence, Negligence
Alternate possibilities, 11, 31–32, 119–27, 145
Amorality, 76
Appraisability, x–xi, 4–5, 7–9, 14–15, Chap. 3 *passim*, Chap. 4 *passim*, 148, 150–52, 154, 165, 168, 173, 180, 184, 186, 188; analyzed, 62–64; conjoint, 60–63, 92–93, 119; degrees of, 56–61, 62–63, 72, 74, 91–92, 95, 97, 133–34, 151, 186; diminished, 10, 68, 93, 95–99; direct, x, 8, 11, 54–58, 62–63, 73, 81, 91–93, 96, 98, 119, 126–27, 138, 188; indirect, x, 8–11, 54–64, 72–73, 75, 81, 91–94, 96–97, 99–100, 108, 112, 117, 119–26, 133, 138, 188; its internalist character, 8–9, 22, 57–58, 61, 64, 72; situational, 138–39; substantial, 9, 54–56, 61, 63, 74–75, 81, 91, 93, 97–99, 113, 122, 138. *See also* Culpability, Indifferenceworthiness, Laudability

Attempts, 6, 10, 22, 35, 87–88, 91–92, 133, 181, 186–87, 193
Belief, 22, 35, 37, 71–72, 87, 91, 139, 142–43, 149–50, 152–53, 165, 176, 184–85; appraisability for, 89, 114–17; as a condition of appraisability, 43–44, 49, 51, 54, 62, 67, 75–76, 92, 106–9, 111, 120–21, 123–24, 133, 136, 138, 177. *See also* Foresight, Ignorance
Blameworthiness, x, 1–2, 4. *See also* Censure, Culpability, Reprehensibility
Blaming, x, 3–4, 11, 38–39, 54, 59, 69, 191. *See also* Inculpation

Callousness, 8, 46–47, 49, 71, 90–91, 108. *See also* Recklessness
Causation, 17–19, 34–35, 37, 93–95, 125–27, 130, 140–41, 146. *See also* Consequences, Responsibility
Censure, x, 11–12, 54, 148–54, 157–59, 163–65, 168, 170–79, 182, 189–91, 193
Chance, 53–54, 72. *See also* Likelihood, Risk
Character, 10–11, 38, 112–13, 115–17, 129, 132, 143
Coercion. *See* Compulsion
Commendation, 11–12, 54, 148–54, 157–58, 164–65, 173–74, 189–90
Common practice, 13–15, 43, 55, 74, 81, 83, 91, 95, 105, 107, 111, 114, 133, 137–38, 179–80, 188
Compassion, 51, 114–15, 118

207